The Constitutional Law Dictionary

THE CONSTITUTIONAL LAW DICTIONARY

VOLUME 1: INDIVIDUAL RIGHTS SUPPLEMENT 2

Covering the 1986–87, 1987–88, 1988–89,
and 1989–90 Terms of the Supreme Court

Ralph C. Chandler
Richard A. Enslen
Peter G. Renstrom

ABC-CLIO

Santa Barbara, California
Oxford, England

Library of Congress Cataloging-in-Publication Data

Chandler, Ralph C., 1934–
    The constitutional law dictionary.

    (Clio dictionaries in political science ; #8)
    Vol. 2 has publisher: ABC-Clio.
    Vol. 2 without series numbering.
    Vol. 1 kept up to date by supplements.
    Includes indexes.
    Contents: v. 1. Individual rights—v. 2. Governmental powers.
    1. United States—Constitutional law—Terms and phrases. 2. United States—Constitutional law—Cases. I. Enslen, Richard A., 1931– . II. Renstrom, Peter G., 1943– . III. Title.
KF4548.5.C47   1985   342.73   84-12320
                                347.302

ISBN 0-87436-598-8 (alk. paper)

98 97 96 95 94 93   10 9 8 7 6 5 4 3 2

ABC-CLIO, Inc.
130 Cremona Drive, P.O. Box 1911
Santa Barbara, California 93116-1911

This book is printed on acid-free paper ⊗.
Manufactured in the United States of America

Clio Dictionaries in Political Science

SERIES STATEMENT

Language precision is the primary tool of every scientific discipline. That aphorism serves as the guideline for this series of political dictionaries. Although each book in the series relates to a specific topical or regional area in the discipline of political science, entries in the dictionaries also emphasize history, geography, economics, sociology, philosophy, and religion.

This dictionary series incorporates special features designed to help the reader overcome any language barriers that may impede a full understanding of the subject matter. For example, the concepts included in each volume were selected to complement the subject matter found in existing texts and other books. All but one volume utilize a subject-matter chapter arrangement that is most useful for classroom and study purposes.

Entries in all volumes include an up-to-date definition plus a paragraph of *Significance* in which the authors discuss and analyze the term's historical and current relevance. Most entries are also cross-referenced, providing the reader an opportunity to seek additional information related to the subject of inquiry. A comprehensive index, found in both hardcover and paperback editions, allows the reader to locate major entries and other concepts, events, and institutions discussed within these entries.

The political and social sciences suffer more than most disciplines from semantic confusion. This is attributable, *inter alia*, to the popularization of the language, and to the focus on many diverse foreign political and social systems. This dictionary series is dedicated to overcoming some of this confusion through careful writing of thorough, accurate definitions for the central concepts, institutions, and events that comprise the basic knowledge of each of the subject fields. New titles in the series will be issued periodically, including some in related social science disciplines.

—Jack C. Plano
Series Editor

CONTENTS

A NOTE ON HOW TO USE THIS BOOK

Students of constitutional law know the extent to which the law is ever changing. With each new term of the Supreme Court the justices review their previous decisions and those of their predecessors in light of current legal and social circumstances. The changes that are made are frequently incremental: a nuance here and an adjustment there. The Court may simply wish to apply an established doctrine or more clearly define a standard in a particular case as it weighs real-world situations on the scales of justice. Sometimes it sweeps aside an entire line of precedent in a bold new interpretation of the Constitution. The system is constantly in flux. It is evolutionary, developmental, and responsive to human need. Thus it adds stability to the governmental system as a whole. A systems theorist would say constitutional law has a well-defined dynamic feedback loop.

These conditions create certain problems for writers and publishers of constitutional law books. Given the lead time necessary to prepare such a book, it is out of date in some particulars on the day it is published. In this case, *The Constitutional Law Dictionary, Volume 1: Individual Rights,* was published in early 1985. The material in it had to be completed in the spring of 1984, during the middle of the 1983–84 term of the Supreme Court. Significant decisions yet to be made in that term, plus, of course, those coming since, are not included in the book. To remedy the obvious need to update the general reader and researcher, this second supplement is offered as the Court begins the 1990–91 term. This is the second such supplement we have prepared. The first, published in 1987, covered the 1983–84, 1984–85, and 1985–86 terms. The second supplement spans the 1986–87, 1987–88, 1988–89, and 1989–90 terms. The following guidelines apply:

(1) Chapters 1 and 8 of the original work are not affected. "Constitutionalism" and "Legal Words and Phrases" remain intact as previously published.

(2) The other six chapters are moved up one chapter number each in the contents listing of the supplement. In the original *Dictionary* the First Amendment was Chapter 2, following "Constitutionalism." In this second supplement it is Chapter 1, and so forth.

(3) All *See also* page number references are keyed to the original work. It is therefore a good idea to have the original *Dictionary* and the first supplement at hand when using this supplement.

(4) Rather than include parts of cases that have been modified since publication of the original work and the first supplement, the entire case is included in the supplement and represents the matter as it now stands in constitutional law. When a new case modifies or replaces an older one, the new standards are emphasized in the *Significance* section of the discussion. The alphabetical list of cases at the beginning of the supplement assembles all of the new cases appearing for the first time, plus the older cases they modify. There are 167 cases contained in this list that have not been discussed in either the original *Dictionary* or the first supplement. The reader should bear in mind that in most instances the new cases are introduced in the descriptions of these older cases, which are also listed at the beginning of each chapter with the new cases mentioned under them. Case names appearing entirely in uppercase letters indicate complete new entries. There are 22 such new entries. These new cases frequently overturn previously established doctrine.

(5) In some instances the complete citation is unavailable because reference page numbers have not been assigned by the publishers of these cases. This is particularly true of the cases decided in 1990. The citation from the *Lawyers Edition* is included for every case.

Recent Supreme Court justices have been added to Appendix C and Appendix D, which are included in full in this supplement. We are grateful for the good reception *The Constitutional Law Dictionary: Individual Rights* has received, and we hope this second supplement will make the book even more useful.

—Ralph C. Chandler
Professor of Political Science
Western Michigan University

—Richard A. Enslen
United States District Judge
Western District of Michigan

—Peter G. Renstrom
Professor of Political Science
Western Michigan University

ACKNOWLEDGMENT

The authors have discussed many of these same cases in our *Constitutional Law Deskbook,* published by The Lawyers Co-operative Publishing Company of Rochester, New York. Lawyers Co-op has allowed us to use portions of text from that volume and other material edited from the annual supplements to the *Deskbook.* We greatly appreciate Lawyers Co-op's consideration and cooperation in the preparation of this volume.

ALPHABETICAL LIST OF CASE ENTRIES

The Constitutional Law Dictionary

1. *The First Amendment*

Free Speech

Free Press

Assembly and Protest

Association

ESTABLISHMENT OF RELIGION

Tax Exemptions

Walz v. New York City Tax Commission, 397 U.S. 664, 90 S. Ct. 1409, 25 L. Ed. 2d 697 (1970)   Upheld tax exemptions on church-owned property. *Walz* addressed the question of whether tax exemptions for religious property are compatible with the Establishment Clause of the First Amendment. The exemption authorized by state law included "real or personal property used exclusively for religious, educational, or charitable purposes as defined by law and owned by any corporation or association organized or conducted exclusively for one or more such purposes and not operating for profit." Walz, a property owner and taxpayer, contended that the exemption indirectly compelled him financially to support religious organizations owning exempted properties. The Supreme Court upheld the exemption over the dissent of Justice Douglas. In the majority opinion Chief Justice Burger asserted that the First Amendment "will not tolerate either governmentally established religion or governmental interference with religion." As long as those proscribed acts are avoided, "there is room for play in a benevolent neutrality which will permit religious exercise to exist without sponsorship and without interference." Evaluation of policies using the religion clauses rests on "whether particular acts in question are intended to establish or interfere with religious beliefs and practices or have the effect of doing so." The legislative purpose served here is legitimate, Burger said. Historically, common exemptions recognize the "beneficial and stabilizing influences" of the nonprofit groups exempted from taxation. The policy also responds to the "latent danger inherent in the imposition of property taxes." What New York is doing is "simply sparing the exercise of religion from the burden of property taxation levied on private profit institutions." On considering primary effect, the Court introduced the entanglement criterion, which would become a decisive factor in many subsequent establishment cases. The chief justice argued that government involvement with religion existed with or without the exemption. Indeed, "elimination of the

7

exemption would tend to expand the involvement of government by giving rise to tax valuation of church property, tax liens, tax foreclosures, and the direct confrontations and conflicts that follow in the train of those legal processes." While some indirect economic benefits and some involvements result from granting the exemption, they are lesser involvements than collecting the property tax. Finally, the Court rejected any "nexus between tax exemption and establishment of religion." The tax exemption is clearly not "sponsorship since the government does not transfer part of its revenue to churches but simply abstains from demanding that the church support the state." *See also* BILL OF RIGHTS, p. 7; ESTABLISHMENT CLAUSE, p. 80; FIRST AMENDMENT, p. 77.

Significance   *Walz v. New York City Tax Commission* (397 U.S. 664: 1970) provided the Supreme Court a comparatively easy way to handle the establishment issue. Unlike direct aid programs, tax exemption had a long history. The history created a presumption for the practice. While benefits may be conveyed at least indirectly to religion, such tax exemptions were quite distinct from grant programs. The exemptions were also different politically in that they did not generate the divisive debate often associated with direct grant programs. *Walz* was viewed as a strongly accommodationist decision. The specific reference to "benevolent neutrality" was seen as a signal that the state may assume something other than a strictly neutral position regarding religion. The new "excessive entanglement" test, while not critical to the outcome of *Walz* itself, was to become the principal criterion in many subsequent establishment cases. Indeed, when the Burger Court invalidated practices on establishment grounds, it often did so on the basis of excessive church-state entanglement.

The tax exemption issue reappeared in two cases decided by the Rehnquist Court. In *Texas Monthly, Inc. v. Bullock* (103 L. Ed. 2d 1: 1989), the Court considered a state sales and use tax exemption for religious publications. The law exempted periodicals published or distributed by a "religious faith" that consisted entirely of writings either "promulgating the teachings of the faith" or "sacred to a religious faith." The exemption was challenged by the publisher of a "general interest" periodical not entitled to the exemption. Although the Court was unable to secure consensus on an opinion, it struck down the exemption in a 6–3 decision. First, the exemption had no secular purpose. When exemptions are granted, they must fall to a "wide array of nonsectarian groups as well as religious organizations." That did not occur here. Rather, the exemption was confined exclusively to religious publications, which gave it insufficient "breadth" to serve a secular objective. The Court noted a second establishment problem. Under the exemption, public officials were to determine whether a message or activity is "consistent with the teachings of the faith." Such a requirement produces a level of entanglement between government and religion greater than would occur through enforcement of the tax laws without the exemption. While religious groups would be affected by absence of the exemption, the Court saw no evidence that the taxes "affected religious beliefs" or "inhibited religious activities." Justice Brennan said that when a subsidy is created that "either burdens nonbeneficiaries markedly" or does not remove a "significant state-imposed deterrent" to free exercise, the law provides "unjustified rewards of assistance to religious organizations" and cannot but send a "message of endorsement to slighted members of the community." The second case, *Jimmy Swaggart Ministries v. Board of Equalization* (107 L. Ed. 2d 796: 1990), upheld a state sales and use tax imposed on a religious organization's sale of religious materials. The California law required retail sellers to register with the state. The law also levied a 6 percent tax on in-state sales and a 6 percent use tax on materials purchased outside the state. The Board of Equalization advised the Jimmy Swaggart Ministries that it needed to register itself and pay accumulated taxes on articles sold at its "evangelical crusades" dating back several years. The tax was challenged by the Ministries as a violation of both religion clauses. A unanimous Supreme Court disagreed. The Swaggart Ministries had based its Free Exercise Clause challenge on cases like the license tax ruling in *Murdock v. Pennsylvania* (319 U.S. 105: 1943). The Court, speaking through Justice O'Connor, distinguished the flat license taxes that operated as a "prior restraint on the exercise of religious liberty" from the sales tax in this case. The license taxes acted as a "precondition" to free exercise. That defect is "simply not present where a tax applies to all sales and uses of tangible personal property in a State." The California tax is not a tax on the right to "disseminate religious information, ideas, or beliefs *per se*." Rather, the tax is on the "privilege of making retail sales of tangible personal property." The tax is owed regardless of the motivation of the sale; the sale of a Bible by a religious organization is treated like the sale of a Bible by a bookstore. Consequently, the Court saw "no danger" that religious activity was being "singled out for special and burdensome treatment." Similarly, because no fee was charged for registering as a seller, the Court did not see that requirement as a precondition for the exercise of evangelistic activity. The Court recognized that the Ministries incurred some economic cost, but the tax is "no different" from other "generally applicable laws and regulations" such as health and safety regulations to which the Ministries must adhere. Justice O'Connor did indicate that a "more onerous tax rate, even if generally applicable, might effectively choke off an adherent's religious practices." She said, however, that "we face no such situation in this case," and the tax as imposed by California simply did not create a "constitutionally significant burden." The Establishment Clause challenge focused on whether administration of the tax produced an unacceptable degree of entanglement between government and religion. The Court ruled that the administration and record-keeping burdens involved in collection and payment of the California tax did not "rise to a constitutionally significant level." The contact required only "routine regulatory interaction," a level that was not seen as violating the nonentanglement command. Imposition of the tax, said O'Connor, did not "require the State to inquire into the religious content of the items sold or the religious motivation for selling or purchasing the items, because the materials are subject to the tax regardless of content or motive." From California's standpoint, the central question is not whether the materials are religious, "but whether there is a sale or a use, a question which involves only a secular determination."

Federal Building Grants

Tilton v. Richardson, **403 U.S. 672, 91 S. Ct. 2091, 29 L. Ed. 2d 790 (1971)** Allowed use of federal construction monies for projects at church-affiliated institutions of higher education. *Tilton* upheld in a 5–4 decision Title I of the Higher Education Facilities Act of 1963. The act provided construction grants to church-related colleges and universities for buildings and facilities "used exclusively for secular educational purposes." It also prohibited use of funds for any project that may be used for "sectarian instruction, religious worship, or the programs of a divinity school." Applicants for funds must "provide assurances that these restrictions will be respected," and enforcement was to be accomplished by government on-site inspections. The act had a provision through which the government would retain a 20-year interest in the financed facilities, enabling the government to recover at least a portion of the grant if the facility were to be used for other than secular purposes. The Court, through Chief Justice Burger, found the act to have a "legitimate secular objective entirely appropriate for government action" without having the effect of advancing religion. The 20-year limit on governmental interest in preserving the exclusively secular character of building uses was voided, however. The Court found it "cannot be assumed that a substantial structure has no value after that period and hence the unrestricted use of a valuable property is in effect a contribution of some value to a religious body." Key to upholding the act otherwise was the Court's

opinion that "excessive entanglement did not characterize the relationship between government and church under the Act." The Court
cited three factors that diminished the extent and the potential danger of the entanglement. First, institutions of higher learning are
significantly different from elementary and secondary schools. Since
"religious indoctrination is not a substantial purpose or activity of
these church-related colleges and universities, there is less likelihood
than in primary or secondary schools that religion will permeate the
area of secular education." Second, the aid provided through the
building grants is of a "non-ideological character." The need to monitor buildings would be less than monitoring teachers, for example.
Third, entanglement is lessened because the aid comes in the form of
a "one-time, single purpose construction grant." There are "no continuing financial relationships or dependencies." The inspections that
do occur to monitor use of funds create only minimal contact. These
factors also substantially lessen the potential for diverse religious fragmentation in the political arena. Justices Douglas, Black, Brennan,
and Marshall dissented. They argued excessive entanglement and the
insufficiency of the restrictions cited in the act. The dissenters pointed
out that even if the specific buildings funded under the grant were
used only for secular purposes, religious institutions were aided by
being able to use for religious purposes monies freed by the receipt of
the federal grant. *See also* CPEARL *v.* NYQUIST (413 U.S. 756: 1973), p.
94; FIRST AMENDMENT, p. 77; LEMON *v.* KURTZMAN (403 U.S. 602:
1971), p. 92; WALZ *v.* NEW YORK CITY TAX COMMISSION (397 U.S. 664:
1970), p. 80; WOLMAN *v.* WALTER (433 U.S. 406: 1977), p. 96.

Significance   *Tilton v. Richardson* (403 U.S. 672: 1971) had substantial impact on Establishment Clause standards in two ways. First, the
entanglement criterion introduced the year before in *Walz v. New York
City Tax Commission* (397 U.S. 664: 1970) was decisive in *Tilton*. It
marked the first application of the standard in a school aid case.
Second, Chief Justice Burger developed the distinction between
higher education and the elementary-secondary levels of education as
a key element in determining the degree to which entanglement existed. Combined with the bricks-and-mortar character of the aid, excessive entanglement was not found in *Tilton*. The Court expanded
this view in subsequent cases. In *Hunt v. McNair* (413 U.S. 734: 1973),
for example, the Court upheld a state financing arrangement that
involved making proceeds from the sale of revenue bonds available to
finance building projects at institutions of higher education, including
nonpublic colleges and universities. The monitoring required during
the payback period of the program was more extensive than in *Tilton*,
but not excessive. Similarly, the Court upheld a broad, noncategorical

grant program for private colleges, including religiously affiliated institutions, in *Roemer v. Board of Public Works of Maryland* (426 U.S. 736: 1976). The Court said the Establishment Clause requires "scrupulous neutrality by the State" but not a "hermetic separation." Although the grants were made annually, the need for close surveillance of purportedly secular activities in *Roemer* was limited enough that it did not constitute excessive entanglement.

Title VII of the Civil Rights Act of 1964 prohibits employment discrimination, but contains an exemption for religious organizations. This exemption was challenged on Establishment Clause grounds if applied to secular activities in *Church of Jesus Christ of Latter-Day Saints v. Amos* (483 U.S. 327: 1987). Amos had been discharged from his job at a church-owned facility that was open to the public and that served no religious purpose. He argued that the church should not be able to discriminate on religious grounds in employment practices for nonreligious jobs. The Court unanimously ruled, however, that the exemption did not violate the Establishment Clause. The Court said that the secular purpose test does not mean the law's purpose "must be unrelated to religion." The purpose requirement is aimed at preventing government from abandoning neutrality and acting to promote a particular point of view on religious matters. It is a permissible legislative purpose to "alleviate significant government interference with the ability of religious organizations to define and carry out their religious missions." Neither did the Court find that the exemption advanced religion. A law is not unconstitutional "simply because it allows churches to advance religion." For a law to have forbidden effects, it is necessary for the government itself to "advance religion through its own activities and influence." Here the advancement was attributable to the church and not to the government. Finally, because the exemption effectuated a more complete separation of church and state, it minimized rather than fostered an entanglement of church and state. The Rehnquist Court responded to the challenge of another federal initiative in *Bowen v. Kendrick* (487 U.S. 589: 1988). Congress passed the Adolescent Family Life Act in 1981 in response to the "severe adverse health, social and economic consequences" that frequently come after pregnancy and childbirth among unwed adolescents. The act authorized federal grants to public or nonprofit private organizations for "services and research in the area of premarital adolescent sexual relations and pregnancy." Recipients of grants were required to provide certain services, such as counseling and education, relating to family life. Various individuals and organizations challenged the program on Establishment Clause grounds because funding under the act had gone to religious institutions whose counsel included abstention from sexual relations and rejection of abortion as an option for pregnant women. The Court ruled that the act was not defective on its face, but found that some grants had been used to support religion and remanded the case for determination of how extensive violations might be and how to remedy any violations. The act was aimed at the legitimate and secular objective of "eliminating or reducing social and economic problems caused by teenage sexuality, pregnancy and parenthood." The increased role for religious agencies was viewed as part of a more general attempt to enlist various private sector organizations and reflected the "entirely appropriate aim of increasing broad-based community involvement" to deal with the problem. The act did not require that grantees have religious affiliation, and, in the Court's view, the services provided were "not religious in character." While the approach chosen to deal with adolescent sexuality and pregnancy may "coincide" with those of religious denominations, the approach was not "inherently religious." Once Congress determined that development of close family ties would help prevent adolescent sexual activity, it was "sensible" for Congress to recognize that religious organizations could "influence family life." On its face, nothing in the act suggested to the Court that it was "anything but neutral" with respect to a grantee's status as secular or sectarian. The possibility that grants may go to "pervasively sectarian" organizations was not sufficient to preclude grants to all religious organizations. Finally, the Court concluded that while monitoring of grants was necessary to make sure that funds were spent as Congress intended, no "excessive entanglement" of government and religious institutions was required under the act.

Antievolution Law

***Edwards v. Aguillard*, 482 U.S. 578, 107 S. Ct. 2573, 96 L. Ed. 2d 510 (1987)**   Struck down a state "creation science" law. The Louisiana Legislature enacted the Balanced Treatment for Creation-Science and Evolution-Science in Public School Instruction Act, which prohibited the teaching of the theory of evolution in public schools unless accompanied by instruction in the theory of creation science. No school was required to teach evolution or creation science, but if either theory was taught, the other must be taught as well. The stated purpose of the law was to protect academic freedom. The Court found the law "facially invalid" in *Edwards v. Aguillard* in a 7–2 decision. The opinion of the Court was delivered by Justice Brennan, who first outlined the general parameters of the Court's inquiry. Determination of whether challenged legislation comports with the Establishment Clause is based on the three-prong test first defined in

Lemon v. Kurtzman (403 U.S. 602: 1971). Under this standard, the legislature must have adapted the law for a secular purpose, the law's principal or primary effect may neither advance nor inhibit religion, and the law must not produce an excessive entanglement of church and state. Brennan observed that the Court has been particularly vigilant in monitoring the Establishment Clause in elementary and secondary schools. "Families," he said, "entrust public schools with the education of their children, but condition their trust on the understanding that the classroom will not purposely be used to advance religious views." This vigilance is necessary because students at these levels are impressionable, and because their attendance is involuntary. The Court concluded that the Creationism Act failed the secular purpose test. While noting that the stated purpose of the law was the protection of academic freedom, the Court said it was clear from the legislative history of the law and comments from the law's sponsor that the act was not designed to further that goal. Under the act, teachers "once free to teach any and all facets of this subject are now unable to do so." In addition, the act failed to ensure instruction in creation science. Rather than protecting academic freedom, the Court concluded that the act had the "distinctly different purpose of discrediting evolution by counter-balancing its teaching at every turn with the teaching of creation science." Brennan said the Court "need not be blind to the legislature's preeminent religious purpose," which was "to advance the religious viewpoint that a supernatural being created humankind." The act's legislative history documented the fact that the proposed change in the science curriculum was done in order to "provide persuasive advantage to a particular religious doctrine that rejects the factual basis of evolution in its entirety." As a result, the Court concluded that the primary purpose of the act was to endorse particular religious doctrine through the use of symbolic and financial support of government and therefore violated the Establishment Clause. Justice Scalia, joined by Chief Justice Rehnquist, disagreed, maintaining that a secular purpose existed for the act. Scalia saw "abundant evidence" of the sincerity of the stated secular purpose. He was highly critical of the majority, saying that the constitutionality of the law "cannot rightly be disposed of on the gallop, by impugning the motives of its supporters." *See also* EPPERSON *v.* ARKANSAS (393 U.S. 97: 1968), p. 86; LEMON *v.* KURTZMAN (403 U.S. 602: 1971), p. 92.

Significance　　The decision in *Edwards v. Aguillard* (482 U.S. 578: 1987) reflects the strict separation stance taken since the early 1960s in this kind of establishment case. In *Epperson v. Arkansas* (393 U.S. 97: 1968), a case very similar to *Aguillard,* the Warren Court struck down a prohibition on the teaching of evolution in public schools because the legislation embraced a particular religious doctrine. More than a decade later the Burger Court, in *Stone v. Graham* (449 U.S. 39: 1980), invalidated a state law requiring the posting of the Ten Commandments in every public school classroom. Calling the secular purpose disclaimer attached to all posted copies "self-serving," the Court said the preeminent purpose for posting the Ten Commandments was "plainly religious in nature." The rationale developed in both *Epperson* and *Stone* served as the basis of Justice Brennan's opinion in *Aguillard*. Finally, just two years before *Aguillard*, in *Wallace v. Jaffree* (472 U.S. 38: 1985), the Court struck down the moment of silence law that authorized time for meditation or voluntary prayer in public schools. Each of these decisions focused on the secular purpose element of the three-pronged test from *Lemon*. They make it apparent that states will find it difficult to gain the Court's approval for initiatives that intend to put religious exercises into public school classrooms. A mere statement of secular purpose will not do.

Use of Public Facilities

Widmar v. Vincent, 454 U.S. 263, 102 S. Ct. 269, 70 L. Ed. 2d 440 (1981) Reversed a state university's refusal to grant a student religious organization access to university facilities. *Widmar* provided the Supreme Court an opportunity to examine a limitation on religious speech imposed in the name of the Establishment Clause. The limitation came in the form of a state university denying use of its facilities to a group wishing to use those facilities for religious worship and religious discussion. The university made its facilities generally available to registered student organizations and had previously permitted the respondent group to use university facilities. The Supreme Court, with only Justice White dissenting, held that the denial of access was unjustified. The Court found the university had "discriminated against the student groups and speakers based on their desire to use a generally open forum to engage in religious worship and discussion." Such a discriminatory and content-based exclusion requires that a state demonstrate a compelling interest for the restriction that is advanced by "narrowly drawn regulation." The compelling interest claimed by the university was maintenance of "strict separation of church and state." The Court allowed that "the interest of the university in complying with its constitutional obligations may be characterized as compelling." Nonetheless, it may not follow that "an 'equal access' policy would be compatible with this Court's Establishment Clause cases." While religious groups may benefit from use of university facilities, "enjoyment of merely 'incidental' benefits does not violate the prohibition against the 'primary advancement' of religion." That the benefits would be incidental was based on the Court's view that "an open forum does not confer any imprimatur of state approval on religious sects or practices." Furthermore, the facilities were available to a "broad class of non-religious as well as religious speakers." The provision of benefits to "so broad a spectrum of groups is an important index of secular effect." Finally, the Court noted that the two religion clauses exist in tension with each other, with Establishment Clause provisions "limited by the Free Exercise Clause and in this case by the Free Speech Clause as well." *See also* BILL OF RIGHTS, p. 7; ESTABLISHMENT CLAUSE, p. 80.

Significance   *Widmar v. Vincent* (454 U.S. 263: 1981) resolves the ambiguity between First Amendment expression and First Amendment establishment interests in favor of the former. While a state university must avoid any activity that would have the effect of advancing religion, the Establishment Clause does not provide a compelling enough interest to allow singling religion out for exclusion from access to university facilities. The content-based limitation on expression is particularly suspect. As the Court held in *Carey v. Brown* (445 U.S. 914: 1980), a case involving selective regulation of labor picketing, "government may not grant the use of a forum to people whose views it finds acceptable, but deny use to those wishing to express less favored or more controversial views." Content discrimination was the central factor here, too. The Court concluded that "selective exclusions from a public forum may not be based on content alone, and may not be justified by reference to content alone." Nevertheless, a state may be able to justify time, place, and manner restrictions on expression so long as they are not selective. In *Heffron v. International Society for Krishna Consciousness, Inc.* (449 U.S. 1109: 1981), the Court upheld a state fair regulation that required the sale, exhibition, or distribution of printed material only from assigned locations. The Court found the regulation reasonable and applicable to all groups, not merely religious organizations.

The Equal Access Act of 1984 requires public secondary schools receiving federal educational funds to allow political or religious student groups to meet on school premises provided other noncurriculum-related groups do so. Under the act, a school need not permit any student group to use facilities for any reason beyond those related to the curriculum. If at least one group unrelated to the school curriculum has access, however, the school becomes a "limited open forum," and religious or political groups must be afforded access to facilities as well. The Court upheld the act against Establishment

Clause challenge in *Board of Education of the Westside Community Schools v. Mergens* (110 L. Ed. 2d 191: 1990). The Court first determined that the school district allowed noncurriculum-related groups to meet. The school district had a formal policy recognizing that student clubs are a "vital part of the education program." About 30 student clubs met on a voluntary basis on school premises at the time Mergens sought access for a Christian Bible club. As a result, the act's equal-access "obligations" were "triggered." The question then became whether the act violated the Establishment Clause. It was argued that if a school district permitted religious groups access to school facilities, it would constitute an official recognition or endorsement of religion. The Court disagreed. The Court applied the three-pronged *Lemon* test and extended "the logic of *Widmar*" to the high school setting. Congress's reason for enacting the law was to "prevent discrimination against religious and other types of speech." Such a purpose, said Justice O'Connor, "is undeniably secular." Neither did access to facilities advance religion. There is a "crucial difference between *government* speech endorsing religion, . . . and *private* speech endorsing religion." The Court concluded that high school students were "mature enough and likely to understand that a school does not endorse religion or support student speech that it merely permits on a nondiscriminatory basis." The proposition, O'Connor continued, that "schools do not endorse everything they fail to censor is not complicated." Indeed, Congress specifically rejected the contention that high school students are "likely to confuse an equal access policy with state sponsorship of religion." Furthermore, the act limits participation of school officials at meetings of student religious organizations and requires that meetings occur during noninstructional time. As a result, the act "avoids the problems of 'the students' emulation of teachers as role models' and 'mandatory attendance requirements.'" The Court acknowledged that the possibility of student peer pressure remained. The Court concluded, however, that a school can "make clear" that permitting a religious club to use facilities is not an endorsement of the club members' views. To the extent it does so, students will "reasonably understand that the school's official recognition of the club evinces neutrality toward, rather than endorsement of, religious speech." In addition, the district recognized a "broad spectrum" of organizations and invited the organization of more clubs. This "counteract[s] any possible message of official endorsement of or a preference for religion or a particular belief." Lastly, the Court found little risk of "excessive entanglement" in this situation. Although the act permits assignment of a school staff member to meetings for "custodial purposes," such oversight of a student-initiated religious group is "merely to ensure order and good behavior." This does not "impermissibly entangle government in the day-to-day surveillance or administration of religious activities."

Religious Displays

Allegheny County v. American Civil Liberties Union, **109 S. Ct. 3086, 106 L. Ed. 2d 472 (1989)** Considered the question of religious displays on public property. The case actually involved two displays. The first was a crèche, a depiction of the Christian nativity scene, on the main inside staircase of the Allegheny County Courthouse. With the crèche was a banner saying "Glory to God in the Highest." The crèche was donated by a Roman Catholic group, a fact indicated on a sign attached to the display. The second display was an 18-foot Hanukkah menorah placed next to a Christmas tree and a sign saluting liberty on the steps of the Pittsburgh City Hall. The menorah was owned by a Jewish group, but was stored and placed on display by the city. The ACLU and several local residents sought to enjoin both displays permanently on Establishment Clause grounds. In a 5–4 decision, the Court ruled that the crèche impermissibly advanced religion, but by a 6–3 vote allowed display of the menorah. On the crèche, Justice Blackmun wrote on behalf of Justices Brennan, Marshall, Stevens, and O'Connor. He began by saying that the "essential principle" of the Establishment prohibition is that government does not "take a position on questions of religious belief." Government's use of symbolism becomes unconstitutional if it "has the effect of endorsing religious beliefs." The effect of the government's use of symbolism, Blackmun continued, "depends upon its context." In ruling on the crèche and the menorah display, the task of the Court is to determine whether, in their "particular physical settings," either has the effect of "endorsing or disapproving religious beliefs." The crèche used "words as well as the picture of the nativity scene, to make its religious meaning unmistakably clear." There is nothing in the context of the courthouse display that "detracts from the crèche's religious message." Allegheny County, said Blackmun, sent an "unmistakable message that it supports and promotes the Christian praise to God that is the crèche's religious message." While government may celebrate Christmas "in some manner," it may not do so in a way that "endorses Christian doctrine." Allegheny County "transgressed that line" in this instance. Justice Kennedy issued a dissent on the crèche decision. His dissent was joined by Chief Justice Rehnquist and by Justices White and Scalia. Kennedy viewed the striking down of the crèche as reflecting "unjustified hostility toward religion." He saw the crèche and the menorah display as comparable and equally permissible. The dissenting justices charged the majority with creating an orthodoxy of secularism. "Obsessive, implacable resistance to all but the most carefully scripted and secularized forms of accommodation requires this Court to act as a censor, issuing national decrees as to what is orthodox and what is not." Kennedy objected to government being limited to acknowledging only a Christmas "in which references to religion have been held to a minimum." Such a policy "lends assistance to an Orwellian rewriting of history." The menorah display brought a different result and a different alignment of justices. Here the crèche dissenters joined Blackmun and O'Connor and found no Establishment Clause defect. While the menorah is a "religious symbol," its "message is not exclusively religious." Like Christmas, the menorah has "secular dimensions" as well. As a result, the menorah display presents a "closer constitutional question." Again, setting was the key. At the city hall, the menorah stood "next to a Christmas tree and a sign saluting liberty." This display was not an endorsement of religion, but "simply a recognition of cultural diversity." Thus, for Establishment Clause purposes, the city's "overall display" must be seen as conveying a "secular recognition of different traditions for celebrating the winter holiday season." Justices Brennan, Marshall, and Stevens dissented from the part of the decision allowing display of the menorah. They saw no difference in the religious messages sent by the two displays.

Significance   *Allegheny County v. American Civil Liberties Union* (106 L. Ed. 2d 472: 1989) was not the Court's first experience with religious displays. In *Lynch v. Donnelly* (460 U.S. 668: 1984), a municipality had included a crèche in its Christmas celebration display. When the crèche was challenged as a violation of the Establishment Clause, the Court resisted the challenge in a 5–4 decision, saying it had consistently rejected a "rigid, absolutist view" of the clause throughout its history. Furthermore, it was not completely accurate to speak of a wall of separation dividing church and state. "Our society cannot have segments or institutions which exist in a vacuum or in total isolation from all other parts, much less from government." The Court maintained that history shows unbroken acknowledgment of the role of religion in American life, and the crèche merely depicted the historical origins of Christmas. If the crèche benefited religion at all, it was only in an "indirect, remote, and incidental fashion." The Court concluded that the city's motives for including the crèche were secular, that religion was not impermissibly advanced, and that an excessive entanglement of religion and government was not created. *Allegheny County* departed from *Lynch* largely in its emphasis on the display setting and the extent to which religious messages were integrated with the secular.

FREE EXERCISE OF RELIGION
Unemployment Compensation

Sherbert v. Verner, 374 U.S. 398, 83 S. Ct. 1790, 10 L. Ed. 2d 695 (1963)   Held that a state may not disqualify a person from unemployment compensation because the person refuses to work on Saturdays for religious reasons. *Sherbert* said the protection of free exercise interests may produce an exemption from secular regulation based on religion. Sherbert was a Seventh-Day Adventist who was discharged from her job because she would not work on Saturday. Saturday is the Sabbath Day for Adventists. Failing to find other employment because of her "conscientious scruples not to take Saturday work," Sherbert filed for unemployment compensation benefits under provisions of South Carolina law. The law required that any claimant is ineligible for benefits if he or she has failed, without good cause, to accept suitable work when offered. Through appropriate administrative proceedings, Sherbert's unwillingness to work on Saturdays was determined to disqualify her from benefits. The Supreme Court held for Sherbert in a 7–2 decision. The burdens imposed on her in this case were too great. She was forced to choose between "following the precepts of her religion and forfeiting benefits" and "abandoning one of the precepts of her religion in order to accept work." Facing such a choice "puts the same kind of burden upon the free exercise of religion as would a fine imposed against appellant for her Sunday worship." The Court failed to find that protection of the unemployment compensation fund from fraudulent claims by unscrupulous claimants feigning religious objections to Saturday work was a sufficiently compelling state interest. Even if the fund were threatened by spurious claims, South Carolina would need to demonstrate that no alternative forms of regulation would combat such abuses. In requiring the religion-based exemption for Sherbert, the Court imposed a requirement of possible differential treatment for those seeking unemployment benefits for refusal to work on Saturdays. The Court suggested, however, that such classification was not establishment of religion. The decision "reflects nothing more than the governmental obligation of neutrality in the face of religious differences." The holding requires only that "South Carolina may not constitutionally apply the eligibility provisions so as to constrain a worker to abandon his religious convictions." Justices Harlan and White dissented on the ground that the decision required an exemption based on religion. The decision requires South Carolina to "single out for financial assistance those whose behavior is religiously motivated, even though it denies such assistance to others whose identical behavior (in this case, inability to work on Saturdays) is not religiously motivated." *See also* GILLETTE v. UNITED STATES (401 U.S. 437: 1971), p. 105; SUNDAY CLOSING LAW CASES (366 U.S. 421: 1961), p. 101; WISCONSIN v. YODER (406 U.S. 205: 1971), p. 106.

Significance   Sherbert v. Verner (374 U.S. 398: 1963) was something of a replay of the free exercise issues seen in the *Sunday Closing Law Cases* (366 U.S. 421: 1961). Sherbert was subjected to economic hardship, like the merchants in the *Sunday Closing Cases*, but the burden in the *Sunday Closing Cases* was indirect. In *Sherbert* the Court found the burden to be impermissibly heavy. Even incidental burdens could be justified only by demonstrating a compelling state interest. The compelling interest standard is far more demanding than merely showing secular purpose. Coupled with the alternate means requirement carried over from the *Sunday Closing Cases, Sherbert* substantially expanded the protection afforded by the Free Exercise Clause. At the same time, the broadened protection for free exercise produces serious establishment problems. They can be seen clearly in *Thomas v. Review Board of the Indiana Employment Security Division* (450 U.S. 707: 1981). Thomas was denied unemployment compensation after voluntarily quitting his job for religious reasons. The Court held the denial of benefits to be a violation of Thomas's free exercise rights. Only Justice Rehnquist dissented. The Court was even more emphatic than in *Sherbert,* saying, "Where the state conditions receipt of an important benefit upon conduct proscribed by religious faith, or where it denies such a benefit because of conduct mandated by religious belief," a believer is unduly pressured and a burden upon religion exists. While the compulsion may be indirect, the infringement upon free exercise is nonetheless substantial. Justice Rehnquist was wholly dissatisfied with the Court's preferential treatment of Thomas. He noted the Establishment Clause would preclude Indiana from legislating an unemployment compensation law with the exemption stipulated by the Court. He argued that the balance had now tipped too heavily in favor of free exercise protection. *Thomas* "reads the Free Exercise Clause too broadly and it fails to squarely acknowledge that such a reading conflicts with our Establishment Clause cases." As such, the decision simply "exacerbates the tension" between the two clauses. The Court took a step back from *Thomas* and *Sherbert* in *Estate of Thornton v. Caldor, Inc.* (472 U.S. 703: 1985), invalidating a state law that gave an employee the absolute right to refuse to work on his or her sabbath. The Court said the statute failed the primary effect test of *Lemon v. Kurtzman* (403 U.S. 602: 1971) in that it required religious concerns automatically to control all secular interests in the workplace.

The Court soon returned to the *Thomas* position in *Hobbie v. Unemployment Appeals Commission of Florida* (480 U.S. 136: 1987). Hobbie had been employed some two and one-half years before undergoing the religious conversion that produced the employment conflict. Florida attempted to distinguish Hobbie's situation from *Sherbert* and *Thomas* by arguing that she was the agent of change herself and was responsible for the consequences of the conflict between her job and her religious beliefs, since her conversion came subsequent to her employment. The Court rejected this position by saying that Florida had asked the Court "to single out the religious convert for different, less favorable treatment than that given an individual whose adherence to his or her faith precedes employment." The timing of Hobbie's conversion was characterized as immaterial to the issue of free exercise burden. Justice Brennan said for the majority that the First Amendment protects the free exercise rights of those who "adopt religious beliefs or convert from one faith to another after they are hired." All three cases, the Court concluded, presented a situation in which the employee was forced to choose between fidelity to religious belief and continued employment. The forfeiture of benefits for choosing fidelity brings "unlawful coercion to bear on the employee's choice." Up through *Hobbie,* in all the cases involving denial of unemployment compensation benefits to persons who have refused to work because of religious beliefs, the claimants had been members of established religious sects. In *Frazee v. Department of Employment Security* (103 L. Ed. 2d 914: 1989), the Court considered the case of a claimant who was not such a member. Neither did the claimant's refusal to work rest on a tenet or teaching of an established religious body. The Court ruled that none of the previous decisions required formal membership in an established sect. Neither had prior cases required a tenet of faith that specifically "forbade the work the claimants refused to perform." Rather, said the Court, the previous cases "rested on the fact that each of the claimants had a sincere belief that religion required him or her to refrain from the work in question." Membership in an organized religious organization, especially one with a specific teaching forbidding Sunday work, "undoubtedly" would "simplify the problem of identifying sincerely held religious beliefs," but the Court rejected the notion that to claim free exercise protection "one must be responding to the commands of a particular religious organization." In a related unemployment compensation matter, the Court ruled in *Oregon Employment Division v. Smith* (108 L. Ed. 2d 876: 1990) that a state could withhold benefits from employees terminated from their jobs for use of peyote, a controlled hallucinogen. The state had refused to pay benefits because use of peyote was a crime in the state, and termination for its use made an employee ineligible for benefits. The employees in this case had used the peyote in the rituals of the Native American Church and sought religious exemption. The Court ruled that while the state legislature could have established such an exemption, the Free Exercise Clause did not require it. "We have never held," said Justice Scalia for the majority, "that an individual's religious beliefs excuse him from compliance with an otherwise valid law prohibiting conduct that the State is free to regulate." Release from employment obligations on religious holidays also create problems, as seen in *Ansonia Board of Education v. Philbrook* (479 U.S. 60: 1986). Philbrook, a schoolteacher, was required to miss approximately six school days a year for religious reasons. Collective bargaining agreement provisions allowing leave for religious observances covered three of these days. Philbrook offered several suggestions, including use of his personal business days, to resolve the problem, but the school district rejected them all. As a result, Philbrook was forced either to take unauthorized leave without pay or to schedule hospital visits on religious days to allow full observance of what he considered to be his religious obligations. Failing resolution of the issue administratively, Philbrook brought suit, citing provisions of Title VII of the Civil Rights Act of 1964. Language in Title VII requires employers to "reasonably accommodate" an employee's religious practices. The issue before the Court in this case was whether the employer had met its obligation to adjust the employee's work schedule in light of his beliefs. The Court held that Title VII did not require an employer to choose any particular reasonable accommodation. Where both employer and employee extend reasonable solutions, Title VII does not force an employer to accept any further proposals from the employee. Since Philbrook could fully observe his religious days, albeit by taking unpaid leave or by other means he did not prefer, the Court concluded that the school district had satisfied the reasonable accommodation requirement. Finally, the Court considered the extent to which the Equal Protection Clause can be used to protect Indian religious grounds in *Lyng v. Northwest Indian Cemetery Protective Association* (485 U.S. 360: 1988). The U.S. Forest Service wished to complete a road by building a connecting segment through a national forest. The area through which the road was to be built had historically been used by members of several Indian tribes for a number of religious rituals. A study commissioned by the Forest Service indicated that building a road in the proposed location would cause "serious and irreparable" harm to the privacy of the area. The Forest Service decided to proceed with the project nonetheless, although a route was eventually selected that avoided archaeological sites and passed as far away as possible from the sites used for spiritual activities by the Indians. The Forest Service also adopted a plan allowing for the harvesting of timber in the area, with protective zones established in the areas immediately around the religious sites. A permanent injunction was obtained on First Amendment grounds against both the road construction and the timber harvesting. The Supreme Court reversed the lower federal courts in a 5–3 decision. The Court said that the Free Exercise Clause "simply cannot be understood to require the Government to conduct its own internal affairs in ways that comport with the religious beliefs of particular citizens." The government may not insist that the Indians "engage in any set form of religious observance." Similarly, the Indians may not demand that the government "join in their chosen religious practices." The Free Exercise Clause protects persons from "certain forms of governmental compulsion." It does not afford an individual the right to "dictate the conduct of the Government's internal procedures."

FREE SPEECH

Symbolic Speech

Texas v. Johnson, **109 S. Ct. 2533, 105 L. Ed. 2d 342: (1989)** Upheld the right of persons to express their political views through the burning of the American flag. Johnson was part of a group that gathered in Dallas to demonstrate at the 1984 Republican National Convention. The group marched through downtown Dallas to the city hall, where Johnson set fire to the flag. He was arrested and subsequently convicted for violation of a Texas law prohibiting flag desecration. The Supreme Court voted 5–4 to strike down the law. Reagan appointees Justices Scalia and Kennedy joined Brennan, Marshall, and Blackmun in the majority, with Justice Brennan speaking for the majority. Texas claimed two interests in support of its conviction of Johnson: preservation of the flag as a "symbol of national unity," and deterring breaches of the peace. The latter was dismissed as an interest "not implicated" in this case. Brennan pointed to prior decisions "recognizing the communicative nature of conduct relating to flags." He said that while government generally has a "freer hand in restricting expressive conduct" than the written or spoken word, it may not "proscribe particular conduct because it has expressive elements." Preservation of the flag as a symbol, on the other hand, relates to "suppression of expression." If there is a "bedrock principle underlying the First Amendment," said Brennan, it is that government may not "prohibit expression of an idea simply because society finds the idea itself offensive or disagreeable." Prior cases have not recognized an exception where the flag is involved, nor have they allowed government to "insure that a symbol be used to express only one view of that symbol or its referents." To allow government to "designate symbols to be used to communicate only a limited set of messages would be to enter territory having no discernible or defensible boundaries." The case presented a problem of line drawing. The question, said Brennan, is how the Court should determine which symbols are "sufficiently special" to qualify for this "unique status." Judges would be forced, he said, to consult their own "political preferences, and impose them on the citizenry, in the very way the First Amendment forbids us to do." The First Amendment does not so protect other "sacred concepts" from "going unquestioned in the marketplace of ideas." "We decline . . . to create for the flag an exception to the joust of principles protected by the First Amendment." Brennan concluded by saying that the decision strengthens the flag's "deservedly cherished place in our community." The decision, he said, reflects the conviction that "our toleration of criticisms such as Johnson's is a sign and source of our strength." The way, he said, to "preserve the flag's special role" is not to punish those who "feel differently about these matters." Rather, it is to "persuade them that they are wrong." We do not "consecrate the flag by punishing its desecration, for in doing so we dilute the freedom that this cherished emblem represents." The dissenters argued the unique position of the flag "as the symbol of our nation." A uniqueness, said Chief Justice Rehnquist, that warrants a "governmental prohibition against flag burning." Justice Stevens referred to the "intangible dimension" of this case that makes use of established symbolic expression rules "inapplicable." The flag, he said, is a symbol of more than "nationhood and national unity." In addition, it signifies "ideas that characterize the society . . . as well as the special history that has animated the growth and power of those ideas." The symbolic value of the flag, therefore, "cannot be measured." Nonetheless, Stevens continued, the government has a significant and legitimate interest in "preserving that value." Occasionally, restrictions must prevail over expression interests. Creating a right to post "bulletin boards and graffiti" on the Washington Monument might "enlarge the market for free expression, but at a cost I would not pay." Similarly, Stevens concluded, "sanctioning the public desecration of the flag will tarnish its value." That tarnish is not justified by the "trivial burden on free expression occasioned by requiring an available, alternative mode of expression—including words critical of the flag—be employed." *See also* TINKER *v.* DES MOINES SCHOOL DISTRICT (393 U.S. 503: 1969), p. 113.

Significance   *Texas v. Johnson* (105 L. Ed. 2d 342: 1989) was among the more controversial decisions in recent years. *Johnson* was not the first case involving flags. It has long been recognized that flags have symbolic value in expression. In 1931 the Court struck down a state law in *Stromberg v. California* (283 U.S. 359) that outlawed the display of a red flag because it symbolized "opposition to organized government." The Court felt that if such symbolic expression as this could be restricted, more general political debate would be seriously jeopardized. The Court has also had occasion to review similar cases involving symbolic use of the American flag. While it has recognized the government's authority to punish certain improper conduct regarding the flag, the Court has generally permitted the symbolic uses. *Street v. New York* (394 U.S. 576: 1969), for example, struck down a state law prohibiting flag mutilation. This case involved a flag burning, but the Court focused on the overbroad character of the restriction. In *Smith v. Goguen* (415 U.S. 566: 1974), the Court reversed a conviction for the "contemptuous" conduct of a person who had sewn a small flag to the seat of his pants. That same year, the Court ruled in *Spence v. Washington* (418 U.S. 405) that superimposing a peace symbol on the flag and flying it upside down was protected. These decisions notwithstanding, symbolic expression is subject to regulation. The line is drawn by examining the action or conduct through which the message is conveyed. As the Warren Court said in *United States v. O'Brien* (391 U.S. 367: 1968), "We cannot accept the view that an apparently limitless variety of conduct can be labeled 'speech' whenever the person engaging in the conduct intends thereby to express an idea." Following the Court's decision in *Texas v. Johnson* (105 L. Ed. 2d 342: 1989), Congress enacted the Flag Protection Act of 1989, which made it a crime to "knowingly mutilate, deface, physically defile, burn, maintain on the floor or ground, or trample upon any flag of the United States." Upon passage of the federal law, flags were burned in a number of political demonstrations. *United States v. Eichman* and *United States v. Haggerty* (110 L. Ed. 2d 287: 1990) arose out of prosecution for flag-burning incidents in Seattle and Washington, D.C., respectively. The cases were combined for review by the Supreme Court. The Court held that the federal law, like the state law in *Johnson,* violated the free speech protection of the First Amendment. Justice Brennan spoke for the same five-justice majority found in the Texas case, and his opinion was a substantial reiteration of the *Johnson* rationale. While conceding that flag burning is "expressive conduct," the government sought to have the Court declare flag burning a kind of expression that falls outside the full protection of the First Amendment. This, said Brennan, "we decline to do." In drafting the federal law, an effort had been made to avoid regulating conduct based on the content of the expressive message. This was the key defect in the Texas law. Brennan said that while the Flag Protection Act "contains no explicit content-based limitation on the scope of prohibited conduct, it is nevertheless clear that the Government's asserted interest is related to the suppression of free expression, and is concerned with the content of such expression." The government's interest in "protecting the physical integrity of a privately owned flag" is based on the "perceived need to preserve the flag's status as a symbol of our nation and certain national ideals." The destruction of a flag, by itself, however, does not "diminish or otherwise affect the symbol." Rather, the government's desire to "preserve the flag as a symbol for certain national ideals is implicated only when a person's treatment of the flag communicates a message to others that is inconsistent with those ideals." The "precise language" of the act "confirms" Congress's intent in the "communicative impact of flag destruction." Each of the terms chosen to define the criminal conduct "unmistakably connotes disrespectful treatment of the flag and suggests a focus on those acts likely to damage the flag's symbolic value." Allowing the government to prohibit flag burning when it endangers the flag's symbolic role would permit the state to "prescribe what shall be orthodoxy by saying that one may burn the flag to convey one's attitude toward it . . . only if one does not endanger the flag's representation of nationhood and national unity." While Congress sought to cast the federal law in "broader terms" than the Texas law in *Johnson*, the Flag Protection Act "still suffers from the same fundamental flaw: it suppresses expression out of concern for its likely communicative impact." Finally, Justice Brennan said the Court declines the invitation to "reassess" the earlier ruling "in light of Congress's recent recognition of a purported 'national consensus' favoring a prohibition on flag-burning." Even presuming such a consensus exists, "any suggestion that the Government's interest in suppressing speech becomes more weighty as popular opposition to that speech grows is foreign to the First Amendment." Justice Stevens said for the dissenters that the government should be able to protect the symbolic value of the flag "without regard to the specific content of the flag burners' speech." Following the Court's ruling in *Haggerty* and *Eichman,* the Congress considered a constitutional amendment that would have permitted prosecution of flag burning, notwithstanding First Amendment protection of symbolic expression. The proposed amendment was defeated in the House of Representatives on June 21, 1990. Renewal of efforts to elevate the flag to constitutionally protected status will be a function of congressional election politics.

Offensive Speech

Cohen v. California, **403 U.S. 15, 91 S. Ct. 1780, 29 L. Ed. 2d 284 (1971)** Held that offensive expression is entitled to First Amendment protection. Cohen was arrested in the Los Angeles County Courthouse for wearing a jacket upon which were emblazoned the words "Fuck the Draft." At his trial Cohen testified the jacket was his means of stating his intensely held feelings about the draft and American involvement in Vietnam. Cohen was convicted of violating a statute prohibiting "malicious and willful disturbing of the peace" by conduct that is "offensive." The Supreme Court invalidated the statute in a 5–4 decision. The Court ruled that the words, rather than the conduct, were the issue. It was "speech" that was being prohibited by the statute. Moreover, the majority held that the California law was vague, the words were not personally directed at anyone, and a state cannot excise epithets as offensive by functioning as a guardian of public morality. Justice Harlan, writing for the majority, said the First Amendment is "designed and intended to remove government restraints from the arena of public discussion." A consequence of such freedom "may often appear to be only verbal tumult, discord, and even offensive utterance," but that is the price of freedom. "We cannot lose sight of the fact that, in what otherwise might seem a trifling and annoying instance of individual distasteful abuse of a privilege, fundamental societal values are truly implicated." Further, the majority was troubled by the "inherently boundless" nature of what California was attempting through the statute. "Surely the State has no right to cleanse the public debate to the point where it is grammatically palatable to the most squeamish among us." Finally, Justice Harlan pointed out that language serves a dual communicative function. It conveys not only ideas capable of relatively precise and detailed explication, but otherwise inexpressible emotions as well. Words are often chosen as much for their emotive as their cognitive force. He concluded, "We cannot sanction the view that the Constitution, while solicitous of the cognitive content of individual speech, has little or no regard for that emotive function which, practically speaking, may often be the more important element of the overall message sought to be communicated." Chief Justice Burger and Justices Blackmun, Black, and White dissented. They said Cohen's "absurd and immature antic" was essentially regulatable conduct. *See also* BILL OF RIGHTS, p. 7; FIRST AMENDMENT, p. 77; *TINKER v. DES MOINES SCHOOL DISTRICT* (393 U.S. 503: 1969), p. 113.

Significance Cohen v. California (403 U.S. 15: 1971) involved an attempt to punish offensive speech. Such attempts typically take the form of prosecution for breach of the peace. In *Chaplinsky v. New Hampshire* (315 U.S. 568: 1942), the Court held that some speech, notably that which is obscene, libelous, and insulting, is not protected by the First Amendment. It is of such slight value that any benefit derived from it is clearly outweighed by the social interest in order and morality. In *Terminello v. Chicago* (337 U.S. 1: 1949), the Court reversed the breach of the peace conviction of a highly provocative speaker, holding that a municipal ordinance was inappropriately applied to limit speech that "invites dispute." Two years later, however, the Court upheld the disorderly conduct conviction of a street-corner speaker in *Feiner v. New York* (340 U.S. 315: 1951). The Court said that when "clear and present danger of riot, disorder, interference with traffic upon the public street, or other immediate threat to public safety, peace, or order appears, the power of the State to prevent or punish is obvious." The dissenters in *Feiner* argued that the speaker ought to have been protected from the hostile crowd and allowed to speak rather than suffering arrest. A somewhat different kind of offensive expression was examined in *Federal Communications Commission v. Pacifica Foundation* (438 U.S. 726: 1978). Upon receipt of a listener's complaint, the FCC found that a radio station had aired an indecent program. The FCC issued an order to the station threatening subsequent sanction if such broadcasting reoccurred. The Supreme Court upheld the FCC's authority to issue such an order. The case of *Rankin v. McPherson* (483 U.S. 378: 1987) involved the rights of a public employee to engage in "offensive" speech. McPherson, an employee of a county constable, was fired from her job for saying to a coworker following the assassination attempt on President Reagan that "if they go for him again, I hope they get him." The Court ruled that McPherson's remarks should not have caused her to be fired for two reasons. First, her remarks were made in the course of discussion of a matter of public concern. While a threat to kill the president would not be protected expression, McPherson's statement was not itself a threat and could not be criminalized. The inappropriate or controversial character of a remark is irrelevant to the question of whether it deals with a matter of public concern. Debate on such matters must be given "breathing space" to allow discussion to remain "uninhibited, robust, and wide-open." Second, the Court said McPherson's work responsibilities should be part of an examination of the reasons offered for her termination. Though McPherson made her remarks in the workplace, they did not interfere with the functioning of her office. Neither was there any danger that the comment had discredited her office. Further, McPherson's termination was not based on an assessment that her remark demonstrated a character trait that made McPherson unfit to perform her work. In cases such as these, said the Court, attention must focus on the employee's responsibilities within the agency. The burden of caution an employee bears for words he or she utters "will vary with the extent of authority and public accountability the employee's role entails." Here, McPherson did not serve a confidential, policy-making, or public-contact role. As a result, the danger to the successful functioning of the constable's office from McPherson's private speech was minimal.

Overbreadth Doctrine

Village of Schaumburg v. Citizens for a Better Environment, **444 U.S. 620, 100 S. Ct. 826, 63 L. Ed. 2d 73 (1980)**   Struck down a local ordinance using the overbreadth doctrine. In *Village of Schaumburg v. Citizens for a Better Environment,* the Supreme Court examined a local ordinance that prohibited door-to-door solicitations for contributions by organizations not using at least 75 percent of their receipts for charitable purposes. "Charitable purposes" excluded such items as salaries, overhead, solicitation costs, and other administrative expenses. An environmental group was denied permission to solicit because it could not demonstrate compliance with the 75 percent requirement. The organization sued on First Amendment grounds. The Court struck down the ordinance over the single dissent of Justice Rehnquist. The Court's primary objection was the overbreadth of the ordinance. The Court noted that a class of organizations existed to which the 75 percent rule could not constitutionally be applied. These were organizations "whose primary purpose is not to provide money or services to the poor, the needy, or other worthy objects of charity, but to gather and disseminate information about and advocate positions on matters of public concern." The costs of research, advocacy, or public education are typically in excess of 25 percent of the funds raised. The Court felt that to lump all organizations failing to meet the 75 percent standard together imposed a direct and substantial limitation on protected activity. While the village interest in preventing fraud may generally be legitimate, the means to accomplish that end must use more precise measures to separate one kind from the other. *See also* BILL OF RIGHTS, p. 7; FIRST AMENDMENT, p. 77.

Significance   *Village of Schaumburg v. Citizens for a Better Environment* (444 U.S. 620: 1980) is important because it produced a requirement that statutes distinguish sufficiently between lawful and unlawful expression or behavior. In *Coates v. Cincinnati* (402 U.S. 611: 1971), the

Court struck down a city ordinance that prohibited three or more persons from assembling on public sidewalks and conducting themselves in such a way as to "annoy any police officer or other persons who should happen to pass by." The Court found the ordinance "makes a crime out of what under the Constitution cannot be a crime." It was also impermissibly vague. It conveyed no standard of conduct and "men of common intelligence must necessarily guess at its meaning." Although the overbreadth and vagueness doctrines have often been invoked to invalidate enactments as in *Schaumburg* and *Coates,* some ordinances survive such challenges. In *Grayned v. Rockford* (408 U.S. 104: 1972), the Court allowed an antinoise ordinance prohibiting disturbances in the proximity of schools in session. The specific school context separated the restriction from the typically vague and general breach of the peace ordinance. The enactment was seen as a reasonable time, place, and manner restriction. It was narrowly tailored to further Rockford's compelling interest in having undisrupted school sessions and was not impermissibly overbroad. In *Village of Hoffman Estates v. Flipside, Inc.* (456 U.S. 950: 1982), the Court upheld an ordinance requiring a license to sell items designed or marketed for use with illegal drugs against claims that the ordinance was both vague and overbroad. The Court ruled that the ordinance merely sought to regulate the commercial marketing of illegal drug paraphernalia and did not reach noncommercial speech. The only potential limit on Flipside's conveying of information was confined to the commercial activity related to illegal drug use. The Court also found the vagueness claim unpersuasive. The "designed for use" provision of the ordinance covered at least some of the items sold at Flipside. The "marketed for use" language provided ample warning to the retailer about licensure and the display practices that could produce violation of the ordinance. The *Schaumburg* reasoning was later applied to a state limitation on charity fund-raising expenses in *Secretary of State of Maryland v. J. H. Munson Company* (467 U.S. 947: 1984). Maryland had enacted a statute designed to prevent abusive and fraudulent fund-raising by prohibiting a charity from spending more than 25 percent of its gross income for expenses. The Court invalidated the law, saying fund-raising for charities was so intertwined with speech that it required First Amendment protection. The Maryland statute was based on the "fundamentally mistaken premise" that fund-raising costs that exceed 25 percent are fraudulent. In another case closely resembling *Munson,* the Court struck down a state law that regulated the practices of professional fund-raisers. North Carolina enacted a "charitable solicitation" law to regulate activities of professional fund-raisers. The law divided fees charged by fund-raisers into three categories. A fee of up to 20 percent of receipts was deemed "reasonable." A fee between 20 and 35 percent was "unreasonable" if it could be shown that the solicitation did not involve certain activities such as advocacy on a public issue as directed by the recipient of the solicitation proceeds. A fee of greater than 35 percent was presumed "unreasonable" but was rebuttable by the fund-raiser. The law also required fund-raisers to disclose the amounts of money actually turned over to charities during the past 12 months. This information was to be made available to potential donors before the solicitation campaign began. In addition, licensure of all fund-raisers was mandated. A coalition of fund-raisers and charitable organizations successfully challenged the provisions on free speech grounds. The Supreme Court found the provisions unconstitutional in *Riley v. National Federation for the Blind of North Carolina* (487 U.S. 781: 1988). Chief Justice Rehnquist and Justice O'Connor dissented, with Justice Stevens joining them on the licensure issue. The Court first dealt with the three-tiered fee schedule. The Court said that solicitation of contributions for charities is protected speech. The formula for characterizing fees was "not narrowly tailored to the State's interest in preventing fraud." Neither did the Court see maximizing funds to charities or guarantees of reasonable fees charged as sufficiently "motivating interests" to warrant regulation of this kind. The Court characterized as "unsound" the asserted justification that charities' speech must be regulated "for their own benefit." The First Amendment "mandates the presumption that speakers, not the government, know best what they want to say and how to say it." The Court found the disclosure requirement defective as a content-based regulation mandating speech a speaker would not otherwise make. Even if the speech is regarded as commercial in an "abstract sense," it "does not retain its commercial character" when it is "inextricably intertwined" with the "fully protected speech involved in charitable solicitations." The Court viewed the state's interest in dispelling the possible misperception that fund-raisers receive more compensation than they really do as "not sufficiently weighty" to require the "unduly burdensome" and overly broad means used here. Finally, the Court struck down the licensure requirement. A speaker's rights "are not lost merely because compensation is received." Further, the asserted power to license brings with it, in the Court's view, the "power directly and substantially to affect the speech they may utter." Finally, the Court used the overbreadth doctrine to invalidate two local ordinances in *Board of Airport Commissioners v. Jews for Jesus* (482 U.S. 589: 1987) and *Houston v. Hill* (482 U.S. 451: 1987). *Airport Commissioners* involved an ordinance banning "all First Amendment activities within the Central Terminal area of Los Angeles International Airport (LAX)." The defect in the regulation was that the policy went further than regulating expressive activity that might create problems, such as congestion or disruption, in the airport;

such a regulation might be a permissible time, place, and manner restriction. Instead, the regulation banned all expression in an effort to create a "virtual First Amendment Free Zone." Not only were groups such as Jews for Jesus reached by the regulation, but the ban extended "even to talking and reading, or the wearing of campaign buttons or symbolic clothing." Under such a sweeping ban virtually everyone entering LAX could be found in violation of the ordinance. *Hill* involved an ordinance making it unlawful to interrupt a police officer in the performance of his duty. Since interruptions by assaulting or striking an officer were otherwise proscribed by state law, the only enforceable portion of the ordinance was the prohibition of verbal interruptions, defined as provisions that deal with speech rather than with core criminal conduct. The Court found the ordinance insufficiently focused because it too broadly applied to speech that in any way interrupts an officer. Such a prohibition infringes on the citizen's right to oppose or challenge police action verbally. The effect of the ordinance was to give police officers "unfettered discretion" to arrest persons for using words that are simply annoying.

FREE PRESS

Prior Restraint

Hazelwood School District v. Kuhlmeier, **484 U.S. 260, 108 S. Ct. 562, 98 L. Ed. 2d 592 (1988)** Upheld broad authority of school officials to monitor student publications. Indeed, the Court held that this authority goes so far as to allow censorship of content thought to be objectionable by school officials. Former staff members of a high school newspaper brought suit, claiming Hazelwood School District violated their First Amendment rights by deleting articles from a particular issue of the newspaper. The articles described student pregnancy experiences and the effect on students of parental divorce. The newspaper was produced by a journalism class as a part of the high school curriculum. The procedure established by the school district was that the principal would review all page proofs prior to publication. In this case, the principal objected to the article on pregnancy as inappropriate for some of the school's younger students. The article on divorce was found objectionable because it actually identified a parent by name and included accusations of abusive conduct. The principal ordered the pages on which the two articles appeared to be withheld from the paper even though these pages contained other, nonobjectionable material. In a 5–3 decision, the Court ruled that there was no First Amendment violation. While acknowledging that students do not "shed their constitutional rights to freedom of speech or expression at the schoolhouse gate," the Court said that the rights of students in public schools are not "automatically coextensive with the rights of adults in other settings." Rather, they must be applied in light of the "special characteristics of the school environment." A school "need not tolerate" student speech that is "inconsistent" with its "basic educational mission, even though the government could not censor similar speech outside the school." The Court rejected the assertion that the paper was a forum for public expression. School facilities are public forums only if they are open for "indiscriminate use" by the "general public" or a portion of the general public. On the other hand, if facilities have been "reserved for other intended purposes," no public forum exists and school authorities may impose "reasonable restrictions." In this case, the school district merely adhered to its policy that publication of the newspaper was part of the educational process and an activity subject to the control of the school staff. Since there was no intent to open the paper to "indiscriminate use" by the student body or even the newspaper's student staff, the Court ruled that the school officials were entitled to reasonable regulation of the content of the paper. Educators may exercise greater control over certain kinds of expression to assure that participants "learn whatever lessons the activity is designed to teach," that readers or listeners are not exposed to material that may be "inappropriate for their level of maturity," and that the positions taken are not "erroneously attributed to the school." Educators, said the Court, do not violate the First Amendment by "exercising editorial control over the style and content of student speech in school-sponsored expressive activities" so long as their actions are "reasonably related to legitimate pedagogical concerns." Justices Brennan, Marshall, and Blackmun disagreed, seeing the principal's action as unconstitutional prior restraint. In their view, the expression did not interfere with the educational process and should have been protected. They also objected to the breadth of discretion permitted the school authorities. *See also* FREE PRESS CLAUSE, p. 415; PRIOR RE-STRAINT, p. 444.

Significance   *Hazelwood School District v. Kuhlmeier* (98 L. Ed. 2d 592: 1988) confronted the central prior restraint issue of censorship. The censorship in *Hazelwood* was direct. Government actions may be indirect, however, and still affect the content or dissemination of information. Consider, for example, the vending box case of *Lakewood v. Plain Dealer Publishing Company* (486 U.S. 750: 1988). A municipal ordinance authorized the mayor to grant or deny permits to publishers to place newspaper vending boxes on public property. If an application was denied, the mayor was required to state a reason (or reasons) for the denial. The Court ruled in favor of the facial challenge to the ordinance. Such a challenge must show a "close enough nexus to expression" to pose a "real and substantial threat of censorship risks." The ordinance in this case required annual application, which opened the door for content regulation. The Court also ruled that the ordinance was "directed narrowly and specifically at . . . conduct commonly associated with expression" and established a licensing agency that "might tend to favor censorship over speech." The ordinance could be applied selectively, which raised the "danger of content and viewpoint censorship." Finally, the Court said that it "cannot be presumed" that the mayor will "adhere to standards absent from the ordinance's face." The discretion exercised by the mayor was seen as "unbridled," a flaw that was not corrected by the ordinance's "minimal requirement" that reasons for denial be stated. A more traditional prior restraint issue was examined in *Florida Star v. BJF* (105 L. Ed. 2d 443: 1989). Florida law prohibited publication of identifying information about the victim of a sex crime. The newspaper had been ordered to pay damages for publishing a victim's name, although the name had been obtained lawfully from police records. The information had been included in a police report left in a law enforcement agency press room, and access to the room and to documents located there was not restricted. The police report in which BJF was identified had been discovered by a reporter-trainee who copied the entire report. The information was subsequently published in a story appearing in the *Florida Star*. BJF filed suit against the newspaper, claiming negligent violation of the statute, and was awarded both compensatory and punitive damages. The Supreme Court reversed in a 6–3 decision. The Court chose not to establish the "broad" principle that damages for encroachment on privacy rights could never prevail over truthful publication. Instead, the Court resolved the issue on "limited principles" that "sweep no more broadly" than the "appropriate context" of this particular case. The Court drew heavily on *Smith v. Daily Mail Publishing Company* (443 U.S. 97: 1979), which said that if a newspaper "lawfully obtains truthful information" it may not be punished for publication of that information "absent a need to further a state interest of the highest order." In this case, the newspaper had accurately reported information lawfully obtained from a government agency. The Court saw "ample" and "less drastic means" open to the state to safeguard information than limiting publication. Neither did the Court find that imposing liability on the newspaper served a state interest of the "highest order." While acknowledging that protecting the privacy of sexual assault victims was "highly significant," imposing liability under these circumstances is "too precipitous a means" of protecting those interests. The Court went on to make two other points with respect to application of the *Daily Mail* principle. First, the press ought not be punished for publishing information that is otherwise publicly available. Such punishment is "unlikely to advance" the interest of victim anonymity that the state seeks to protect. Where the government has made information available, it is "highly anomalous to sanction persons other than the source of the release." Second, the Court indicated that punishment of truthful publication in this situation may result in press "timidity and self-censorship." A final example of government restraint of dissemination of information concerns a state law that permanently prohibited a grand jury witness from disclosing his or her testimony. To the extent the prohibition applied to a person's own testimony after the grand jury term ended, a unanimous Supreme Court struck down the regulation in *Butterworth v. Smith* (108 L. Ed. 2d 572: 1990). The Court recognized the "tradition of secrecy" that has evolved as one of the ways to ensure grand jury impartiality and protect against "overreaching" by the state. At the same time, mere "invocation of grand jury interests is not 'some talisman that dissolves all constitutional protections.'" In this case, the state sought to prevent Smith, a reporter, from "publication of information relating to alleged government misconduct—speech which has traditionally been recognized as lying at the core of the First Amendment." Preservation of grand jury secrecy was not seen as a sufficient interest here to warrant a "permanent ban on disclosure by a witness of his own testimony once a grand jury had been discharged." In contrast to any state interests, the effect of the prohibition on the witness is "dramatic." The law extends "not merely to the life of the grand jury, but to the indefinite future." The "potential for abuse" of the prohibition "through its employment as a device to silence those who know of unlawful conduct or irregularities on the part of public officials, is apparent."

Libel

***Hustler Magazine v. Falwell*, 485 U.S. 46, 108 S. Ct. 876, 99 L. Ed. 2d 41 (1988)**   Held that a public figure cannot be awarded damages for the "intentional infliction of emotional distress" caused by the publication of a parody. Campari Liqueur conducted an advertising campaign in which celebrities discussed their first experiences with the liqueur—their "first times." *Hustler* published an advertisement parody, so labeled in small print at the bottom of the page, in which Falwell, a prominent religious and political personality, was represented as recalling his "first time" as a drunken and incestuous affair with his mother in an outhouse. Falwell brought suit against *Hustler* in

U.S. district court, claiming that publication of the parody entitled him to damages for libel, invasion of privacy, and intentional infliction of emotional distress. The Court directed a verdict for *Hustler* on the invasion of privacy issue. As later characterized by the court of appeals, the jury found that the parody could not reasonably be understood as representing actual facts, and it ruled for the magazine on the libel claim. The jury did, however, award Falwell damages on the emotional distress claim. The court of appeals affirmed, saying that when the libel standard of actual malice is applied in a tort action for emotional distress, knowing or reckless falsity need not be demonstrated. The court of appeals further held that even if the ad parody was constitutionally protected opinion, the only relevant factor was whether the publication was sufficiently outrageous to constitute the intentional infliction of emotional distress. The Supreme Court unanimously reversed the court of appeals (with Justice Kennedy not participating). The opinion of the Court was offered by Chief Justice Rehnquist. The case, he said, presented the Court with a "novel" First Amendment question: whether a public figure may recover damages for "emotional harm" caused by publication of material "offensive to him, and doubtless gross and repugnant in the eyes of most." Falwell was asking the Court to find that a state's interest in protecting public figures from emotional distress is "sufficient to deny First Amendment protection to speech that is patently offensive and is intended to inflict emotional injury even when that speech could not reasonably be interpreted as stating actual facts about the public figure involved." This, said Rehnquist, "we decline to do." The sort of "robust" political debate encouraged by the First Amendment will necessarily produce expression that is "critical" of public figures who are "intimately involved in the resolution of important public issues." Such criticism will not always be "reasoned or moderate," and public figures will be subjected to "vehement, caustic, and sometimes unpleasantly sharp attacks." Only defamatory falsehoods uttered with knowledge that they are false or with "reckless disregard" for the truth provide a public figure with an opportunity to hold a speaker liable for damage to reputation. False statements uttered without actual malice may have little or no value, but they are "inevitable in free debate." Legal rules imposing stricter liability would have a "chilling effect" on expression and would not give freedoms of expression the "breathing space" they require. Rehnquist characterized Falwell's arguments as urging a different standard because the state is trying to prevent severe emotional distress to people subjected to offensive publication. In Falwell's view, said Rehnquist, so long as the utterance was "intended to inflict emotional distress, was outrageous, and did in fact inflict serious emotional distress," it is of "no constitutional import" whether the statement was fact or opinion or whether it was true or false. The Court rejected this contention. Rather, it is "intent to cause injury that is the gravamen of the tort." In response, Rehnquist said that while the law does not regard the intent to inflict emotional distress as one that should "receive much solicitude," many things done with motives that are "less than admirable are protected by the First Amendment." Accordingly, while bad motives may be "deemed controlling for purposes of tort liability" in other areas of the law, the First Amendment prohibits such a result in the "area of public debate about public figures." Were the court to hold otherwise, said Rehnquist, there can be "little doubt" that political cartoonists and satirists "would be subject to damages awards without any showing that their work falsely defamed its subject." Rehnquist examined the history of political cartoons and caricatures. He concluded that despite their "sometimes caustic nature . . . , graphic depictions and satirical cartoons have played a prominent role in public and political debate." From a historical perspective, it is "clear that our political discourse would have been considerably poorer without them." He then rejected Falwell's contention that the *Hustler* parody was "so outrageous as to distinguish it from more traditional political cartoons." Rehnquist acknowledged that the *Hustler* caricature of Falwell was "at best a distant cousin" of the traditional political cartoon. If it were possible, he said, to lay down a "principled standard" to separate them, "public discourse would probably suffer little or no harm." Rehnquist doubted, however, that such a standard existed and "was certain" that the "pejorative description 'outrageous' does not supply one." "Outrageousness," in the field of political and social discourse, has "an inherent subjectiveness" that would allow a jury to "impose liability on the basis of the jurors' tastes or views, or perhaps on the basis of their dislike of a particular expression." An "outrageousness" standard thus "runs afoul" of the "long-standing refusal" to permit damages to be awarded because expression may have an "adverse emotional impact on the audience." Rehnquist concluded the Court's opinion by saying that public figures may not recover damages for the tort of intentional infliction of emotional distress without showing that the publication "contains a false statement of fact which was made with 'actual malice.'" This conclusion, said Rehnquist, "reflects our considered judgment that such a standard is necessary to give adequate 'breathing space' to freedoms protected by the First Amendment." *See also* LIBEL, p. 433.

Significance   The Court's decision in *Hustler Magazine v. Falwell* (485 U.S. 46: 1988) was important for two reasons. First, the decision indicates that the Court is not interested in making it easier for public figures to collect damages when subjected to criticism and satire. On the contrary, the decision ought to discourage plaintiffs who feel offended by media treatment from resorting to litigation as a means of recovery. Second, the decision dispels speculation that the Court was on the verge of abandoning the "actual malice" rule established in *New York Times v. Sullivan* (376 U.S. 254: 1964). The so-called *Sullivan* rule has served as the basis for publications defending themselves in libel actions. During the last decade, the Court seemed to be in doubt as to whether the *Sullivan* rule provided public figures with enough room to protect themselves. The Court's decision in the *Hustler* case was squarely founded on *Sullivan,* and it seems apparent that the Court is satisfied, at least for now, with the *Sullivan* rule serving as the basis for limiting libel actions against the media. For the quarter century since *Sullivan,* statements of opinion, as opposed to statements of "fact," have enjoyed virtual protection from libel actions. In addition to *Sullivan,* further support for a privilege for "comment" can be found in *Gertz v. Robert Welch, Inc.* (418 U.S. 323: 1974), where the Court said that under the First Amendment, "there is no such thing as a false idea. However pernicious an opinion may seem, we depend for its correction not on the conscience of judges and juries, but on the competition of other ideas." In *Milkovich v. Lorain Journal* (111 L. Ed. 2d 1: 1990), the Court clarified this point and ruled that opinions are not categorically insulated from being found defamatory. Chief Justice Rehnquist said that the Court did not think that "this passage from *Gertz* was intended to create a wholesale defamation exception for anything that might be labeled opinion." Such an interpretation is not only contradictory to the "tenor and context" of the *Gertz* passage, but would "ignore the fact that expressions of opinion may often imply an assertion of objective fact." The Court was satisfied that the "breathing space" needed for free expression was "adequately secured . . . without the creation of an artificial dichotomy between 'opinion' and 'fact.'" A statement as a matter of public concern "must be provable as false before there can be liability under state defamation law." The key in these cases is separating "pure" opinion from opinion that "contains actionable assertions of fact." Under the terms of this ruling, then, the statement "In my opinion Mayor Jones is a liar" is actionable. In contrast, the statement "In my opinion Mayor Jones shows his abysmal ignorance by accepting the teachings of Marx and Lenin" would not. The First Amendment, concluded Rehnquist, ensures that "a statement of opinion relating to matters of public concern which does not contain a provable false factual connotation will receive full constitutional protection."

Commercial Press

Pittsburgh Press Company v. Human Relations Commission, **413 U.S. 376, 93 S. Ct. 2553, 37 L. Ed. 2d 669 (1973)** Declared that particular kinds of commercial speech may be regulated. The Pittsburgh Press Company was found to be in violation of a Human Relations Commission ordinance because it placed help-wanted advertisements in sex-designated columns. The commission ordered the newspaper to end the gender-referenced layout of the advertisements. The order was affirmed in Pennsylvania's judicial system. The Supreme Court ruled the order was not prior restraint in a 5–4 decision. The Court first determined the advertisements were commercial speech, not merely because they were advertisements, but because of their commercial content. They were, in fact, "classic examples of commercial speech" because of the proposal of possible employment. They were therefore unlike the political advertisement in the *New York Times v. Sullivan* (376 U.S. 254: 1964). The Pittsburgh Press Company argued that editorial judgment about where to place an advertisement should control, rather than its commercial content. The Court majority answered that a "newspaper's editorial judgments in connection with an advertisement take on the character of the advertisement and, in those cases, the scope of the newspaper's First Amendment protection may be affected by the content of the advertisement." The kind of editorial judgment involved in this case did not strip commercial advertising of its commercial character. Even more crucial was the fact that the commercial activity involved was illegal employment discrimination. In the Court's view advertisements could be forbidden in this instance just as advertisements "proposing the sale of narcotics or soliciting prostitution" could be forbidden. The justices concluded their opinion by ruling that any First Amendment interest that applies to an ordinary commercial proposal is "altogether absent when the commercial activity itself is illegal and the restriction on advertising is incidental to a valid limitation on economic activity." Dissents were entered by Chief Justice Burger and Justices Douglas, Stewart, and Blackmun. The chief justice wrote that the First Amendment "includes the right of a newspaper to arrange the content of its paper, whether it be news items, editorials, or advertising, as it sees fit." Justice Douglas argued that employment discrimination can be otherwise handled. No ordinance justifies censorship. Justice Stewart felt that, given the Court's holding, there is "no reason why Government cannot force a newspaper publisher to conform in the same way in order to achieve other goals thought socially desirable." If government can "dictate the layout of a newspaper's classified advertising pages today, what is there to prevent it from dictating the layout of the news pages tomorrow?" *See also* BILL OF RIGHTS, p. 7; FIRST AMENDMENT, p. 77; *NEW YORK TIMES v. SULLIVAN* (376 U.S. 254: 1964), p. 121.

Significance   The commercial speech holding in *Pittsburgh Press Company v. Human Relations Commission* (413 U.S. 376: 1973) had its origin in *Valentine v. Chrestensen* (316 U.S. 52: 1942). The latter decision clearly put commercial speech outside First Amendment coverage. *New York Times v. Sullivan* (376 U.S. 254: 1964) substantially narrowed the *Chrestensen* concept of commercial speech, and following *Pittsburgh Press,* the Burger Court narrowed the definition even further. In *Bigelow v. Virginia* (421 U.S. 809: 1975), the Court protected the publication of an advertisement by an organization offering services related to legal abortions in another state. The Court held the advertisement "conveyed information of potential interest and value to a diverse audience," not merely a commercial promotion of services. The next year, in *Virginia State Board of Pharmacy v. Virginia Citizens Consumers Council, Inc.* (425 U.S. 748: 1976), the Court struck down a statute that made advertising of prescription drugs a form of conduct possibly leading to a suspension of license. The Court argued that even if the advertiser's interest is a purely economic one, such speech is not necessarily disqualified from protection. The consumer and society in general have a "strong interest in the free flow of commercial information." Such a free flow is indispensable in a predominantly free enterprise economy that requires many private economic decisions. Regulation of commercial content by professional associations was at issue in *Shapero v. Kentucky Bar Association* (486 U.S. 466: 1988). Lawyers are able to advertise, but are not permitted by rules of the profession to solicit legal business directly. Shapero wished to send a letter to potential clients threatened with foreclosure, but approval was withheld by the state bar association on the ground that the letter violated a state court rule barring targeted advertising. The court rule was based on Rule 7.3 of the American Bar Association's Model Rules of Professional Conduct, which prohibits such solicitation. The Supreme Court held that the comprehensive ban on targeted, direct-mail solicitation violated the First Amendment. The Court saw the sending of "truthful and nondeceptive" letters to potential clients as protected commercial speech. Such speech, said the Court, can be restricted only in order to pursue "substantial governmental interests" and only in ways that "directly advance" such interests. The Court distinguished between written and in-person solicitation and concluded that the former did not require a categorical ban. The "possibility of improper conduct and the improbability of effective regulation" are diminished in the direct-mail situation.

The direct-mail approach, said the Court, is less "coercive" than the in-person solicitation and can be scrutinized as are other forms of advertising.

Obscenity Standards

Miller v. California, **413 U.S. 15, 93 S. Ct. 2607, 37 L. Ed. 2d 419 (1973)** Tightened definitional standards for obscenity. In *Miller* the Burger Court remodeled and reinterpreted the Warren Court obscenity holdings. Miller had been convicted of distributing obscene material. His offense was that he had conducted an aggressive book sales campaign by sending unsolicited brochures through the mail. A five-justice majority upheld Miller's conviction and offered a redefinition of the test from *Roth v. United States* (354 U.S. 476: 1957). The Court found no fault with *Roth,* but said that subsequent decisions had "veered sharply away from the *Roth* concept." Thus the need existed to restore its original intent. While many cases had brought about such a need, the major offender in Chief Justice Burger's view was *Memoirs v. Massachusetts* (383 U.S. 413: 1966), in which a plurality of the Court produced a "drastically altered test" that required the prosecution to prove a negative. The prosecution had to prove that material was "utterly without redeeming social value—a burden virtually impossible to discharge." In establishing the revised standard, the Burger Court drew heavily from *Roth.* An obscenity statute must be limited to works that, taken as a whole, appeal to the prurient interest in sex or portray sexual conduct in a patently offensive way. The material when taken as a whole must lack serious literary, artistic, political, or scientific value. The Court specifically rejected the social value standard from *Memoirs*. It also proposed some flexibility in applying its guidelines to specific cases. The nation is "simply too big and too diverse" for a uniform standard of prurient interest or patently offensive sexual conduct. The Court viewed it as unrealistic to base proceedings around an abstract formulation. To require a state to try a case around evidence of a national community standard would be an exercise in futility. The Court asserted that people in different states vary in their tastes and attitudes, and "this diversity is not to be strangled by the absolutism of imposed uniformity." State obscenity trials can therefore base evaluation of materials on the contemporary community standards of the particular state. Justices Brennan, Marshall, and Stewart dissented. They argued that obscenity regulations ought to be confined to the distribution of obscene materials to juveniles and unwilling audiences. In his dissent in *Paris Adult Theatre I v. Staton* (413 U.S. 49:

1973), a companion case to *Miller,* Justice Brennan also warned of another expression problem. He said, "The State's interest in regulating morality by suppressing obscenity, while often asserted, remains essentially unfocused and ill-defined." When attempts are made to curtail unprotected speech, protected speech is necessarily involved as well. Thus the effort to serve this speculative interest through regulation of obscene matter "must tread heavily on the rights protected by the First Amendment." Justice Douglas also dissented, offering an absolutist argument for expression in all circumstances. *See also* FIRST AMENDMENT, p. 77; *MEMOIRS v. MASSACHUSETTS* (383 U.S. 413: 1966), p. 133; *ROTH v. UNITED STATES* (354 U.S. 476: 1957), p. 131.

Significance   *Miller v. California* (413 U.S. 15: 1973) represented the first consensus statement on obscenity standards since *Roth* in 1957. *Miller* is of consequence primarily because the Court's rejection of national community standards prompted highly diverse outcomes relative to obscenity regulations. It also removed the social value criterion as an insurmountable obstacle to prosecution. *Miller* provided examples of the kinds of materials that may be offensive enough to be regulated, but a lack of doctrinal clarity remained. Just a year after *Miller,* the Court unanimously reversed an obscenity conviction in *Jenkins v. Georgia* (418 U.S. 153: 1974), overturning a local judgment that the film *Carnal Knowledge* was obscene. The Court cautioned that local juries and their application of community standards are not without First Amendment boundaries. *Miller* did prompt greater regulation, however, and such regulated activities have generally been supported by the Court. In *New York v. Ferber* (458 U.S. 747: 1982), for example, the Court unanimously upheld a statute prohibiting "persons from knowingly promoting a sexual performance by a child under the age of 16." The Court said the states are "entitled to greater leeway in the regulation of pornographic depictions of children." Because state-defined morality "bears so heavily and pervasively on the welfare of children, the balance of compelling interests is clearly struck, and it is permissible to consider these materials as without First Amendment protection." In *Brockett v. Spokane Arcades, Inc.* (472 U.S. 491: 1985), however, the Court held that a state obscenity law could not ban lustful material. Just because sexual response is aroused, expression may not therefore automatically be regulated. The Court said that material that does no more than "arouse 'good old-fashioned, healthy' interest in sex" is constitutionally protected. In *Pope v. Illinois* (481 U.S. 497: 1987), the Court ruled that when evaluating the value element, a jury should not be instructed to apply contemporary community standards. Such community standards, said the Court, are appropriately used only when the prurient interest and patent offensiveness elements are considered. There is no suggestion in *Miller* or subsequent cases that the value of an allegedly obscene work is to be determined by reference to community standards. *Miller* itself points out that the First Amendment protects works of value regardless of whether the government or a majority of people approve of the ideas these works represent. Just as the ideas represented in a work need not obtain majority approval, neither does the value of a work depend on the degree of local acceptance it has won. The proper question is not whether an ordinary member of a given community would find serious literary, artistic, political, or scientific value in any work, but whether a reasonable person would find such value in the material taken as a whole. A nonlocal and more uniform standard must be used in applying the value element of the *Miller* test.

A 1988 amendment to the Federal Communications Act made it a crime to use a telephone to send an "indecent" as well as an "obscene" message for commercial purposes. While the objective of earlier regulations had been to protect minors from such communications, the 1988 amendment banned "obscene and indecent" communications to any recipient. Challenge to the amendment was considered by the Court in *Sable Communications of California, Inc. v. Federal Communications Commission* (106 L. Ed. 2d 93: 1989). The Supreme Court ruled for Sable Communications with respect to the regulation of "indecent" messages, but upheld the authority of Congress to impose a total ban on "obscene" messages. Obscenity, said the Court, is not protected expression under the First Amendment, and a prohibition on the interstate transmission of obscene commercial messages is permissible. Neither did the federal prohibition on obscene messages conflict with the Court's holding in *Miller*. It had been argued by Sable that the law created a "national standard of obscenity" in a manner incompatible with *Miller*. While *Miller* allows localities to enforce their own "community standards," it did not preclude Congress from prohibiting "communications that are obscene in some communities under local standards even though they are not obscene in others." The sender, while obligated to comply with the ban, said the Court, is free to "tailor its messages, on a selective basis, to the communities it chooses to serve." The Court was unanimous in striking down the regulation of "indecent" content as an overly broad restriction. The amendment was designed to protect minors from the messages, an interest the Court acknowledged to be "compelling." The ban, however, denied adult access to messages that are "indecent but not obscene," a policy that "far exceeds that which is necessary to limit the access of minors to such messages." The Court distinguished regulation of "indecent" radio broadcasts from the "dial-it medium" because the latter requires the listener to take "affirmative steps to receive the communications." The government's contention that only a total ban could protect against access by minors was, accordingly, seen as "unpersuasive" by the Court.

Obscenity: Zoning

Young v. American Mini Theatres, Inc., **427 U.S. 50, 96 S. Ct. 2440, 49 L. Ed. 2d 310 (1976)** Upheld zoning ordinances regulating locations of adult theaters. *Young* approved amendments to Detroit zoning ordinances providing that adult theaters be licensed. They could not be located within 1,000 feet of any two other "regulated uses" or within 500 feet of any residential area. The other "regulated uses" included some 10 categories of adult entertainment enterprises. An adult theater was defined as one that presented material characterized by emphasis on "specified sexual activities" or "specified anatomical areas." *Young* was a 5–4 decision against several lines of challenge. First, the Court rejected assertions of vagueness in the ordinance because "any element of vagueness in these ordinances has not affected the respondents." The application of the ordinances to the American Mini Theatres "is plain." As for the licensure requirement, the Court noted that the general zoning laws of Detroit imposed requirements on all motion picture theaters. The Court said, "We have no doubt that the municipality may control the location of theaters as well as the location of other commercial establishments." Establishment of such restrictions in themselves is not prohibited as prior restraint. The "mere fact that the commercial exploitation of material protected by the First Amendment is subject to zoning and other licensing requirements is not sufficient reason for invalidating these ordinances." The Court also considered whether the 1,000-foot restriction constituted an improper content-based classification. The Court said that "even within the area of protected speech, a difference in content may require a different government response." Citing the public figure category in libel law and prohibitions on exhibition of obscenity to juveniles and unconsenting adults, the Court held that the First Amendment did not foreclose content distinctions. They "rest squarely on an appraisal of the content of the material otherwise within a constitutionally protected area." Even though the First Amendment does not allow total suppression, the Court held that a state may legitimately use the content of Mini Theatre materials as the basis for placing them in a different classification from other motion pictures. Finally, the Court upheld the regulated use classification on the basis of the city's interest in preserving the character of its neighborhoods. Detroit has a legitimate interest in attempting to preserve the quality of urban life. It is an interest that "must be accorded high respect," and the city must be allowed "a reasonable opportunity to experiment with solutions to an admittedly serious problem." Justices Brennan, Stewart, Marshall, and Blackmun dissented, basing their opinion on the vagueness and content orientation of the ordinance. *See also* BILL OF RIGHTS, p. 7; FIRST AMENDMENT, p. 77; *MILLER v. CALIFORNIA* (413 U.S. 15: 1973), p. 134.

Significance   *Young v. American Mini Theatres, Inc.* (427 U.S. 50: 1976) represents a new wave of cases raising issues about local regulation of "adult" entertainment. The Court has generally supported local regulation provided expression is not completely prohibited and a compelling interest can be demonstrated. Meeting these conditions is not always easy, however. In *Erznoznick v. Jacksonville* (422 U.S. 205: 1975), the Court struck down an ordinance that prohibited the exhibition of films containing nudity if the screen could be seen from a public street. The Court cited the limited privacy interest of persons on the streets, but it also stressed the overly broad sweep of the ordinance. In *Schad v. Borough of Mount Ephraim* (452 U.S. 61: 1981), the Court invalidated a zoning ordinance that banned live entertainment in a borough establishment. Convictions under the ordinance had been secured against an adult bookstore operator for having live nude dancers performing in the establishment. The borough argued that permitting such entertainment would conflict with its plan to create a commercial area catering only to the immediate needs of residents. The Court considered such justification "patently insufficient." The ordinance prohibited a "wide range of expression" that has long been held to be within the protection of the First and Fourteenth Amendments. Ten years after *Young*, the Court once again reviewed a local attempt to regulate the location of adult theaters in *City of Renton v. Playtime Theatres, Inc.* (475 U.S. 41: 1986). Using the same rationale stated in *Young*, the Court upheld a municipality's authority to require dispersal of such establishments. Since the municipal ordinance did not bar adult theaters entirely, it was reviewed as a time, place, and manner regulation. Such regulations are acceptable so long as they serve a substantial interest and do not unreasonably limit avenues of communication. Justice Rehnquist said for the Court that the First Amendment requires only that a local unit refrain from denying individuals a "reasonable opportunity to open and operate an adult theater within the city." He said the city of Renton easily met that requirement in the ordinance under review. *FW/PBS, Inc. v. City of*

Dallas (107 L. Ed. 2d 603: 1990) reviewed a comprehensive city ordinance regulating "sexually oriented" businesses, including bookstores. The city sought to regulate such businesses through a variety of licensing and zoning requirements. All owners of sexually oriented businesses were required to obtain a license from the city as well as to pay an annual fee. The ordinance contained civil disability provisions that prohibited people convicted of certain crimes from obtaining a license. Licenses could also be revoked or not renewed if the owner (or his or her spouse) was convicted of certain specified offenses. The ordinance also defined "adult motels" as those renting rooms for periods under 10 hours. An adult motel was a "sexually oriented" business and thus subject to the licensure provisions of the ordinance. Such establishments also had to be more than 1,000 feet from parks, churches, and residential or business structures. The Court found that no party had standing to challenge several ordinance provisions and confined itself to the licensing issue and the 10-hour room-rental definition. The Court struck down the former in a 6–3 decision while unanimously upholding the latter. The defect in the licensing provisions was that they operated as a prior restraint. Any system of prior restraint, said the Court, carries a "heavy presumption against its constitutional validity" for two reasons. First, such schemes give government "unbridled discretion" that may result in censorship. Second, prior restraint systems seldom impose stringent time limits on the decision maker. The Dallas ordinance created the possibility not only that protected speech could be censored through the licensing requirements, but that the licensor has "unlimited time within which to issue a license" as well. This creates the "risk of indefinitely suppressing permissible speech." The 10-hour definition was challenged on two grounds. First, it was argued that Dallas had insufficient basis to conclude that rental of motel rooms for periods of less than 10 hours actually produced "adverse impacts." The Court found the legislative judgment that short rental periods are likely to "foster prostitution" to be reasonable. Second, it was contended that this ordinance provision violated privacy rights by impinging on the right to intimate association. The Court rejected this contention by saying that limiting motel room rentals will not have any "discernible effect on the sorts of traditional personal bonds" referred to in previous right of association cases. Such "personal bonds" that are formed through the use of a motel room for less than 10 hours, the Court concluded, are not those that have "played a critical role in the culture and traditions of the Nation by cultivating and transmitting shared ideals and beliefs."

Private Obscenity

Stanley v. Georgia, **394 U.S. 557, 89 S. Ct. 1243, 22 L. Ed. 2d 542 (1969)** Held that a state could not prohibit private possession of obscene materials. Stanley was convicted of possessing obscene films. The films were discovered while federal and state agents searched Stanley's home under authority of a warrant issued in connection with an investigation of Stanley's alleged involvement in bookmaking. The Supreme Court unanimously reversed Stanley's conviction. Justices Stewart, White, and Brennan reversed exclusively on improper search grounds. Stanley's First Amendment claim was based on his "right to read or observe what he pleases—the right to satisfy his intellectual and emotional needs in the privacy of his own home, and the right to be free from state inquiry into the contents of his library." Georgia's statute was based on the view that there are "certain types of materials that the individual may not read or even possess." The Court was unpersuaded, saying that "mere categorization of these films as 'obscene' is insufficient justification for such drastic invasion of personal liberties." Although privacy was a key consideration, the Court stressed the First Amendment aspects of *Stanley.* Justifications for regulation of obscenity "do not reach into the privacy of one's own home. If the First Amendment means anything, it means that a State has no business telling a man, sitting alone in his house, what books he may read or what films he may watch. Our whole constitutional heritage rebels at the thought of giving government the power to control men's minds." The interests of the state are insufficient to protect individuals from obscenity in this fashion. "Whatever the power of the State to control public dissemination of ideas inimical to the public morality, it cannot constitutionally premise legislation on the desirability of controlling a person's private thoughts." Neither may the state justify the prohibition of privately held obscene materials as a means of forestalling antisocial conduct. The state "may no more prohibit mere possession of obscenity on the ground that it may lead to anti-social conduct than it may prohibit possession of chemistry books on the ground they may lead to the manufacture of homemade spirits." The Court also rejected the argument that outlawing possession of obscenity is required to allow enforcement of prohibitions against its distribution. The right to read or observe is dominant and "its restriction may not be justified by the need to ease the administration of otherwise valid criminal laws." *See also* BILL OF RIGHTS, p. 7; FIRST AMENDMENT, p. 77; *MILLER v. CALIFORNIA* (413 U.S. 15: 1973), p. 134.

Significance   *Stanley v. Georgia* (394 U.S. 557: 1969) decided that privately held obscene material is a protected right. The Burger Court followed *Stanley*, however, by closing off the means of delivering obscene material. *United States v. Reidel* (402 U.S. 351: 1971) held that obscene material was unprotected expression and could constitutionally be excluded from the mail. On the same day, in *United States v. Thirty-Seven Photographs* (402 U.S. 363: 1971), the Court allowed a prohibition on the importation of obscenity from abroad even if it is intended for private use. The following year, in *United States v. 12 200-ft. Reels of Super 8mm. Film* (413 U.S. 123: 1972), the Court allowed seizure of materials coming into the country from Mexico. The justices declared that the right to private possession of obscene materials did not afford a "correlative right to acquire, sell, or import such material even for private use only." The most noteworthy modification of *Stanley* came in *Paris Adult Theatre I v. Staton* (413 U.S. 49: 1973), a companion to *Miller v. California* (413 U.S. 15: 1973). *Paris* held that obscene films do not "acquire constitutional immunity from state regulation simply because they are exhibited for consenting adults only." The Court recognized the "legitimate state interests at stake in stemming the tide of commercialized obscenity." It is an interest that includes protecting the "quality of life and the total community environment." The Court ruled in *Osborne v. Ohio* (109 L. Ed. 2d 98: 1990) that states can outlaw the private possession of pornographic materials featuring minors. Crucial to the decision was the choice of *New York v. Ferber* (458 U.S. 747: 1982) rather than *Stanley* as the controlling precedent. The law struck down in *Stanley*, however, was intended to prevent "poison[ing] the minds" of those who observed such material. In this case, the state did not "rely on a paternalistic interest in Osborne's mind." Rather, Ohio enacted the law in an attempt to "protect the victims of child pornography; it hopes to destroy a market for the exploitive use of children." The Ohio legislature made the judgment that using children as subjects in pornographic materials is "harmful to the physiological, emotional, and mental health of the child." That judgment, said the Court, "easily passes muster" under the First Amendment. Furthermore, it is "surely reasonable" for Ohio to conclude that it will "decrease the production of child pornography if it penalizes those who possess and view the product, thereby decreasing demand." Given the importance of Ohio's interest in protecting the child victims, "we cannot fault Ohio for attempting to stamp out this vice at all levels in the distribution chain." Osborne also challenged the Ohio law as overbroad. The Court rejected this contention, finding that the state supreme court had interpreted the law in such a way as to focus or confine sufficiently the materials that could be reached under the regulation. Justices Brennan, Marshall, and Stevens felt the Ohio law was overbroad. Brennan said he shared the majority's concerns on the issue, but was dissatisfied with the way the interests were balanced. In his view, the majority was "so disquieted by the possible exploitation of children" in the production of pornographic materials that it was "willing to tolerate the imposition of criminal penalties for simple possession."

ASSEMBLY AND PROTEST

Public Premises

Adderley v. Florida, **385 U.S. 39, 87 S. Ct. 242, 17 L. Ed. 2d 149 (1966)** Held that demonstrators may be barred from assembly on the grounds of a county jail. *Adderley* considered whether certain locations might be put off-limits to demonstrations or assemblies. Adderley and a number of others were convicted of trespass for gathering at a county jail to protest the arrest of several students the day before, as well as local policies of racial segregation at the jail itself. When the demonstrators would not leave the jail grounds when asked, they were warned of possible arrest for trespass. Adderley and others remained on the premises, were arrested, and were subsequently tried and convicted. The Court upheld the conviction in a 5–4 decision. The Court focused on the question of whether the trespass convictions deprived the demonstrators of their freedom of speech. Through Justice Black, the Court majority concluded that "nothing in the Constitution of the United States prevented Florida from even-handed enforcement of its general trespass statute against those refusing to obey the sheriff's order to remove themselves from what amounted to the curtilage of the jailhouse." The fact that the jail was a public building did not automatically entitle the protesters to demonstrate there. The state, no less than a private owner of property, has power to preserve the property under its control for the use to which it is lawfully dedicated. The security purpose to which the jail was dedicated outweighed the expression interests of the protesters. The justices felt that to find for Adderley would be to endorse "the assumption that people who want to propagandize protests or views have a constitutional right to do so whenever and wherever they please." The Court categorically rejected that premise and concluded its opinion by saying that the Constitution does not forbid a state to control the use of its own property for its own lawful nondiscriminatory purposes. Justice Douglas dissented, joined by Chief Justice

Warren and Justices Brennan and Fortas. Douglas considered the jailhouse "one of the seats of government" and an "obvious center for protest." *See also* FIRST AMENDMENT, p. 77; *PRUNEYARD SHOPPING CEN-TER v. ROBINS* (447 U.S. 74: 1980), p. 144; *TINKER v. DES MOINES SCHOOL DISTRICT* (393 U.S. 503: 1969), p. 113.

Significance   *Adderley v. Florida* (385 U.S. 39: 1966) illustrated the "speech plus" test. In certain situations speech is defined as conduct beyond oral expression itself. The additional conduct is subject to regulation at a cost to expression. In *Cox v. Louisiana* (379 U.S. 536: 1965), the Court upheld a state statute that prohibited picketing near a courthouse. It said a state could legitimately insulate its judicial proceedings from demonstrations. While restrictions were said to be warranted in *Adderley* and *Cox,* breach of the peace convictions of persons demonstrating on the grounds of a state capitol were reversed in *Edwards v. South Carolina* (372 U.S. 229: 1963). Similarly, a peaceful sit-in at a library was protected in *Brown v. Louisiana* (383 U.S. 131: 1966). More recently, the Court struck down an ordinance that prohibited picketing in the proximity of school buildings when classes were in session in *Chicago Police Department v. Mosley* (408 U.S. 92: 1972). The ordinance was invalidated largely because it excepted labor picketing from the ban. The Court did suggest the city had a legitimate interest in preventing school disruption, however. Time, place, and manner restrictions have generally been recognized by the Court, provided that significant governmental interests can be demonstrated. Trespass on private property was subject to punishment for many years, although civil rights sit-ins forced a legislative reevaluation of that policy. The Supreme Court successfully avoided dealing with the sit-in issue directly until passage of the Civil Rights Act of 1964, which prohibited the discriminatory practices in public accommodations that had triggered the sit-in demonstrations in the first place. In a case involving another use of public property, the Court held in *City Council of Los Angeles v. Taxpayers for Vincent* (466 U.S. 789: 1984) that a municipality could ban the posting of political campaign signs on utility poles. The ban was seen to be content-neutral and directed toward a legitimate aesthetic interest. The purpose of the regulation was "unrelated to the suppression of ideas," and interfered with expression only to the extent necessary to eliminate visual clutter. The Court noted that the ban on posting signs did not impinge on any alternative modes of communication.

Congress passed a law in the late 1930s that made it unlawful (1) to display any sign within 500 feet of an embassy that might bring a foreign government into disrepute or (2) to congregate within 500 feet of an embassy and refuse to disperse upon order of the police.

The law exempted picketing as a result of bona fide labor disputes. This law, now part of the District of Columbia Code, was reviewed in *Boos v. Barry* (485 U.S. 312: 1988) after Boos and others had sought to display signs critical of the Soviet Union and Nicaragua. The Supreme Court upheld the congregation provisions, but reversed on the display portion of the law. While recognizing the need to shield foreign governments from criticism, the Court found the display provision to be a content-based regulation on particular expression in a public forum. The Court did not find the restriction narrowly enough focused and suggested that less restrictive alternatives were "readily available." The Court also said that while regulations may permissibly be aimed at "secondary effects," those that focus on the "direct impact of speech on its audience represent a different situation." The "emotive impact of speech on its audience is not a secondary effect." The congregation provision, on the other hand, had been confined by the lower courts to dispersal of only those assemblies that are "directed at an embassy" and only when security was threatened. This construction did not allow the provision to reach a "substantial amount of constitutionally protected conduct." Its reach was limited to security-threatening situations and was site specific. Accordingly, the Court ruled that the provision was not overbroad; neither did it permit the police too much enforcement discretion. Finally, the Court rejected an Equal Protection Clause challenge on the labor-nonlabor congregation distinction. The Court ruled that the effect of the distinction was muted by the striking down of the display provision and the narrow interpretation of the congregation provision. Since only congregation that threatens an embassy's security can be restrained, any peaceful congregation, including peaceful labor congregation, is permitted. A city's authority to regulate concerts held in a municipal park was before the Court in *Ward v. Rock Against Racism* (105 L. Ed. 2d 661: 1989). An association called Rock Against Racism (RAR) had sponsored annual concerts at a band shell in New York City's Central Park. The city received many complaints about the excessive noise associated with RAR concerts, but had also experienced similar problems with other band shell events as well. The complaints were typically about substandard equipment and technicians unskilled at mixing sound. In response to these difficulties, the city issued a set of use guidelines governing all band shell concerts. Among other things, it was specified that the city would furnish the amplification equipment and employ an experienced sound technician to operate it. RAR sought a declaratory judgment against the guidelines as an interference with the association's First Amendment expression rights. The Supreme Court ruled the guidelines to be a valid place and manner regulation. Government is not permitted to adopt a regulation of speech because of "disagreement with the message it conveys." The city had two objectives in instituting the guidelines: controlling noise and ensuring sound quality. Neither of these purposes, concluded the Court, had anything to do with content. The Court also found sufficient safeguards in the guidelines to reject the contention that the city possessed too much enforcement latitude under the regulations. The Court further concluded that the regulations were tailored narrowly enough to serve a significant government interest. Here the Court disagreed with the court of appeals "sifting through" all the "available or imagined" alternative means of regulation. The restrictive means approach, said the Court, has historically not been used in examining time, place, and manner regulations. All that is required under the narrow tailoring standard is that the regulation "promotes a substantial governmental interest that would be achieved less effectively absent the regulation" while at the same time not being "substantially broader than necessary to achieve that interest." The question in *United States v. Kokinda* (111 L. Ed. 2d 571: 1990) was whether a U.S. Postal Service regulation banning solicitation on sidewalks located entirely on Postal Service property violated the First Amendment. The Court upheld the regulation in a 5–4 decision. The Court first determined the standard by which the regulation would be assessed. It applied the tripartite forum analysis for this purpose. Under this framework, regulation of speech on government property that has been "traditionally open to the public for expressive activity, such as public streets or parks, is examined under strict scrutiny." Similarly, regulation of expression on property the government "has expressly dedicated for speech activity" is subject to strict scrutiny. On the other hand, expressive activity where the government "has not dedicated its property to First Amendment activity is examined only for reasonableness." The Court rejected the argument that all sidewalks be regarded as a traditional public forum. The "mere physical characteristics of the property cannot dictate forum analysis." The "location and purpose" of a public sidewalk "is critical to determining whether such a sidewalk constitutes a public forum." The sidewalk subject to regulation in this case did not have the "characteristics of public sidewalks traditionally open to expressive activity." Rather, this particular sidewalk was constructed "solely to provide for the passage of individuals engaged in postal business," thus it was not a traditional public forum sidewalk. Even if the sidewalk had some recognized First Amendment uses, "regulation of the reserved nonpublic uses would still require application of the reasonableness test." Under this standard, not only must the regulation be "reasonable," but it must not be an "effort to suppress expression merely because public officials oppose the speaker's view." Two factors were key to the Court's finding this regulation reasonable. First, Congress had directed the Postal Service to become self-sufficient and to provide service "responsive" to the "needs of the American people." This mission was drawn for the Postal Service "at a time when the mail service is becoming much more competitive." The Court was thus deferential to regulations designed to facilitate the efficient conduct of Postal Service business. Second, solicitation is different from other forms of expression. It is "confrontation," and is "inherently more intrusive and intimidating than an encounter with a person giving out information." These factors led the Court to conclude that it is reasonable to limit access to Postal Service property for solicitation, because solicitation is "inherently disruptive of the Postal Service's business." And because the regulation excludes all groups from engaging in solicitation, it was viewed as content-neutral and could not be regarded as an "effort to suppress expression because officials oppose the views."

ASSOCIATION

Keyishian v. Board of Regents, **385 U.S. 589, 87 S. Ct. 675, 17 L. Ed. 2d 629 (1967)** Required that more than "mere membership" in organizations be demonstrated before the imposition of restrictions on associational rights. *Keyishian* examined New York statutory provisions known collectively as the Feinberg Law, which authorized the Board of Regents to monitor organizational memberships of state employees. The board was required to generate a list of subversive organizations. Membership in any one of them was prima facie evidence of disqualification from public employment, including appointments to academic positions. While the person being terminated could have a hearing, the hearing could not address the matter of the subversive classification of the organization. Keyishian and several other faculty members in the state university system were dismissed because of their membership in the Communist party. The Court struck down the Feinberg Law in a 5–4 decision. The majority rejected the premise that "public employment, including academic employment, may be conditioned upon the surrender of constitutional rights which could not be abridged by direct government action." The Court found "mere membership" to be an insufficient basis for exclusion. "Legislation which sanctions membership unaccompanied by specific intent to further the unlawful goals of the organization or which is not active membership violates constitutional limitations." The Court also said the statutes "sweep overbroadly in association which may not be proscribed." The regulations "seek to bar employment both for association which legitimately may be proscribed and for association which may not be sanctioned." The flaw of overbroad sweep was as fatal as the flaw of vagueness. The dissenters, Justices Clark, Harlan, Stewart, and White, reacted strongly by saying the Court majority "has by its broadside swept away one of our more precious rights, namely the right of self-preservation." *See also DENNIS v. UNITED STATES* (341 U.S. 494: 1951), p. 111; *NAACP v. ALABAMA* (357 U.S. 449: 1958), p. 147; *WHITNEY v. CALIFORNIA* (274 U.S. 357: 1929), p. 149.

Significance   *Keyishian v. Board of Regents* (385 U.S. 589: 1967) over-turned *Adler v. Board of Education* (342 U.S. 485: 1952), decided 15 years earlier. *Adler* had found the Feinberg Law constitutional, decid-ing that teachers "have no right to work for the State in the school system on their own terms." The state may inquire into the fitness and suitability of a person for public service, and past conduct may well relate to present fitness. In addition, one's associates, past and present, may properly be considered in determining fitness and loy-alty. "From time immemorial, one's reputation has been determined in part by the company he keeps." Shortly after *Keyishian,* in *United States v. Robel* (389 U.S. 258: 1967), the Court voided a McCarron Act provision that prohibited any member of a Communist action orga-nization from working in a defense facility. As in *Keyishian,* the Court found the statute "casts its net across a broad range of associational activities, indiscriminately trapping membership which can be consti-tutionally punished and membership which cannot be so proscribed." In a decision predating *Keyishian* and *Robel* by a year, but using similar rationale, the Court struck down a loyalty oath provision that imposed penalties upon anyone taking the oath who might later become a member of a subversive organization. The case was *Elfbrandt v. Russell* (384 U.S. 11: 1966). The Burger Court did uphold a loyalty oath in *Cole v. Richardson* (405 U.S. 676: 1972), which required public em-ployees to uphold and defend the federal and state constitutions and to oppose the overthrow of federal or state governments by illegal means. *Cole* found the oath sufficient in that it did not impose specific action obligations on persons taking it. It required only a general commitment to abide by constitutional processes.

The Rehnquist Court has taken at least three other opportunities to speak to associational freedom. Two of these cases were brought by labor unions. Section 109 of the Omnibus Budget Reconciliation Act of 1981 provided that the household of a striking worker cannot become eligible for food stamps unless eligibility was established prior to the strike. These provisions were upheld by the Court in *Lyng v. International Union, United Automobile, Aerospace and Agricultural Im-plement Workers of America* (485 U.S. 360: 1988). The law was challenged on the ground that it interfered with the right of strikers to associate with their families, unions, and fellow union members. It was further contended that the provisions violated the strikers' right of expression about union affairs free of governmental coercion. The Court said the statute did not "directly or substantially interfere" with either family living arrangements or the right of workers to associate with each other. Indeed, the Court said, it is "exceedingly unlikely" that relatives would choose to live apart simply to increase food stamp allotments since the additional costs would exceed the "incremental value of the additional stamps." Neither did the law "prevent" or "burden" workers' ability to "associate together in unions to promote their lawful objectives." Any impact that might exist here results from the government's refusal to extend benefits to those with diminished income. Such a policy does make it more difficult for workers to sustain themselves and possibly their strike. The Court said, however, that the strikers' right of association "does not require the Government to furnish funds to maximize the exercise of that right." Similarly, the Court did not find a free expression violation. The statute does not coerce political belief or action. Rather, it declines to extend benefits. The Constitution "does not confer an entitlement to such funds as may be necessary to realize all the advantages of that freedom." In *Communications Workers of America v. Beck* (487 U.S. 735: 1988), the Court ruled that unions cannot compel nonmembers to pay "agency fees" if those fees are used for political or other purposes that are not directly related to collective bargaining. Prior to this decision, unions were free to use such agency fees for non–collective-bargaining activities. A number of nonmember employees of the Communication Workers of America (CWA) challenged the CWA's use of agency fees to, for example, support endorsed political candidates, organize employees at other companies, and conduct various lobbying activities. They contended that use of fees for such purposes violated the CWA's "duty of fair representation." The issue in this case was whether the "financial core" includes the obligation to "support union activities beyond those germane to collective bargaining, contract administration, and grievance adjustment." The Court ruled that it did not. A similar decision was rendered in a case involving a state bar association. The State Bar of California is integrated. That is, those who wish to practice law in California are statutorily required to become dues-paying members of the state bar. Virtually all state bar activities are financed by the membership dues. Among these were activities that could be characterized as political or ideological. In the case of *Keller v. State Bar of California* (110 L. Ed. 2d 1: 1990), the Court had to determine whether state bar associations are analogous to government agencies or to private organizations, such as labor unions. Action was brought by Keller and other California State Bar members who wished to prevent use of the mandatory dues for those political activities with which they disagreed. Had the Court viewed the state bar as a governmental entity, the state bar would have been free to use dues revenue for activities beyond its traditional professional regulating functions. A unanimous Court, however, ruled that state bar use of compulsory dues for political purposes violated the free speech rights of members who might disagree. The decision effectively limited bar association expenditures to those activities required for the effective regulation of the profession and the improvement of the quality of legal services. Finally, the Court reviewed a city ordinance that authorized restriction of the use of certain dance halls to persons between the ages of 14 and 18. The ordinance was challenged by the owner of one of the "teenage" dance halls on right of association grounds. The Supreme Court upheld the ordinance in *City of Dallas v. Stanglin* (104 L. Ed. 2d 18: 1989). The Court said that associational freedom extends to "intimate human relationships" and those activities that involve "expressive association." The large numbers of teens who patronized Stanglin's dance hall were neither members of any "organized association" nor engaged in a "form of intimate association." They were essentially strangers who had in common only the price paid for admission. There was no evidence that patrons "take positions on public issues" or anything resembling that kind of activity. The generalized right to "social association," concluded the Court, does not include "chance encounters in dance halls."

Electoral Process

Buckley v. Valeo, 424 U.S. 1, 96 S. Ct. 612, 46 L. Ed. 2d 659 (1976) Examined the constitutionality of the Federal Election Campaign Act of 1974. *Buckley* considered the act against various First Amendment challenges, including the possibility that regulation of the electoral process impinges upon individual and group expression. The Federal Election Campaign Act was passed in the wake of the Watergate scandal. It sought to protect the electoral process by (1) limiting political campaign contributions, (2) establishing ceilings on several categories of campaign expenditures, (3) requiring extensive and regular disclosure of campaign contributions and expenditures, (4) providing public financing for presidential campaigns, and (5) creating a Federal Election Commission to administer the act. Suit was filed by a diverse collection of individuals and groups, including U.S. Senator James Buckley, the Eugene McCarthy presidential campaign, the Libertarian party, the American Conservative Union, and the

New York Civil Liberties Union. By differing majorities, the Court upheld those portions of the act that provided for campaign contribution limits, disclosure, public financing, and the Election Commission. The section imposing limits on expenditures was invalidated. In a *per curiam* opinion, the Court said the act's contribution and expenditure ceiling "reduces the quantity of expression because virtually every means of communicating ideas in today's society requires the expenditure of money." The Court distinguished, however, between limits on contributions and limits on those things for which the contributions might be spent. While the latter represent substantial restraint on the quantity and diversity of political speech, limits on contributions involve "little direct restraint." The contributor's freedom to discuss candidates and issues is not infringed in any way. Even though contributions may underwrite some costs of conveying a campaign's views, the contributions must be transformed into political expression by persons other than the contributor. The Court acknowledged a legitimate governmental interest in protecting the "integrity of our system of representative democracy" from quid pro quo arrangements that might arise from financial contributions. Expenditure limits, on the other hand, severely burden one's ability to speak one's mind and engage in vigorous advocacy. Neither is the First Amendment to be used to equalize political influence. "The concept that government may restrict the speech of some elements of our society in order to enhance the relative voice of others is wholly foreign to the First Amendment." By striking the expenditure limits, the Court allowed unlimited use of personal wealth or expenditures made on behalf of campaigns separate from the actual campaign organization of a candidate. On the matter of disclosure, the Court agreed that the requirement might deter some contributions, but viewed it as a "least restrictive means of curbing the evils of campaign ignorance and corruption." The Court also upheld the act's public financing provisions by rejecting a claim that a differential funding formula for major and minor parties was unconstitutional. *See also* FIRST AMENDMENT, p. 77; *NAACP v. ALABAMA* (357 U.S. 449: 1958), p. 147; *WHITNEY v. CALIFORNIA* (274 U.S. 357: 1927), p. 149.

Significance   *Buckley v. Valeo* (424 U.S. 1: 1976) generated important follow-up questions regarding regulation of the electoral process. In *First National Bank of Boston v. Bellotti* (435 U.S. 765: 1978), the Court struck down a state statute prohibiting the use of corporate funds for the purpose of influencing a referendum question. Without showing that the corporation's advocacy "threatened imminently to undermine democratic processes," the state has no interest sufficient to limit a corporation's expression of views on a public issue. In

Consolidated Edison Company v. Public Service Commission of New York (447 U.S. 530: 1980), the Court overturned a state commission order prohibiting utilities from enclosing inserts discussing public policy issues in billing envelopes. The Court said the order was aimed at the pro–nuclear energy content of the insert and was not justifiable as a time, place, and manner restriction on speech. Neither may corporations be forced to disseminate messages with which they disagree. In *Pacific Gas and Electric Company v. Public Utilities Commission* (484 U.S. 853: 1987), the Court ruled that a state regulatory agency could not order a privately owned utility to send inserts from a consumer group in their quarterly billing envelopes. The Court said freedom of speech "includes within it the choice of what not to say." The Court added that such freedom of choice is not dependent on whether the protection is sought by an individual or a corporation. In *Citizens Against Rent Control/Coalition for Fair Housing v. City of Berkeley* (450 U.S. 908: 1981), the Court struck down a municipal ordinance limiting contributions to organizations formed to support or oppose ballot issues. With only Justice White dissenting, the Court drew heavily on *Buckley* and concluded that the ordinance went too far in restraining individual and associational rights of expression. The Court extended the *Buckley* reasoning in *Federal Election Commission v. National Conservative Political Action Committee* (470 U.S. 480: 1985), saying the Federal Election Campaign Act could not limit political action committees (PACs) to an expenditure of $1,000 for promoting candidacies of publicly funded presidential aspirants. Such an expenditure limit impermissibly infringed on First Amendment speech and associational rights.

The Federal Election Campaign Act came under further review in *Federal Election Commission v. Massachusetts Citizens for Life* (479 U.S. 238: 1986). Under challenge was the section prohibiting corporations from using general funds to make expenditures related to an election to any public office. Massachusetts Citizens for Life (MCFL), a nonprofit, nonstock corporation, was formed to promote pro-life causes. MCFL used its general treasury to prepare and distribute a special election edition of its newsletter. This publication categorized all candidates for state and federal offices in terms of their support or opposition to MCFL's views. The Supreme Court ruled unanimously that the special edition of the newsletter fell within the scope of the prohibition of the law, but that the provision created unacceptable First Amendment violations for corporations such as MCFL. In order to sustain a burden on First Amendment rights, a compelling state interest must be demonstrated. Most of the rationale supporting regulations of this kind stems from the special characteristics of the corporate structure. The Court reiterated the reasoning from previous decisions permitting restrictions. The "integrity of the marketplace of political ideas" must be protected from the "corrosive influence of corporate wealth." Direct corporate spending "raises the prospect that resources amassed in the economic marketplace may be used to provide an unfair advantage in the political marketplace." The availability of resources may make a corporation a "formidable political presence, even though the power of the corporation may be no reflection of the power of its ideas." The Court held that groups such as MCFL simply do not pose that danger of corruption. MCFL was formed for the express purpose of promoting political ideas, and its activities cannot be considered as business activities. This ensures that its political resources reflect political support. Because the group sells no shares, persons affiliated with MCFL will have no economic disincentive for disassociating if they disagree with its political activity. In addition, MCFL's own policies prohibit taking contributions from business corporations or labor unions. This prevents it from becoming a "conduit for that kind of spending which threatens the political marketplace." The Court upheld, however, the power of the federal and state governments to regulate the campaign expenditures of business corporations in *Austin v. Michigan Chamber of Commerce* (108 L. Ed. 2d 652: 1990). The Michigan Campaign Finance Act prohibited corporations from using general treasury funds for independent expenditures for state political candidates. Rather, corporations were required to use funds specifically segregated for political purposes. The state regulation did allow business corporations to establish political action committees to make such independent expenditures. The Michigan Chamber of Commerce wished to use general treasury funds on behalf of a specific candidate for state office, and it sought to enjoin enforcement of the restriction. The Supreme Court ruled that the regulation did not violate the First Amendment. The Court found that protecting the electoral process from the "corrosive and distorting effects of immense aggregations of wealth" was a sufficiently compelling interest to justify the regulation. Corporate wealth can "unfairly influence elections when it is deployed in the form of independent expenditures." The Court then turned to the Chamber's claim that, like Massachusetts Citizens for Life, it, too, was a nonprofit ideological corporation. The Court disagreed, citing the organizational characteristics developed in the *MCFL* decision. MCFL was formed for the "express purpose of promoting political ideas, and cannot engage in business activities." Its "narrow political focus" ensures that its political resources "reflect its political support." The Chamber, on the other hand, had "more varied purposes." Second, MCFL had no shareholders or similarly affiliated members; thus no one connected with the organization had "economic disincentive for disassociating with it if they disagree with its political activity." While the Chamber lacked shareholders as such, many of its members may be "reluctant to withdraw as members if they disagree with the Chamber's political expression, because they wish to benefit from the Chamber's nonpolitical programs and to establish contacts with other members of the business community." Third, MCFL was "independen[t] from the influence of business corporations." Indeed, it was on this basis that the Court found the Chamber to differ "most greatly from the Massachusetts organization." MCFL did not accept contributions from business corporations, thus it could not serve as a "conduit for the type of direct spending that creates a threat to the political marketplace." In "striking" contrast, the Chamber's members are largely business corporations, whose "political contributions and expenditures can be constitutionally regulated by the State." Business corporations therefore could "circumvent the Act's restrictions by funneling money through the Chamber's general treasury." Justices Kennedy, Scalia, and O'Connor dissented. They pointed to the majority's "hostility to the corporate form," and saw the regulation of corporate wealth as far too "imprecise to justify the most severe restriction on political speech ever sanctioned by this Court." *Meyer v. Grant* (100 L. Ed. 2d 425: 1988) examined a Colorado law that makes it a felony to pay circulators of initiative petitions. Proponents of a state constitutional amendment challenged the prohibition on First Amendment grounds. The Supreme Court unanimously held that the regulation abridged political expression protections. The circulation of an initiative petition, said the Court, "necessarily involves both the expression of a desire for political change and a discussion of the merits of the proposed change." The activity involves the kind of "interactive communication" that is "appropriately described as core political speech." The Court saw the Colorado regulation as restricting expression in two ways. First, it limits the "number of voices" who could convey the message and restricts the size of the audience that can be reached. Second, it reduces the chances of obtaining sufficient signatures to access the ballot, which, in turn, limits the opportunity to make the issue the "focus of statewide discussion." Colorado argued that other avenues of expression remain open and that the state retains authority to regulate the scope of the "state-created right to legislate by initiative." The Court rejected both contentions. That other means of expression remain available "does not take their speech through petition circulators outside the bounds of First Amendment protection." The regulation, said the Court, limits access to the "most effective, fundamental, and perhaps economical avenue of political discourse, direct one-to-one communication." The First Amendment protects not only advocacy, but also the right to choose the "most effective means for doing so." The Court also failed to find that the prohibition was necessary to ensure that an initiative has "sufficient grass roots support" to warrant ballot access or to protect the integrity of the initiative process. The interest of ballot access is sufficiently addressed by the signature requirement. The issue of process integrity revolved around the circulator duty of verifying the authenticity of signatures. In the Court's view, paid circulators were not likely to be less vigilant than volunteers "motivated entirely by an interest in having the proposition placed on the ballot."

Tashjian v. Republican Party of Connecticut, 479 U.S. 208, 107 S. Ct. 544, 93 L. Ed. 2d 514 (1986)   Ruled that states may not require political parties to hold primary elections open only to registered party members. Under a state law enacted in 1955, Connecticut required that voters in a party primary must be registered members of that party. In an effort to broaden it own electoral base, the Republican Party of Connecticut changed its rules of participation in primaries for federal and state offices. Possessing insufficient strength to amend state law, the organization brought suit in federal court, asserting that enforcement of the law substantially burdened the First Amendment right of association. In a 5–4 decision, the Supreme Court ruled for the party. Justice Marshall delivered the opinion of the Court. He began by saying that challenges to election law provisions cannot be resolved by any litmus-paper test that separates valid from invalid restrictions. Rather, courts must first consider the character and magnitude of the asserted injury to protected rights, and then evaluate the precise interests offered by the state as justification for any burden. Finally, courts must weigh the extent to which those interests make it necessary to burden a plaintiff's rights. The party's First Amendment interest was clearly evident to the Court. The freedom to engage in association is an inseparable aspect of the liberty embraced by freedom of speech. The freedom of association includes partisan political organization, and the right to associate with the party of one's choice is an integral part of this basic constitutional freedom. Accordingly, the party's attempt to broaden its base is conduct "undeniably central to the exercise of the right to association." The statute in this case limits who the party may invite to participate in the basic function of selecting the party's candidates. The law thus limits the party's "associational opportunities at the crucial juncture at which the appeal to common principle may be translated into concerted actions, and hence to political power in the community." Connecticut attempted to justify restriction of the party's associational interest on four grounds. First, the state claimed the administration of primaries under the party rule would cost too much. Even if the state were accurate in its projections, the Court said that the possibility of future cost increases in administering the election policy is not a sufficient basis in this case for interfering with the party's associational rights. Second, Connecticut contended that the state law prevented raiding, a practice whereby voters sympathetic to one party participate in another party's primary in hope of influencing the result. While acknowledging a legitimate state interest in preventing raiding and thereby protecting the integrity of the electoral process, the Court felt that the interest was not involved here. A raid on the Republican primary by independents was seen as a curious concept only distantly related to the kinds of raiding that might appropriately be regulated. Third, the Court was unpersuaded by the state's contention that the law prevented voter confusion. Connecticut argued that the public might not understand what a candidate stands for when he or she is nominated by an "unknown, amorphous body outside the party, while nevertheless using the party name." The Court deferred, however, to the ability of voters to remain sufficiently informed without the state's assistance. Finally, Connecticut contended that its law protected the integrity of the two-party system and the responsibility of party government. Here the Court refused to consider the wisdom of open versus closed primaries and was unwilling to let the state substitute its own judgment for that of the party, even if the latter's course of conduct was destructive to its own interests. Speaking for himself and Chief Justice Rehnquist and Justice O'Connor, Justice Scalia said the majority view exaggerates the importance of the associational issue involved. He said the party's only complaint was that it could leave selection of its candidates to persons unwilling to become party members. He thought it "fanciful" to see an associational linkage between the party and putative independent voters, where there was no meaningful connection. If the concept of freedom of association is extended to such casual contacts, it ceases to be of any analytic use. Scalia also suggested that the state is not bound to honor the party's choice of method in determining its nominees. He felt the state is entitled to protect the party against itself. *See also* RIGHT OF ASSOCIATION, p. 386.

Significance   The Court's ruling in *Tashjian v. Republican Party of Connecticut* (479 U.S. 208: 1986) permitted a state party to determine the rules by which it conducted its own primary. A similar ruling was made in *Eu v. San Francisco County Democratic Central Committee* (103 L. Ed. 2d 271: 1989). California election law contains a provision that forbids governing bodies of political parties from endorsing or opposing candidates in primary elections. Another provision makes it a misdemeanor for a primary candidate to claim official party endorsement. Additional portions of the law regulate organization and composition of parties' governing bodies, limit terms of officers, and establish residency requirements for party chairs. The Court invalidated these provisions on associational grounds. The ban on primary endorsements keeps a party from "stating whether a candidate adheres to the tenets of the party or whether party officials believe that the candidate is qualified" for office. The law "directly burdens," said the Court, the party's capacity to "spread its message," and it "hamstrings" voters as they attempt to inform themselves about issues and candidates. The party's associational rights allow it to "identify the people who constitute the association," and to select candidates who best represent the party's "ideologies and preferences." Interfering with the party's power to endorse "suffocates this right." The Court has generally steered clear of intervention in partisan political processes. In *O'Brien v. Brown* (409 U.S. 1: 1972), for example, the Court invoked the political question doctrine when it held that federal courts did not possess the authority to interject themselves into the deliberative processes of a presidential nominating convention. A decade later the Court ruled in *Democratic Party v. LaFollette* (450 U.S. 351: 1981) that a state could not require national party convention delegates to support the candidacy of the winner of the state's presidential primary. Notwithstanding this generally noninterventionist tendency, the Court has found state interest in some restrictions on the electoral process to be compelling. In *Rosario v. Rockefeller* (410 U.S. 752: 1973), it upheld a requirement that voters register in a party at least 30 days prior to a general election in order to participate in the next primary. Similarly, the Court upheld a California law that denied ballot access to independents who had been registered party members within 17 months prior to an election (*Storer v. Brown*, 415 U.S. 724: 1974). Both of these cases were explicitly distinguished from Connecticut's law in *Tashjian*. Justice Marshall said the regulations upheld in *Rosario* and *Storer* were designed to protect parties from the "disorganizing effect of independent candidacies launched by unsuccessful putative nominees." This action was undertaken to protect the disruption of the political parties from without, and not to prevent parties from taking internal steps affecting their own process for the selection of candidates. Marshall was careful to point out, however, that *Tashjian* should not be read as blanket support for open primaries, or as meaning that no state regulation of primary voting qualifications could be sustained. In a footnote (13), Marshall said that party rules seeking to open primaries to anyone would pose a different set of considerations from those involved in *Tashjian*. The Court has generally steered away from the practices of political parties.

The Burger Court, however, rendered two rulings on political appointments. In *Elrod v. Burns* (427 U.S. 347: 1976), the Court held that an incoming county official could not fire department employees because they belonged to the wrong party. *Branti v. Finkel* (445 U.S. 507: 1980) involved assistant public defenders. The rationale shared by these two cases was that firings based on party affiliation penalized political thought. The principle of these cases was substantially broadened by the Rehnquist Court in *Rutan v. Republican Party of Illinois* (111 L. Ed. 2d 52: 1990), in which the Court ruled that hiring decisions for public positions could not be based on party affiliation. Justice Brennan, speaking for a five-justice majority, said that political victors are entitled to "only those spoils that may be constitutionally obtained." Unless party affiliation is an "appropriate requirement" for a position, the First Amendment precludes use of party affiliation in hiring, promotion, recall, and transfer decisions. Employees who do "not compromise their beliefs" stand to lose in a variety of ways. For example, an employee may lose "increases in pay or job satisfaction attendant to promotion." These are "significant penalties . . . imposed for the exercise of rights guaranteed by the First Amendment." So, too, is denial of a state job on the basis of partisan affiliation. State jobs are "valuable," and the inability to secure one "is a serious privation." Unless use of patronage is "narrowly tailored" to further a "vital" governmental interest, it encroaches on the First Amendment. Illinois asserted that patronage both produces a more effective work force and protects political parties. The Court disagreed. Brennan said that government can secure "effective" employees by sanctioning workers whose work is "deficient." Party affiliation is not a proxy for deficient performance as such. Neither is the democratic process furthered by patronage. Parties are "nurtured by other, less intrusive and equally effective methods." To the contrary, patronage "decidedly impairs the elective process by discouraging free political expression by public employees." Justice Scalia said in dissent that a legislature could determine that patronage "stabilizes political parties and prevents excessive political fragmentation—both of which are results in which states have a strong governmental interest." Scalia said he did not wish to endorse patronage himself. Rather, he regarded it as a "political arrangement that may sometimes be a reasonable choice, and should therefore be left to the judgment of the people's elected representatives."

Munro v. Socialist Workers Party, **479 U.S. 189, 107 S. Ct. 533, 93 L. Ed. 2d 499 (1986)**   Upheld a state law limiting general election ballot access to those candidates receiving at least 1 percent of the primary vote total. The state of Washington established a two-step process for minor party candidates seeking to get on the general election ballot. Any such candidate must first secure the convention nomination of his or her party. As the nominee, the candidate would appear on the primary election ballot. In order to access the general election ballot, the candidate needed to receive at least 1 percent of all votes cast for that office in the primary election. Candidate Dean Peoples was placed on the primary election ballot as the nominee of the Socialist Workers party. Peoples received only 596 of the 681,690 votes cast in the primary, or .09 percent. Accordingly, his name was not placed on the general election ballot. Action was brought in federal court by Peoples, the party, and two registered voters, claiming abridgment of rights secured by the First Amendment. In a 7–2 decision, the Supreme Court upheld the restrictions on ballot access. The opinion of the Court was delivered by Justice White. He established a general framework at the outset by indicating that restrictions on ballot access for political parties impinge on both the rights of individuals to associate for political purposes and the rights of qualified voters to cast their votes efficaciously. Such rights are not absolute, however, and are necessarily subject to qualification if elections are to be run fairly and effectively. In reviewing the restrictions of this type, White said it is clear that states may condition access to the general election ballot by minor party or independent candidates upon a showing of a modicum of support among the potential voters for the office. Generally, deference will be extended to state regulations in this area. When states attempt to justify access restrictions, there is no requirement of a "particularized showing of the existence of voter confusion, ballot overcrowding, or the presence of frivolous candidates prior to the imposition of reasonable restrictions." To require actual proof of these conditions would invariably lead to lengthy disputes over the sufficiency of the evidence offered by a state in support of the restriction. In addition, such a requirement would necessitate that a state's electoral processes sustain some level of damage before the legislature could act. The Court preferred that legislatures be able to respond to potential deficiencies with foresight rather than reactively as long as the response is reasonable and does not significantly impinge on protected rights. In this case, the Court concluded that Washington had created no impediment to voting in primary elections. Candidates and members of any organization, regardless of size or duration of existence, were viewed as wholly free to associate, to proselytize, to speak, to write, and to organize campaigns for any school of thought they wish. States do not have a constitutional imperative to reduce voter apathy or assist unpopular candidates to enhance their chances of gaining access to the general election ballot. All Washington did here was to require a candidate to demonstrate a significant modicum of voter support, a condition it was entitled to impose. Justice Marshall, joined by Justice Brennan, dissented. He spoke to the role of minor parties in the American political system and argued that their contributions cannot be realized if they are unable to participate meaningfully in the phase of the electoral process where policy choices are most seriously considered. In Marshall's view, the state had impermissibly preempted participation by minor parties and allowed them to be "excised from the electoral process before they have fulfilled their central role in our democratic political tradition: to channel dissent into that process in a constructive fashion." *See also* RIGHT OF ASSOCIATION, p. 386.

Significance   The ballot access issue examined in *Munro v. Socialist Workers Party* (479 U.S. 189: 1986) is not new. For years the Court refrained from engaging in direct supervision of state electoral processes. That policy began to change with the Warren Court's decision to address the issue of legislative apportionment. Regulations that made it difficult for new or minor parties to get on the ballot began to be scrutinized more carefully. In *Williams v. Rhodes* (393 U.S. 23: 1968), for example, the Court voided an Ohio statute that required new parties to file a substantial number of petition signatures to access the ballot. Established parties were exempt from the requirement, and the Court ruled that the policy unfairly burdened new parties. Similarly, the Court struck down an early filing date for candidates other than those nominated by the two major parties in *Anderson v. Celebrezze* (460 U.S. 780: 1983). But as Justice White said in *Munro,* there were cases decided during this same period that established with unmistakable clarity that states may, as a manifestation of their interest in preserving the integrity of the election process, require candidates to make a preliminary showing of support to qualify for ballot access. In *Jenness v. Fortsen* (403 U.S. 431: 1971), for example, the Court sustained a Georgia requirement that independent and minor party candidates submit petitions signed by at least 5 percent of those eligible to vote in the election for the office involved. Likewise, the Court upheld a state requirement in *American Party of Texas v. White* (415 U.S. 767: 1974) that minor party candidates demonstrate support through signatures of voters numbering at least 1 percent of the total votes cast in the most recent gubernatorial election. What is clearly reflected in such cases as *Jenness, White,* and *Munro* is that the Court will permit states significant latitude in restricting ballot access as long as access conditions are not excessive.

2. The Fourth Amendment

Good Faith Exception

United States v. Leon, 468 U.S. 897, 104 S. Ct. 3405, 82 L. Ed. 2d 677
(1984)   Upheld a "good faith" exception to the exclusionary rule.
United States v. Leon involved an attempt to suppress evidence obtained through a search conducted under warrant. It was determined
that the affidavit supporting the application for a warrant did not
actually establish probable cause. The lower courts ruled that despite
the fact that police officers acted in good faith and pursuant to what
they felt was a legally sufficient warrant, the evidence had to be suppressed. In a 6–3 decision, the Supreme Court reversed. The opinion
of the Court was written by Justice White, who defined the issue in
Leon as whether the exclusionary rule should be modified to allow
admission of evidence seized "in reasonable, good faith reliance" on a
search warrant that is subsequently held to be defective. White commented on the exclusionary rule itself, saying there is no provision in
the Fourth Amendment "expressly precluding the use of evidence
obtained in violation of its commands." The exclusionary rule operates as a judicially created remedy to protect Fourth Amendment
rights generally rather than as a "personal constitutional right of
the person aggrieved." White pointed to the "substantial social cost"
exacted by the rule, and argued that unbending application of it
"impedes the truth-finding functions of judge and jury." An objectionable collateral consequence is that some guilty defendants go free
or receive reduced sentences through plea bargaining. Indiscriminate
application of the rule also generates disrespect for the law and the
administration of justice. This is more likely when law enforcement
officers have acted in good faith or their transgressions have been
minor. For these reasons, recent Court decisions have focused on the
remedial objectives of the rule, and the Court has become more in-
clined to adopt a balancing approach. White said that application of
the rule must continue where a Fourth Amendment violation is substantial and deliberate, but the rule should be modified to allow use of
evidence obtained by officers reasonably relying on a warrant. The
courts must be sure that affidavits supporting the warrant are not

knowingly or recklessly false, and that the magistrate issuing the warrant has functioned in a neutral and detached manner. To extend the rule further serves no deterrent function. The rule is designed to limit police misconduct rather than punish errors of judges and magistrates. It is contrary to the rule's purpose to apply it to diminish objectively reasonable police misconduct. Once the warrant has been issued, there is "literally nothing more the policeman can do in seeking to comply with the law." Penalizing the officer for a magistrate's error rather than his own "cannot logically contribute to the deterrence of Fourth Amendment violations." In the case of Leon, since the reliance of officers on the judge's determination was objectively reasonable, the exclusion of evidence based on their activity was not necessary. Justices Brennan, Marshall, and Stevens dissented. Brennan called the decision one of a series aimed at the "gradual but determined strangulation of the exclusionary rule." Brennan felt the Court ignored the fundamental constitutional importance of what was at stake in *Leon*. He said fighting crime will always be a sufficiently critical and pressing concern to present "temptations of expediency" leading to "forsaking our commitment to the protection of individual liberty and privacy." Stevens said the Court should not so easily concede the existence of a constitutional violation for which there is no remedy. He said to do so is to convert the Bill of Rights into an unenforceable honor code that the police may follow at their discretion. *See also* EXCLUSIONARY RULE, p. 409; FOURTH AMENDMENT, p. 159; *MAPP v. OHIO* (367 U.S. 643: 1961), p. 172; *STONE v. POWELL* (428 U.S. 465: 1976), p. 173.

Significance   The Court said in *United States v. Leon* (454 U.S. 869: 1984) that the exclusionary rule may be modified to permit use of evidence seized by police officers as long as they reasonably relied on a warrant subsequently found to be defective. *Leon* represents a substantial alteration of the exclusionary rule, but the Court was careful to point out that the "good faith" exception does not apply under all conditions. The police may not mislead a magistrate or knowingly offer false information in support of an affidavit, for example. Neither may police officers claim good faith when it is clear the magistrate is not neutral. Further, reasonable reliance on a warrant cannot exist where it lacks specificity or is otherwise facially defective. Similarly, the Court held in *Maryland v. Garrison* (480 U.S. 79: 1987) that search evidence obtained by police through an "honest mistake" could be used in a c.iminal prosecution. The Baltimore police obtained and executed a search warrant for a third-floor apartment believing there was only one apartment on the floor. The third floor actually contained two apartments. One was occupied by the party named in the warrant, the other by Garrison. Before it was apparent to the police that they were in Garrison's apartment, they discovered and seized drugs that subsequently were introduced as evidence in the successful prosecution of Garrison. The Court said the constitutionality of police conduct must be judged in light of the information available to them at the time they acted. Information that emerges after the warrant is issued has no bearing on the validity of the warrant. Just as finding illegal items cannot validate a warrant invalid when issued, it is equally clear that a later determination that a valid warrant was too broad does not retroactively invalidate the warrant. Execution of this warrant presented other problems. Had the officers been aware that there were two apartments and that the warrant was in error, they would have been obligated not to search Garrison's apartment. The limits of the search were based on the information available as the search proceeded. While the purpose justifying a search limits the scope of the search, the Court recognized the need to "allow some latitude for honest mistakes that are made by officers in the dangerous and difficult process of making arrests and executing search warrants." The validity of a search such as this depends on whether the officers' failure to realize the overbreadth of the warrant was objectively understandable and reasonable. In this instance, the Court concluded that it was.

In *Oliver v. United States* and *Maine v. Thornton* (466 U.S. 170: 1984), the Court said that police officers do not need a warrant to search for drugs in open fields. An open field was not found to be a person, a house, or effect entitled to Fourth Amendment protection. It possessed no expectation of privacy. Similarly, the Court upheld warrantless aerial observations and aerial photography in two cases decided in 1986. In *California v. Ciraolo* (476 U.S. 207: 1986), the Court permitted aerial surveillance of a fenced backyard. The police suspected that marijuana was being grown on the property. In a 5–4 decision, the Court said any citizen flying in the airspace over the yard could have seen what a police office observed. The Fourth Amendment does not require that police officers flying in public airspace must obtain a warrant to observe what is visible to the naked eye. In *Dow Chemical Company v. United States* (476 U.S. 227: 1986), the Court permitted the Environmental Protection Agency to use aerial photographic equipment for measuring emissions at Dow's production facilities to determine whether Dow was in compliance with Clean Air Act standards. The Court said that open areas of an industrial complex are comparable to open fields, for which persons cannot demand privacy. *Florida v. Riley* (102 L. Ed. 2d 835: 1989) extended *Ciraolo* to helicopters. *Ciraolo* had involved surveillance from a higher altitude (1,000 feet) from a fixed-wing aircraft. Key to extending *Ciraolo* to *Riley* was the conclusion that police do not need a warrant when they make "naked eye" observations from public airways. The Court also weighed the expectations of privacy for a greenhouse. Riley had taken precautions against ground-level observations, but because the sides and top of his greenhouse were at least partially open, the greenhouse was subject to view from above. Using *Ciraolo,* the Court concluded that Riley "could not reasonably have expected" the contents of the greenhouse to be "immune" from official inspection from the air. Riley also argued that the helicopter had been too low, at least 100 feet below the minimum for fixed-wing aircraft. The Court pointed out that different regulations apply to helicopters, and that the helicopter used by the police had not been in violation of existing altitude restrictions applicable to helicopters. Anyone, said the Court, "could have been flying over Riley's property at the altitude of 400 feet and could have observed Riley's greenhouse." Neither, said the Court, was there "any intimation" that the observations "interfered with [Riley's] normal use of the greenhouse or other parts of the curtilage." A variation on the open fields doctrine was examined in *United States v. Dunn* (480 U.S. 294: 1987). Through the use of electronic tracking devices and aerial surveillance, drug enforcement agents traced supplies used in drug manufacture to a barn on Dunn's ranch. The ranch was encircled by a perimeter fence and several barbed-wire fences. Around the front of the barn was a wooden fence. Without a warrant, but prompted by the smell of chemicals and the sound of a motor coming from the barn, the officers traversed the fences and moved to a point outside the barn. They did not enter the barn, but instead shone a flashlight into it from outside and observed what they believed to be a drug laboratory. The agents then left the ranch, but entered it twice the following day to confirm their judgment that it was a place of drug preparation. A warrant was subsequently obtained and executed. The Court ruled that there was no Fourth Amendment violation. One question before the Court was whether the barn was within the ranch house's curtilage, that area immediately surrounding a residence that is afforded the same protection as the house itself. The Court said that four factors apply to extent-of-curtilage situations. First is proximity of the area claimed to be curtilage. In this case, the barn was 50 yards from the fence surrounding the house and 60 yards from the house itself. Second is whether the area is within any enclosure surrounding the house. Dunn's barn did not lie within the area surrounded by the fence. Third is the nature of the uses to which the area is put. Here law enforcement officers had objective data indicating the barn was not being used for intimate activities of the home. Fourth is the matter of what steps were taken by the resident to prevent the area from being observed. In this instance, Dunn had taken no action to protect the barn from observation by those standing in the open fields. The Court concluded that for Fourth Amendment purposes the barn was not within the curtilage of the ranch house. Dunn also asserted that he possessed an expectation of privacy distinct from the curtilage matter because his barn was an essential part of his business. The Court rejected his assertion on open field grounds. The mere erection of a fence in open fields does not create a constitutionally protected privacy interest. The term *open fields* may include any unoccupied or undeveloped area outside the curtilage. The officers in this case did not enter any structure, but merely stood in open fields outside the curtilage of the house and peered into the barn's open front. Neither did the use of a flashlight directed through the open front of Dunn's barn transform their observations into an unreasonable search. In *Thompson v. Louisiana* (469 U.S. 17: 1984), the Court opined that a search was not entitled to a warrant exception simply because it occurred at a murder scene. Thus the Court's general opinion in recent years does not appear to support claims of Fourth Amendment violations. Finally, the good faith immunity issue was raised in *Malley v. Briggs* (475 U.S. 335: 1986). On the basis of approved telephone monitoring, Officer Malley prepared felony complaints against the Briggs. Malley presented arrest warrants to a judge, who signed them. The Briggs were subsequently arrested, but a grand jury failed to find cause to indict them. They then brought a damage action against Malley, claiming he violated their rights by applying for the warrants. Malley in turn claimed absolute immunity from such a suit. The Court held that Malley was entitled only to limited immunity from damage liability. Such cases must be judged by the objective reasonableness standard, which provides "ample protection to all but the plainly incompetent or those who knowingly violate the law."

Warrantless Arrest

***Welsh v. Wisconsin*, 466 U.S. 740, 104 S. Ct. 2091, 80 L. Ed. 2d 732 (1984)**   Held that police officers may not enter a person's home at night without a warrant to make an arrest for a nonjailable traffic violation unless there are exigent circumstances. *Welsh v. Wisconsin* involved an erratic driving incident reported to authorities by a witness. The driver abandoned the car, but officers learned of his address by checking the registration. Without a warrant, they went to Welsh's residence, entered, and found him in bed. He was arrested and taken to police headquarters, where he refused to take a breath test. The trial court ruled his arrest to be lawful and suspended his license for failure to take the test. The Wisconsin Supreme Court upheld the arrest. The Supreme Court reversed the state court in a 6–3 decision. The opinion of the Court was delivered by Justice Brennan. In 1980, the Court held in *Payton v. New York* (445 U.S. 573) that a warrantless arrest in a person's home was prohibited unless both probable cause and exigent circumstances existed. *Welsh* examined one aspect of the question of what constitute exigent circumstances. Brennan said it was axiomatic that the "physical entry of the home is the chief evil against which the wording of the Fourth Amendment is directed." Accordingly, warrantless searches and arrests that occur inside a home are presumptively unreasonable, and exceptions are few and carefully delineated. The police bear a heavy burden when attempting to demonstrate an urgent need that might justify a warrantless search or arrest. Brennan said the Court's hesitation in finding exigencies is especially appropriate where the offense for which there is probable cause to arrest is relatively minor. When the government's interest is only to arrest for such an offense, the presumption of unreasonableness is difficult to rebut. Furthermore, the government usually should be able to make such arrests with a warrant issued by a neutral and detached magistrate. When an officer undertakes to act as his or her own magistrate, he or she ought to be able to point to some real, immediate, and serious consequence if seeking the warrant is postponed. The nature of the underlying offense is an important factor in the exigent circumstances calculus. Most courts have refused to permit warrantless home arrests for non-felonious crimes. The warrant exception for exigent circumstances is narrowly drawn to cover real and uncontrived emergencies. The exception is thus limited to the investigation of serious crimes. Misdemeanors are excluded. It is difficult to conceive of a warrantless home arrest that would not be unreasonable when the underlying offense is minor. In this case, the only potential emergency claimed was the need to ascertain the petitioner's blood-alcohol level. The state's classification of the first offense for driving while intoxicated as a noncriminal, civil forfeiture offense is the best indication of the state's interest in precipitating an arrest. Given this expression of the state's interest, a warrantless home arrest cannot be upheld simply because evidence of the petitioner's blood-alcohol level might have dissipated while the police obtained a warrant. Justices White and Rehnquist dissented, feeling the state had a substantial enough interest to justify a warrantless, exigent circumstance search, despite the noncriminal classification. They saw the need to prevent the deterioration of evidence as an exigent circumstance. Chief Justice Burger said he would have preferred to examine the questions presented by the dissenters in a "more appropriate case." *See also* EXIGENT CIRCUMSTANCE, p. 410; FOURTH AMENDMENT, p. 159; PROBABLE CAUSE, p. 446.

Significance   The Court established in *Welsh v. Wisconsin* (466 U.S. 740: 1984) that a warrantless entry of a house to make an arrest for a civil traffic offense was prohibited by the Fourth Amendment unless exigent circumstances existed. The matter of how much authority officials possess to enter private homes to make a warrantless arrest has always been troublesome. In *Payton v. New York* (445 U.S. 573: 1980), the Court said that the authority to enter a private residence without a warrant was absolutely contingent on the presence of probable cause and an emergency. In *Payton,* the police were attempting to make a routine arrest for a felony-level offense, but the Court held that the arrest was unreasonable. *Payton* did not attempt to define what constitutes a sufficiently exigent circumstance to support a warrantless arrest, however. The pursuit of a fleeing suspect into a private residence was permissible, but beyond that the contours of judicial policy remained vague. *Welsh* thus attempted to clarify the nature of an emergency. The Court insisted that the state show an urgent need for a warrantless arrest, suggesting that the demonstration of an actual exigency may be virtually impossible if the underlying offense is minor. If a state has classified an offense as minor, not even the preservation of evidence produces a sufficiently compelling need for a warrantless arrest. The Court ruled in *Minnesota v. Olson* (109 L. Ed. 2d 85: 1990) that a warrantless arrest of a guest in a friend's residence violates the Fourth Amendment. The Court held that the guest had an expectation of privacy sufficient to protect him from warrantless arrest. Such a finding "merely recognizes the everyday expectations of privacy we all share." Staying overnight in another's home "is a longstanding social custom that serves functions recognized as valuable by society." That the host possesses "ultimate control" is not incompatible with a guest having a legitimate expectation of privacy. The house guest is there "with the permission of the host, who is willing to share his house and his privacy with his guest." All guests share the expectation of privacy "despite the fact that they have no legal interest in the premises and do not have the legal authority to determine who may or may not enter the household." Warrantless entry can occur only under exigent circumstances. In other words, there must be probable cause to believe, among other things, that destruction of evidence is imminent, the suspect will escape, or danger to the officer(s) or others is likely. Under *Payton,* incriminating statements made following a warrantless in-house arrest are inadmissible. The question in *New York v. Harris* (109 L. Ed. 2d 13: 1990) was whether the existence of probable cause and administration of the *Miranda* warnings might overcome the taint of the unlawful arrest. Police had probable cause to believe that Harris had committed murder. They entered Harris's house without a warrant and advised him of his rights. By police accounts, Harris then confessed to the crime. He was arrested and taken to the police station, where he was again given the *Miranda* warnings. He then signed a written confession. A state appellate court ruled that both the in-home and police station statements were inadmissible under *Payton.* The Supreme Court permitted use of those statements made outside the house despite the defective arrest. *Payton,* said the Court, was intended to "protect the physical integrity of the home." It was not intended to grant suspects "protection from statements made outside their premises where the police have probable cause to arrest the suspect for committing a crime." Presence of probable cause was controlling here. Police had cause to question Harris prior to his arrest. Thus statements made at the police station were not an "exploitation of the illegal entry into his home." Suppressing the station house statement would, in the Court's view, not serve the purpose of *Payton,* because evidence stemming from the defective arrest was already inadmissible under *Payton.* In-home statements made following warrantless entry remain inadmissible, thus the principal incentive to follow *Payton* remains. Suppression of Harris's station house statements would have only "minimal" value in deterring *Payton* violations.

Warrantless Search

Michigan v. Tyler, **436 U.S. 499, 98 S. Ct. 1942, 56 L. Ed. 2d 487 (1978)** Applied the exigent circumstances exception to the inspection of a fire site. A fire began about midnight in a store co-owned by Tyler. Before the fire was fully extinguished, the fire chief made a cursory inspection of the fire scene. Among the things noted at the time were containers of flammable liquid. The police were immediately informed, and a fuller investigation commenced. After leaving the scene for several hours, both police and fire officials returned to the unsecured location around 8:00 a.m., examined the scene more systematically, and seized evidence. In the days that followed, additional visits to the scene were made and additional evidence, largely in the form of photographs, was obtained. None of the inspections, either those taking place during the fire itself or those occurring up to 30 days after the fire, was conducted with a warrant or with Tyler's consent. The Supreme Court, with Justice Brennan not participating, unanimously ruled that the searches occurring during and immediately after the fire had satisfied the conditions of the exigency exception. Those occurring more than nine hours after the fire did not satisfy the exigent circumstance conditions, however. The Court rejected the arguments that no privacy interests remained, as the badly burned premises had been abandoned, and that searches by officials other than police are not encompassed by the Fourth Amendment. Warrants are generally required, and an official must show more than "the bare fact that a fire has occurred." Even though there is a "vital social objective in ascertaining the cause of the fire, the magistrate can perform the important function of preventing harassment by keeping that invasion to a minimum." However, this search was subject to the exigent circumstance exception. The Court said, "A burning building clearly presents an exigency of sufficient proportions to render a warrantless entry 'reasonable.'" The authorities were properly on the premises, and could thus seize evidence in plain view. Justice Stewart argued that "it would defy reason to suppose that a fireman must secure a warrant or consent before entering a burning structure to put out the blaze. And once in the building for that purpose, fire fighters may seize evidence of arson that is in plain view." Justices Marshall and White would have restricted the warrantless search up to the point the fire was extinguished. They would have required a warrant for the return inspection the morning after the fire. Justice Rehnquist considered the search of a "routine and regulatory" nature and would have placed it outside the conventional Fourth Amendment coverage. *See also* FOURTH AMENDMENT, p. 159; *UNITED STATES v. EDWARDS* (415 U.S. 800: 1974), p. 176.

Significance   Warrantless searches are permitted if exigent or emergency circumstances can be demonstrated. *Michigan v. Tyler* (436 U.S. 499: 1978) examined the exigent circumstance exception associated with entry into burning property. The exigent circumstance exception is based upon the recognition that prior authorization through a warrant may simply be impossible under the conditions. To expect an officer to interrupt "hot pursuit" of a suspect, for example, to obtain a warrant to continue the chase onto private property is generally regarded as unreasonable. Key to proceeding without a warrant is demonstration of a compelling emergency. In *Tyler,* the Court found the presence of fire fighters on the burning property to be justified. Once legally on the property, the officers could reasonably investigate the origin of the fire. The investigation was permitted not only because it could be related to the preservation of potential evidence of crime, but also because it was necessary to reduce the likelihood of the fire recurring. Thus the fire was viewed as an emergency sufficient to allow the fire officials to be on the premises legally.

The legal presence also allowed warrantless investigation for a reasonable time following the onset of the fire. Those searches that occurred in the days following the fire were not seen as contemporaneous with the exigency that permitted the initial legal entry onto the property. Once property can be secured, the exigency ends and no necessity for proceeding without a warrant remains. In a more recent arson search case, *Michigan v. Clifford* (464 U.S. 287: 1984), the Court held that where "expectations of privacy" remain for fire-damaged premises, administrative warrants are required for searches intended to determine the cause and place of origin of the fire. Privacy expectations are "especially strong" for a private home, and a delay between the fire and the search brings with it warrant requirements. Once the cause and place of origin of the fire have been determined, the scope of the search is limited, and the search for additional evidence of criminal conduct can proceed only under a search warrant obtained on a showing of probable cause.

The Court reiterated the limited character of the plain view warrant exception in *Arizona v. Hicks* (480 U.S. 321: 1987). A shot was fired through the floor of Hicks's apartment, injuring a man on the floor below. Police entered Hicks's apartment without a warrant to search for the shooter and to determine if there were other victims. While there, an officer noticed two sets of stereo equipment. Suspecting they were stolen, the officer recorded their serial numbers and telephoned them to headquarters. In order to read some of the numbers, however, the officer had to move the equipment. The numbers revealed that the stereos had indeed been stolen in an armed robbery. The Supreme Court ruled that no lawful seizure could occur. The Court said that merely recording the numbers did not constitute a seizure, but moving the equipment was a search separate and apart from the search for the shooter, victims, and weapons that was the lawful objective of the entry. By moving the stereo sets, an action unrelated to the objective of the lawful entry, a new invasion of Hicks's privacy was produced. It was unjustified by the exigent circumstance that validated the entry. The Court went on to consider whether the plain view doctrine might allow the search to stand as reasonable. It concluded that it did not in absence of probable cause. To say otherwise would be to cut the plain view doctrine loose from its theoretical and practical moorings. The doctrine was used to avoid some of the inconvenience and risk that may be associated with obtaining a warrant under certain circumstances. "Dispensing with the need for a warrant is worlds apart from permitting a lesser standard of cause for the seizure than a warrant would require." The search of a dwelling, no less than a dwelling place seizure, requires probable cause, and there is "no reason why application of the plain view doctrine would supplant that requirement." The issue in *California v. Greenwood* (100 L. Ed. 2d 30: 1988) was whether the Fourth Amendment prohibits warrantless searches and seizures of trash left for collection outside a residence. Believing Greenwood to be engaged in drug trafficking, the police obtained from Greenwood's regular trash collector garbage bags left by him in front of his house. Largely on the basis of material found in the bags, warrants were obtained to search the house. The Supreme Court allowed the search. The Court said that Greenwood had "voluntarily" left the trash for collection in an area "particularly suited for public inspection." Having done so, his claimed "expectation of privacy" in the discarded items was not "objectively reasonable." The Court called it "common knowledge" that garbage bags left along a public street are "readily accessible to animals, children, scavengers, snoops, and other members of the public." In addition, the Court said that when Greenwood left the garbage at the curb for the collector, he was conveying it to a "third party" who might then sort through it or permit others, including the police, to do so. The police cannot "reasonably be expected to avert their eyes from the evidence of criminal activity that could have been observed by any member of the public."

Washington v. Chrisman, **455 U.S. 1, 102 S. Ct. 812, 70 L. Ed. 2d 778 (1982)**   Involved a plain view seizure of evidence located in a residence some distance from the place of a legitimate arrest. Chrisman was stopped by a campus police officer for illegally possessing liquor. The officer asked Chrisman for identification. Chrisman had no identification on him and requested that he be permitted to return to his dormitory room to obtain it. The officer agreed and accompanied him to the residence hall. The officer stood at the open door of Chrisman's room and watched him look for identification. While waiting, the officer noticed what he believed to be marijuana lying "in plain view" on the desk in the room. The officer entered the room, confirmed that the substance was marijuana, and advised Chrisman and his roommate of their rights. The students consented to a broader search of the room, which yielded more marijuana and LSD. The students subsequently sought to have the evidence suppressed on the ground that the officer was not entitled to enter the room and either examine or seize the marijuana and LSD without a warrant. In a 6–3 decision, the Supreme Court upheld the search. The plain view doctrine was critical for the majority. The doctrine "permits a law enforcement officer to seize what clearly is incriminating evidence or contraband when it is discovered in a place where the officer has a right to be." The majority concluded that the officer had properly accompanied Chrisman to his room, and that remaining at the doorway was irrelevant to sustaining the warrantless search. The officer had "an unimpeded view of and access to the area's contents and its occupants." The officer's "right to custodial control did not evaporate with his choice to hesitate briefly in the doorway." He had a "right to act as soon as he discovered the seeds and the pipe." This is a classic instance of incriminating evidence found in plain view when a police officer, "for unrelated and entirely legitimate reasons, obtains lawful access to an individual's area of privacy." Justices Brennan, Marshall, and White dissented, saying the plain view doctrine "does not authorize an officer to enter a dwelling without a warrant to seize contraband merely because the contraband is visible from outside the dwelling." For them, the failure of the officer to enter the room with Chrisman was a fatal defect. Further, the exigency of custody pursuant to arrest did not justify entry into the room. *See also COOLIDGE v. NEW HAMPSHIRE* (403 U.S. 443: 1971), p. 162; FOURTH AMENDMENT, p. 159.

Significance   *Washington v. Chrisman* (455 U.S. 1: 1982) rested upon the plain view exception to the warrant requirement. *Chrisman* drew heavily from *Harris v. United States* (390 U.S. 234: 1968) and *Coolidge v. New Hampshire* (403 U.S. 443: 1971). *Harris* involved the discovery of evidence while securing an impounded car as defined in department regulations. *Harris* held that evidence may be seized that is "in the plain view of an officer who has the right to be in a position to have that view." Controlling in *Harris* was the recognition that the officer had legally opened the door to Harris's car before finding the seized evidence. The *Harris* decision does not permit warrantless entry of a residence, however, simply because an officer notes contraband through a window. *Coolidge* sharpened *Harris* by saying that "plain view alone is never enough to justify the warrantless seizure of evidence." The exigent circumstance, however, can provide the basis for the warrantless seizure of evidence in plain view. *Coolidge* also established that plain view discoveries "must be inadvertent." The inadvertence requirement was dropped in *Horton v. California* (110 L. Ed. 2d 112: 1990), however. The Court found the inadvertence rationale from *Coolidge* flawed in two ways. First, law enforcement standards ought not to "depend upon the subjective state of mind" of an officer. That an officer "is interested" in particular evidence and "expects to find it" during the search "should not invalidate its seizure if the search is confined in area and duration by terms of the warrant." If an officer has a valid warrant to search for one item, and "merely a suspicion" concerning a second item, "we fail to see why that suspicion should immunize the second item from seizure if it is found during a lawful search for the first." Second, the Court was not persuaded that the inadvertence requirement prevented general searches or the conversion of specific warrants into general warrants. That interest, said Justice Stevens, "is already served by the requirement that no warrant issue unless it 'particularly describes the place to be searched and the person or things to be seized.'" "Scrupulous adherence to these requirements," Stevens continued, "serves the interests in limiting the area and duration of the search that the inadvertence requirement inadequately protects." Once those requirements have been met and lawful access has been established, no other Fourth Amendment interest is "furthered by requiring that the discovery of evidence be inadvertent." *Chrisman* does reiterate that legal entry by an officer must occur prior to the plain view discovery and seizure. Standing in the doorway of the students' room was a legal crossing of the "constitutionally protected threshold"; thus the seizure of evidence noticed in plain view was permissible. A variation on the plain view theme was developed in *United States v. Jacobsen* (466 U.S. 109: 1984). Several bags of a white powder were found concealed in a tube by freight company employees as they examined a damaged package. The employees notified authorities, who subjected the powder to tests without a warrant. The substance was confirmed to be cocaine. A warrant was subsequently obtained to search the location to which the package was addressed. The Court held that a warrant was not necessary for the chemical test. The original discovery had been made by private persons, thus it was not seen as official conduct subject to Fourth Amendment limitations. The subsequent inspection by law enforcement agents did not materially expand the scope of the search conducted by the freight company personnel. The law enforcement search "impinged no legitimate expectation of privacy." The Court saw the seizure of the bags as appropriate because it was apparent the bags contained contraband. Given what the agents came to know about the package, the Court found the contents to be virtually in plain view and thus seizable. Conducting the test was not seen as compromising a legitimate privacy interest because it merely disclosed whether or not the substance was cocaine.

Automobile Searches

***Chambers v. Maroney*, 399 U.S. 42, 90 S. Ct. 1975, 26 L. Ed. 2d 419 (1970)** Considered the distinction between residences and automobiles in applying Fourth Amendment protections. Following an armed robbery a description of the robbers and their car was broadcast. Police stopped a car meeting the description and arrested the occupants. The car was taken to the police station and subsequently searched without a warrant. The search produced both weapons used and property taken in the robbery. Following his conviction Chambers sought habeas corpus relief on the grounds of unconstitutional search. The Supreme Court unanimously (Justice Blackmun not participating) rejected Chambers's claim. The majority cited prior cases that recognized "a necessary difference between a search of a store, dwelling house or other structure . . . and a search of a ship, motor boat, wagon or automobile." The Court said that the "circumstances that furnish probable cause to search a particular auto for particular articles are most often unforeseeable; moreover, the opportunity to search is fleeting, since a car is readily movable." Given this situation, an "immediate search is constitutionally permissible." The Court could have chosen to require immobilization of the car until a warrant could be obtained, but it rejected this course as only a "lesser" intrusion. In the Court's view there was no difference between "seizing and holding a car before presenting the probable cause issue to a magistrate and . . . carrying out an immediate search without a warrant." As long as probable cause exists, either course is permitted. Since Chambers's car was properly under the control of the police, there was "little to choose in terms of practical consequences between an immediate search without a warrant and the car's immobilization until a warrant is obtained." *See also* FOURTH AMENDMENT, p. 159; HABEAS CORPUS, p. 419; *SOUTH DAKOTA v. OPPERMAN* (428 U.S. 364: 1978), p. 185; *UNITED STATES v. ROBINSON* (414 U.S. 218: 1973), p. 183.

Significance   *Chambers v. Maroney* (399 U.S. 42: 1970) provided a contemporary reiteration of the "moving vehicle" exception to the warrant requirement first introduced in 1925 in *Carroll v. United States* (267 U.S. 132). The moving vehicle doctrine allows a warrantless vehicle search because the mobility of vehicles creates a particular exigency, that is, the possibility that the vehicle could be moved out of the jurisdiction. The same standards of probable cause exist, however, as would apply if a warrant could be feasibly sought. The searching officer must be able to support a belief that the vehicle contains seizable articles. *Carroll* thus created a key distinction between vehicles and places of residence. Mobility of the former creates a generally applicable warrant exception. *Chambers* expanded upon *Carroll* by allowing the mobility exigency to pertain if the vehicle was first taken to the police station. *Chambers* rejected the need to obtain a warrant once the vehicle had been secured, which broadens the scope of the exception. It is also clear from *Chambers* that the rationale that applies to automobiles extends to other movable conveyances, such as trucks, ships, and planes. Examination of the vehicle exception in the special case of mobile homes was undertaken in *California v. Carney* (471 U.S. 386: 1985). Carney argued that his mobile home was more like a dwelling than a vehicle and thus should not fall within the vehicle warrant exception. The Supreme Court disagreed. Though recognizing that the vehicle possessed many of the attributes of a home, it was also readily mobile, a characteristic that made the mobile home comparable to an automobile. In addition, since the mobile home was a vehicle, there were diminished expectations of privacy. Because it was licensed to operate on public streets and highways, it was more subject than a residence to extensive regulation and inspection. Carney also contended that mobile homes should be distinguished from other vehicles because they are capable of functioning as residences. The Court refused to distinguish worthy from unworthy vehicles because to do so would require application of the exception depending on vehicle size and the quality of its appointments. The Court chose to retain the established basis for application of the exception—ready mobility and the presence of the vehicle in a setting that objectively indicates the vehicle is being used for transportation. These two exception conditions ensure that police officers are not unnecessarily hamstrung and that the legitimate privacy interests of the public are protected.

South Dakota v. Opperman, **428 U.S. 364, 96 S. Ct. 3092, 49 L. Ed. 2d 1000 (1978)** Involved a warrantless inventory search of an impounded automobile. Opperman's car was impounded for numerous parking violations. A police officer noted some personal property in the car, and, following established practices, inventoried the car's contents. During the inventory, marijuana was discovered in the unlocked glove compartment. Opperman was subsequently prosecuted for possession of marijuana. He sought to have the evidence suppressed, but his motion was denied and he was convicted. The Supreme Court affirmed the conviction 5–4. In addition to the mobility dimension involved with automobiles, the majority stressed that there is a diminished "expectation of privacy with respect to one's automobile" as distinct from "one's home or office." The primary function of automobiles is transportation, and a car "seldom serves as one's residence or as the repository of personal effects." In the course of their "community caretaking functions," police officers often take automobiles into custody. Impounded cars are routinely secured and inventoried in order to protect the owner's property, minimize claims against the police officers over lost or stolen property, and protect police officers from potential danger. The majority found these "caretaking procedures" to be an established practice within state law.

The search was not unreasonable because the inventory was "prompted by the presence in plain view of a number of valuables inside the car." Opperman never suggested that this "standard practice, essentially like that followed throughout the country, was a pretext concealing an investigatory police motive." A dissent authored by Justice Marshall was joined by Justices Brennan, Stewart, and White. It emphasized there was "no reason to believe that the glove compartment of the impounded car contained any particular property of any substantial value." In addition, the minority deferred to Opperman's locking of the car as adequate protection of his property. The police could show no further need for protection. Finally, police officers made no attempt to secure Opperman's consent. In short, the dissenters objected to the result of the holding that "elevates the conservation of property interests—indeed mere possibilities of property interests—above the privacy and security interest protected by the Fourth Amendment." *See also* FOURTH AMENDMENT, p. 159.

Significance   *South Dakota v. Opperman* (428 U.S. 364: 1978) broadened permissible seizures under the plain view doctrine by approving the warrantless entry into an impounded car for purposes of conducting a standard inventory. While the Court limited the *Opperman* holding to the facts of that case, two points stand out in the opinion. First, authorities were allowed to seize criminal evidence from a car that was entered with neither a warrant nor probable cause to believe that evidence of a crime was contained therein. The rationale was the "diminished expectation of privacy" attached to a car and the various needs served by conducting the inventory. Second, the Court suggested that such inventories ought not be evaluated in probable cause terms. In a footnote, the Court observed that the "probable cause approach is unhelpful when analysis centers upon the reasonableness of routine administrative caretaking functions." The majority maintained that *Opperman* represented "standard practice" for the police, and there existed no suggestion of any investigatory motive. Had there been such a motive, the investigation would have been a "subterfuge for criminal investigation" and would not have been permitted. Since *Opperman,* the Court has broadened the scope of permissible impoundment searches without warrant. In *Michigan v. Thomas* (458 U.S. 259: 1982), the Court upheld the warrantless search of an impounded automobile made subsequent to a routine inventory. The *Thomas* decision was reiterated in *Florida v. Myers* (466 U.S. 380: 1984). At the time of Myers's arrest, his car was searched by authorities and taken to an impound lot. Some eight hours later, a second search was conducted without a warrant. The Court upheld the second search because police officers had cause to believe

evidence was still located in the car. The Court said the impoundment search was justified on the same grounds as the initial search
incident to the arrest. The Court ruled in *Florida v. Wells* (109 L. Ed.
2d 1: 1990) that law enforcement officials do not have unlimited
discretion to search closed containers found while conducting an inventory search of a vehicle. Wells had been arrested for driving under
the influence of alcohol. He gave his permission to open the trunk of
his impounded car. A locked suitcase was found in the trunk. The
suitcase was opened and found to contain marijuana. The Court
ruled that the opening of the suitcase violated the Fourth Amendment.
The Court held that the key defect was the absence of specific department policy on closed containers that would govern the officers in
conducting inventory searches. Individual officers must not have so
much discretion in those situations that inventory searches can become
a "purposeful and general means of discovering evidence of crime."
The Court did not say, however, that all officer discretion must be
removed. In prohibiting "uncanalized discretion" in the inventory
situation, there is "no reason to insist that they be conducted in a totally
mechanical 'all or nothing' fashion." Police policies that mandate the
opening of all containers or no containers are "unquestionably permissible." It would be, said the Court, "equally permissible to permit
officers sufficient latitude" to determine whether a particular container may be opened "in light of the nature of the search and the
characteristics of the container itself." The "allowance of the exercise
of judgment based on concerns related to the purpose of an inventory
search does not violate the Fourth Amendment."

Stop and Frisk

Terry v. Ohio, **392 U.S. 1, 88 S. Ct. 1868, 20 L. Ed. 2d 889
(1968)** Examined the practice of stop and frisk and established
basic guidelines for a limited warrantless search conducted on persons
behaving in a suspicious manner. A police officer of 39 years' service
observed two men, later joined by a third, acting "suspiciously." Specifically, the officer felt the men were "casing" a particular store. The
officer approached the men, identified himself as a police officer, and
requested identification. Upon receiving an unsatisfactory response
to his request, the officer frisked the men. Terry was found to have a
gun in his possession, and was subsequently charged and convicted
for carrying a concealed weapon. The Supreme Court upheld the
validity of the stop and frisk practice, with only Justice Douglas dissenting. It was admitted in *Terry* that the officer did not have "probable cause" to search. Indeed, this is why *Terry* is an important Fourth

Amendment ruling. The majority distinguished between a frisk and a full search. The Court concluded that the officer was entitled to conduct a cursory search for weapons. Such a search is "protective," and while it constitutes an "intrusion upon the sanctity of the person," it is briefer and more limited than a full search. The frisk was justified by the need to discover weapons that may be used to harm the officer or others. Thus, where the officer "observes unusual conduct which leads him reasonably to conclude in light of his experience that criminal activity may be afoot," where he identifies himself as a police officer, and where "nothing in the initial stages of the encounter serves to dispel his reasonable fear for his own or others' safety," he is entitled to conduct a cursory search. Justice Douglas argued that probable cause had not been satisfied with respect to the weapons charge, i.e., the officer had no basis to believe Terry was carrying a weapon; thus the search was invalid. *See also* BROWN *v.* TEXAS (443 U.S. 47; 1979), p. 190; FOURTH AMENDMENT, p. 159; STOP AND FRISK, p. 455.

Significance   *Terry v. Ohio* (392 U.S. 1: 1968) provided law enforcement authorities with the capability of executing preventive actions. Not only did *Terry* allow police to stop a person in situations deemed to be "suspicious," but *Terry* authorized a limited weapons pat-down. Controlling in *Terry* was observed behavior that would justify or give cause for making the stop. Given cause to stop, the officer was entitled to conduct at least a cursory search. *Terry* does not allow a full search unless the cursory search yields a weapon that leads to an actual custodial arrest. In *Sibron v. New York* (392 U.S. 40: 1968), a case decided with *Terry,* the Court disallowed a stop and frisk that netted a package of narcotics, because the searching officer could not demonstrate cause for the stop. There was no reason to infer that Sibron was armed at the time of the stop or presented a danger to the officer. The Court felt the search of Sibron was a search for evidence, not for weapons. The Burger Court expanded upon *Terry* in *Adams v. Williams* (407 U.S. 143: 1972) when it permitted a frisk based upon an informant tip as opposed to an officer's own observations. In *Pennsylvania v. Mimms* (434 U.S. 106: 1977) the Court held that an officer could order a lawfully detained driver out of his automobile. Once out, the *Terry* standard must still be met. The Court concluded that considerations of an officer's safety justify having a driver leave a car, and if cause exists to proceed with a frisk, a pat-down is permissible. *Terry* and other cases that build upon it authorize substantial latitude for a cursory weapons search if observed or reported behavior can focus sufficient suspicion.

Recent cases further define the scope of *Terry*. In *United States v. Place* (462 U.S. 696: 1983) the Court held that suspicious luggage may be seized at an airport and subjected to a sniff test by narcotics detection dogs. In this case the permissible limits of a *Terry* search were exceeded, however, when the luggage was kept for 90 minutes, the suspect was not informed of where the luggage would be taken, and detention officers failed to specify how the luggage might be returned. *Terry* was extended in *Michigan v. Long* (463 U.S. 1032: 1983) when the Court allowed a protective search of the passenger compartment of a stopped car. The majority ruled that "*Terry* need not be read as restricting the preventive search to the person of the detained suspect." Search of the passenger compartment of a car is permissible as long as the police "possess an articulable and objectively reasonable belief that the suspect is potentially dangerous." Contraband discovered in the course of such a protective search is admissible evidence. The Court used the reasonable suspicion standard of *Terry* to uphold searches by school officials in *New Jersey v. T.L.O.* (469 U.S. 325: 1985). The Court held that searching a student's handbag is justified if there are "reasonable grounds for suspecting" the search will yield evidence that laws or school rules are being violated. Such searches are permissible if they are related to the objectives of the search and are not excessively intrusive, given the age and sex of the student and the nature of the infraction. The Court recognized that searches are a "severe violation" of the student's privacy. It therefore urged school officials to limit their conduct "according to the dictates of reason." But the Court said society must recognize that drug use and crime are "major social problems," and that searches are justified as a means of maintaining school discipline. Although it noted that constitutional protections did not apply in this case, the Court permitted the search based on the existence of reasonable suspicion. Further evolution of *Terry* occurred in *United States v. Sharpe* (470 U.S. 675: 1985), in which the Court upheld short-term (i.e., 20-minute) investigative detention where reasonable suspicion exists. In *Hayes v. Florida* (470 U.S. 811: 1985), however, the Court said that police officers may not take a suspect to police headquarters for fingerprinting in the absence of probable cause, a warrant, or the person's consent. The Court left the door open for a brief detention for field administration of fingerprinting when reasonable suspicion exists. It said such detention "is not necessarily impermissible."

The reasoning from *Terry* was extended to "protective sweeps" in *Maryland v. Buie* (108 L. Ed. 2d 276: 1990). A "protective sweep" is a "quick and limited search of a premises incident to an arrest." Such a sweep is conducted to "protect the safety of police officers or others."

The sweep is "narrowly confined to a cursory visual inspection of those places in which a person might be hiding." The Court emphasized that the sweep is not to be a "full search of the premises." Rather, it may extend only to those "spaces where a person may be found," and it may last no longer than necessary to "dispel the reasonable suspicion of danger." The Court acknowledged that an arrestee has an "expectation of privacy" in the remaining areas of his residence, but this did not mean that "such rooms were immune from entry." Determinations of reasonableness of a search require a balancing of the intrusion on individual Fourth Amendment interests against the "protection of legitimate governmental interests." The "ingredients to apply the balance struck in *Terry*," said the Court, "are present in this case." In *Terry*, the Court was concerned with the interest of the officers in "taking steps to assure themselves that the persons with whom they were dealing were not armed with or able to gain immediate control of weapons that could unexpectedly and fatally be used against them." The Court saw an "analogous interest" in law enforcement officers' taking steps to assure themselves that "the house in which a suspect is being or has just been arrested is not harboring other persons who are dangerous and who could expectedly launch an attack." Furthermore, the Court said that neither a warrant nor probable cause was required for such a protective sweep. Rather, the sweep can commence with a "reasonable, articulable suspicion that the house is harboring a person posing a danger to those on the arrest scene." Justices Brennan and Marshall dissented. They argued that because of the "special sanctity" of a house, and the "highly intrusive nature of a protective sweep," officers must have "probable cause to fear that their personal safety is threatened by a hidden confederate of an arrestee before they may sweep through the entire house." The key issue in most stop and frisk situations is how much information is needed to establish reasonable suspicion. The question in *Alabama v. White* (110 L. Ed. 2d 301: 1990) is whether an anonymous tip, uncorroborated by evidence of criminality, can provide the basis for a stop and frisk. The Court ruled an anonymous tip, if sufficiently supported by independent evidence, could provide reasonable suspicion. Like probable cause, said Justice White, reasonable suspicion is "dependent upon both the content of information possessed by the police and its degree of reliability." If a tip has a "relatively low degree of reliability," more corroborative information is necessary to "establish the requisite quantum of suspicion that would be required if the tip were more reliable." A tip's reliability is determined by application of the totality of circumstances approach. In this case, police were able to corroborate "significant aspects" of the informer's tip, which, in turn, imparted some degree of reliability to the other allegations. In addition, the tip contained a "range of details" related not only to "easily obtained facts and conditions existing at the time of the tip," but also to "future actions of third parties ordinarily not easily predicted." This information of future conduct "demonstrated inside information," and a "special familiarity" with White's activities. This familiarity, said the Court, made it reasonable for police to believe that a person "with access to such information is likely to also have access to reliable information about the individual's illegal activities." Although Justice White characterized the judgment as "close," the majority concluded that the tip, as corroborated, "exhibited sufficient indicia of reliability to justify the investigatory stop" of White. The dissenters, Justices Stevens, Brennan, and Marshall, felt the anonymous tip provided "anything but a reliable basis" for suspicion of criminal conduct.

Consent Searches

United States v. Matlock, **415 U.S. 164, 94 S. Ct. 988, 39 L. Ed. 2d 242 (1974)** Considered whether a third party may consent to a search. Matlock was convicted of bank robbery. Part of the evidence used against him was stolen money found during a warrantless search in a bedroom Matlock shared with someone else. Consent for the search yielding the stolen money was obtained from the other person, not Matlock. The Supreme Court upheld the search in a 6–3 decision. The majority stressed the decisive element in determining the adequacy of a third-party consent was joint occupancy or control. The Court found such control present in this case because (1) Matlock had often represented the other person as his wife, (2) the consenting person "harbored no hostility" toward Matlock, and (3) the person admitted cohabitation out of wedlock with Matlock, a criminal offense in the state of the search. The majority concluded that she was in a position to give valid consent to the search. The dissent offered by Justices Douglas, Brennan, and Marshall argued that consent cannot be obtained unless the consenting party is informed of the right to refuse consent. Their central thrust was that waiver of the right to privacy cannot be effectively made if a person "is totally ignorant of the fact that, in absence of his consent, such invasions of privacy would be constitutionally prohibited." Justice Douglas also pointed out that no exigent circumstance prevailed here; thus authorities had every opportunity to secure a warrant prior to the conduct of the search. *See also* EXIGENT CIRCUMSTANCE, p. 410; FOURTH AMENDMENT, p. 159; *SCHNECKLOTH v. BUSTAMONTE* (412 U.S. 218: 1973), p. 191.

Significance   *United States v. Matlock* (415 U.S. 164: 1974) provided guidance in the matter of third-party consent searches. If the suspect does not offer consent, the question becomes whether anyone may legally consent to the search of the suspect's premises. In *Matlock,* the Court targeted the "common authority" criterion. If a third party shares common authority over a place or items within a place, that person may properly consent to the search. Generally, common authority would cover consent by a spouse or persons otherwise living together such as in *Matlock.* Consent in these situations, however, may be limited if there are places or items within the shared premises that are "exclusively used" by the nonconsenting other party. Parents may generally consent to searches of rooms occupied by minor children within the parents' premises. Minors, on the other hand, typically may not provide consent to search shared premises. The ability to consent is independent from possessing title to the premises to be searched. Accordingly, a landlord may not legally consent to the search of a leased room or rooms, nor may the employee or agent of any landlord consent to a search on behalf of a tenant. This applies also to short-term renters in hotels or motels. *Matlock* permits third-party consent searches if the third party has common authority over the premises to be searched. The question before the Court in *Illinois v. Rodriguez* (111 L. Ed. 2d 148: 1990) was whether a warrantless entry is lawful if based on the consent of a third party the police reasonably believe to have common authority over the premises, but who does not in fact possess such authority. The Court upheld the entry. Justice Scalia said there are "various elements" that can make the search of a person's home "reasonable," one of which is "consent of the person or his cotenant." The "essence" of Rodriguez's argument is that "we should impose upon this element a requirement that we have not imposed upon other elements that regularly compel government officials to exercise judgment regarding the facts; namely the requirement that their judgment be not only responsible, but correct." The Court refused to do so and pointed out that warrants need only be "supported by 'probable cause,' which demands no more than a proper assessment of probabilities in particular factual contexts." The general rule, said Scalia, is that factual determinations made by agents of government be reasonable, but not necessarily correct. The Constitution is no more violated in this case than it is when police "enter without a warrant because they reasonably (though erroneously) believe they are in pursuit of a violent felon who is about to escape." The Court said its decision "does not suggest that law enforcement officials may always accept a person's invitation to enter premises." As with other factual judgments bearing on searches and seizures, consent entries must be judged against the objective standard: "would the facts available to the officer at the moment . . . warrant a man of reasonable caution in the belief that the consenting party had authority over the premises?" If not, a warrantless entry "without further inquiry is unlawful unless authority actually exists. But if so, the search is valid." The dissenters, Justices Brennan, Marshall, and Stevens, said that so long as the third party does not have authority to consent, the privacy expectation of the suspect remains undiminished.

Prisoners' Rights

Block v. Rutherford, **468 U.S. 576, 104 S. Ct. 3227, 82 L. Ed. 2d 438 (1984)** Held that persons detained in a pretrial circumstance do not have the right to contact visits and can have their cells searched in their absence. *Block v. Rutherford* involved a policy of the Los Angeles County Jail that denied any contact visits with relatives or friends of pretrial detainees. Also under review was the practice of jail authorities of conducting irregularly scheduled searches of individual jail cells when the occupants were not present. A number of pretrial detainees brought a class action challenging the policy and practice. The lower federal courts sustained the challenge. The Supreme Court reversed, however, in a 6–3 decision. The opinion of the Court was written by Chief Justice Burger. First, the chief justice described the security concerns that attended the case. The Los Angeles County Jail houses some 200,000 persons annually while they await trial. Those who must be detained before trial constitute a serious security problem, "given the ease with which one can obtain release on bail or personal recognizance." Holding a person before trial thus becomes a "significant factor bearing on the security measures that are imperative to proper administration of a detention facility." The Court defined the inquiry as being whether or not the challenged condition or policy constitutes punishment. Is the disability imposed for the purpose of punishment, or is it incidental to some other legitimate governmental purpose? Without proof of intent to punish, the issue hinges on whether there is an alternative purpose for the restriction and whether the restriction is excessive. Before applying these guidelines to *Block,* the Court expressed its belief that courts should play a very limited role in the administration of detention facilities. Prison administrators should be accorded wide-ranging deference in the adoption and execution of policies and practices that in their judgment are needed to preserve internal order and discipline and maintain institutional security. In considering the ban on contact visits, the Court focused on the question of legitimate government objective since it was conceded the prohibition was not intended as punishment. The Court found a "rational connection" between the ban and internal security at the facility. Contact visits "invite a host of security problems." They open the institution to the introduction of drugs, weapons, and other contraband. The visits also pose the danger of exposing visitors to risk from detainees awaiting trial for serious, sometimes violent, offenses. In this respect, pretrial detainees are as much a security risk as convicted prisoners. The Court did not find a total ban on contact visits excessive. To attempt limited visitation for low security risk detainees would offer a difficult identification problem exacerbated by the constantly changing nature of the inmate population. Burger reiterated the Court's unwillingness to "substitute our judgments on these difficult and sensitive matters" for that of persons charged with and trained in the running of such facilities. The Court concluded that the prohibition was "an entirely reasonable, nonpunitive response to legitimate security concerns." The Court simply deferred to the "informed discretion of prison authorities" by upholding the shakedown searches of cells conducted in the absence of detainees. Justices Brennan, Marshall, and Stevens dissented. Brennan said the Court appeared willing to sanction any prison condition for which one could imagine a "colorable rationale," no matter how oppressive or ill justified that condition is in fact. *See also* FOURTH AMENDMENT, p. 159.

Significance   Security reasons prompted the Court in *Block v. Rutherford* (468 U.S. 576: 1984) to hold that detention facility officials may prohibit all contact visits. For similar reasons the Court also upheld searches of detention facility cells in the absence of the detainee. While prisoners are constitutionally protected, recent decisions such as *Block* clearly indicate that the scope of their protection is more severely restricted than that of the general public. The first major case in this area was *Bell v. Wolfish* (441 U.S. 520: 1979), in which the Court upheld a variety of practices at a short-term custodial facility. Included in the permitted practices were (1) "double-bunking," or the assignment of two detainees to a cell originally designed for single occupancy, (2) limiting receipt of hardcover books to those mailed directly from publishers or bookstores, (3) prohibiting receipt of all packages from outside the detention facility, (4) strip and body cavity searches following contact visits, and (5) unobserved cell searches. As in *Block,* the Court was highly deferential to the security and management interests of detention facility officials. The Court also noted a diminished privacy expectation for persons in such detention facilities. Two years after *Bell v. Wolfish,* the Court upheld in *Rhodes v. Chapman* (452 U.S. 337: 1981) long-term double-celling against claims that it constituted cruel and unusual punishment. In *Whitley v. Albers* (475 U.S. 312:

1986), the Court ruled that the shooting of an inmate by a prison guard while the guard was trying to halt a prison riot was not cruel and unusual punishment either. The Court concluded that it is "obduracy and wantonness, not inadvertence or error in good faith" that characterizes conduct prohibited by the Cruel and Unusual Punishment Clause. The infliction of pain during an attempt to restore order is not prohibited "simply because it may appear in retrospect" that the measures taken may have been unreasonable, and hence unnecessary in the strict sense. The Court said the general requirement that a claimant establish the unnecessary and wanton infliction of pain should be applied with due regard for differences in the kind of conduct involved. In *Hudson v. Palmer* (468 U.S. 517: 1984), decided the same day as *Block,* the Court said prisoners could be subjected to random searches. If a prisoner's lawfully possessed property is destroyed during such a search, a constitutional violation occurs only if the state provides no mechanism to obtain remedy for the property lost. Chief Justice Burger said in *Hudson* that "the recognition of privacy rights for prisoners in their individual cells simply cannot be reconciled with the need for incarceration and the needs of penal institutions." These words epitomize the Burger Court's general stance in response to prisoner challenges to detention facility practices.

Three Rehnquist Court decisions reflect the same position. Regulations on prison visitation were challenged in *Kentucky Department of Corrections v. Thompson* (104 L. Ed. 2d 506: 1989). A class action was filed by a number of inmates after several visitors had been denied admission under the institution's regulations. The issue before the Court was whether the state and institutional policies created a liberty interest protected by the Fourteenth Amendment. Among other things, the inmates asserted that the regulations violated their due process rights under the Fourteenth Amendment. The Court ruled otherwise, saying that no liberty interest was established through the policies. Liberty interests, said the Court, arise from two sources—the "Due Process Clause itself and the laws of the States." The Court said it could not "seriously be contended" that an "inmate's interest in unfettered visitation is guaranteed directly by the Due Process Clause." State law, however, may create "enforceable liberty interests in the prison setting." A state creates a protected liberty interest by "placing substantive limitations on official discretion." This may occur in a number of ways, but takes place most often when the state establishes "substantive predicates" to govern decision making and by "mandating the outcome to be reached upon a finding that the relevant criteria have been met." While the regulations in this case provided certain substantive predicates, they lacked the "requisite relevant mandatory language." The Court referred to the language in the institution's memorandum that provided that the staff "reserves the right to allow or disallow visits." Such language, said the Court, "is not mandatory." Visitors "may" be excluded if they fall within a defined category, "but they need not be." Nor is being in one of the categories a necessary element of exclusion. The "overall effect" of the regulations is "not such that an inmate can reasonably form an objective expectation that a visit would necessarily be allowed absent the occurrence of one of the listed conditions." Put another way, the regulations were not found to be worded in such a way that "an inmate could reasonably expect to enforce them against prison officials." In 1974, the Supreme Court ruled in *Procunier v. Martinez* (416 U.S. 396) that the censoring of prisoners' outgoing mail could be done only to advance a "substantial governmental interest." Because of the First Amendment implications of such actions by prison officials, *Martinez* required "heightened" judicial scrutiny. In *Thornburgh v. Abbott* (104 L. Ed. 2d 459: 1989), the Court refused to use the *Martinez* standard in reviewing restrictions on materials coming into a prison. Rather, the Court ruled that the reasonableness standard was sufficient in this situation. Under Federal Bureau of Prison regulations, wardens are authorized to reject certain publications if they are judged to be "detrimental to the security, good order, or discipline of the institution," or if they might "facilitate criminal activity." Publications may not be rejected solely on the basis of religious, philosophical, political, social, or sexual content or solely because the material may be "unpopular or repugnant." The Court distinguished incoming material from outgoing mail, saying the problems associated with the latter were of a "categorically lesser magnitude." Materials received by a prison can circulate and become disruptive, thus a more deferential standard than *Martinez* is appropriate. The Court characterized the prison environment as "volatile" and said it was necessary to give prison officials "broad discretion to prevent . . . disorder." The Court agreed that the process used to review materials would "raise grave First Amendment concerns outside the prison context," but was permissible for prisons given the primacy of protecting prison security. Finally, the Court ruled in *Washington v. Harper* (108 L. Ed. 2d 178: 1990) that a state prisoner could be administered antipsychotic drugs against his will without a judicial hearing. The Court recognized a prisoner's "significant liberty interest" in avoiding unwanted drug treatment, but said that due process rights must be "defined in the context of the inmate's confinement." State policy required demonstration of medical need to treat the inmate. Coupled with the state's interest in maintaining prison safety and security, the Court was satisfied that Due Process Clause needs had been met. There can be "little doubt," said Justice Kennedy for the six-justice majority, as to "both the legitimacy and importance of the government interest presented here." There are few cases in which the state's interest in "combating the danger posed by a person to both himself and others is greater than the prison environment." Indeed, said Kennedy, the state has an "obligation to provide prisoners with medical treatment consistent with their own medical interest, but also the needs of the institution." Prison administrators have not only an interest in "ensuring the safety" of their own personnel, but the "duty to take reasonable measures for the prisoners' own safety." Where the prisoner's mental illness is the "root cause of the threat he poses," the state's interest in "decreasing the danger to others necessarily encompasses an interest in providing him with medical treatment for his illness." Involuntary treatment of prisoners could commence only after a finding of medical need. Under policy provisions, a psychiatrist's determination of medical need and recommendation for involuntary medication are reviewed by a three-person committee consisting of a psychiatrist, a psychologist, and an institution official. None of the committee members can have any direct involvement in the diagnosis or treatment of the inmate. The involuntary drug treatment cannot commence without concurrence of the committee. In addition, procedural protections exist, such as right to notice of the hearing, right to attend the hearing, right to cross-examine all witnesses, right to be represented by a "lay adviser versed in the psychological issues," and right to appeal. The Court was satisfied that these processes satisfied procedural due process notwithstanding the absence of a judicial hearing. The Court saw the administrative hearing as a more suitable forum than a judicial hearing for review of the medical questions. The decision to medicate is complex because of the risks associated with certain antipsychotic drugs. It was the Court's view that the inmate's interests are "perhaps better served" by allowing the judgment to medicate to be made by "medical professionals rather than a judge."

Drug Testing

Skinner v. Railway Labor Executives' Association, **489 U.S. 602, 109 S. Ct. 1402, 103 L. Ed. 2d 639 (1989)** Upheld drug testing as a condition of employment. The epidemic of drug abuse has generated several constitutional questions. The Rehnquist Court has responded to a number of these since 1989. In *Skinner,* the Court upheld a drug testing program, but its support was not unqualified. The Court rested its decision on the nature of the job responsibilities. At issue were regulations issued by the Federal Railroad Administration under authority given the secretary of transportation (Skinner) to adopt industry safety standards. Two particular regulations were challenged. The first required blood and urine tests of covered employees following major train accidents or incidents. The second authorized administration of breath and urine tests to employees who violate certain safety rules. The court of appeals ruled that the Fourth Amendment requires "particularized suspicion" prior to testing. The Supreme Court disagreed. The Court ruled the regulations reasonable under the Fourth Amendment despite the absence of warrant or reasonable suspicion requirements. The Court saw the government interest in regulating conduct of railroad employees as critical. Such employees have "safety-sensitive" responsibilities that bear directly on the traveling public. This creates a "special needs" interest that "plainly justifies" prohibiting covered employees from drug or alcohol use while on duty. In addition, these "special needs" create an interest that "goes beyond normal law enforcement" that may justify "departures from" usual probable cause and warrant requirements. The Court held that neither the requirements for warrant nor individualized suspicion was "essential to render the intrusions reasonable." After reviewing the purposes of warrants, the Court concluded that in this context the use of warrants would "do little to further those aims." The intrusions are "narrowly and specifically defined" and "well known to the covered employees." Furthermore, the warrant requirement would "significantly hinder" and otherwise "frustrate" the purposes of testing in the time needed to obtain a warrant and would result in "destruction of valuable evidence." As for individualized suspicion, the Court saw the testing as posing only "limited threats" to employee privacy expectations. This is especially true in an industry already subject to "pervasive" safety regulation at both the federal and state levels. The government interest in testing without individualized suspicion was also seen as compelling because employee impairment may not become noticeable before an accident. Employees subject to test, said the Court, "discharge duties fraught with such risks of injury to others that even a momentary lapse of attention can have disastrous consequences." Accordingly, the regulations that produce effective deterrence are reasonable. The testing under review in *Skinner* was upheld 7–2, with Justices Brennan and Marshall dissenting. Both argued that testing should not occur without individualized suspicion that an employee is using drugs or alcohol. Justice Marshall also refused to defer to the public safety rationale. "History teaches," he said, "that grave threats to liberty come in times of urgency, when constitutional rights seem too extravagant to endure." *See also* FOURTH AMENDMENT, p. 159.

Significance   In addition to *Skinner v. Railway Labor Executives' Association* (489 U.S. 602: 1989), the Court ruled on two other drug testing cases in 1989. The Court's decision in *National Treasury Employees' Union v. von Raab* (489 U.S. 656: 1989) was similar to *Skinner,* but varied somewhat because of differences in job responsibilities. Here the Customs Service required urinalysis of employees seeking transfer or promotion to positions having direct involvement with drug interdiction, or if the position required the carrying of firearms, or if the person would be handling "classified" information. The Court ruled that requiring mandatory urine samples as a condition of promotion or transfer must meet Fourth Amendment standards of reasonableness, but held the drug screening requirement was reasonable even without warrant or individualized suspicion provisions. The warrant requirement would "divert valuable agency resources" and provide "little or no protection of personal privacy," given that the testing purpose is "narrowly and specifically" defined. Moreover, the Court reasoned that affected employees are aware of the testing requirement and the procedures used. The procedures are specifically set forth and are not subject to discretion. As a result, there is no determination to be made by a judicial officer, because "implementation of the process becomes automatic" upon the employee's pursuit of one of the defined Customs Service positions. In assessing the reasonableness of the process, the Court had to balance the public interest in the program against the individual privacy concerns of the employees. The Court referred to the Customs Service as our nation's "first line of defense against one of the greatest problems affecting the health and welfare of our population." Many of the service's employees are "often exposed" to both the criminal element involved with drug smuggling and the controlled substances they attempt to bring into the country. Because of this exposure, the government has a "compelling interest in ensuring that front-line interdiction personnel are physically fit, and have unimpeachable integrity and judgment." The Court compared this interest with that of searching travelers entering the country, and said it was "at least as important." The Court also said that Customs Service employees who carry firearms or are directly involved in interdiction have a "diminished expectation of privacy" with regard to the required urine testing. Unlike private citizens or other government personnel, Customs Service employees engaged in interdiction "reasonably should expect effective inquiry into their fitness." The same is true of those carrying firearms. Successful performance of their job responsibilities depends "uniquely on their judgment and dexterity," and these employees cannot reasonably expect to "keep from the Service information that bears directly on their fitness." While screening designed to elicit this information "doubtless infringes on some privacy expectations," the Court concluded "we do not believe these expectations outweigh the Government's interest in safety and the integrity of our borders." Justices Brennan and Marshall were joined in dissent in the Customs case by Justices Stevens and Scalia. The dissenters focused on the same individual suspicion issue discussed in the railroad case. Justice Scalia said that without evidence of Customs Service personnel abusing drugs or alcohol, the screening was "particularly destructive of privacy and offensive to personal dignity." The third drug testing decision came in the Conrail case, *Consolidated Rail Corporation v. Railway Labor Executives' Association* (105 L. Ed. 2d 250: 1989), and examined the narrow issue of whether federal labor law required railroads to bargain with their employees prior to implementation of a compulsory testing program. The Court ruled that the drug testing represented only a "minor dispute" under law and could be undertaken within the scope of an existing contract. Had the Court ruled the testing to be a "major" dispute, the matter would have required a bargained resolution. Conrail has, as a standard practice, required employees to undergo physical examinations. Such exams were performed for several reasons, each of which had its own purposes and associated standards for evaluation. As medical procedures changed in some of these exams, the changes and adjustments in standards were unilaterally implemented by Conrail. The Court saw drug testing as generally analogous to the other medical testing. The union that challenged the testing programs was entitled, said the Court, to seek arbitration on the matter. The Court acknowledged that drug testing may be different in kind from the other medical examinations because Conrail's "true motive is disciplinary" with respect to the former. Such an argument "could carry the day in arbitration," but did not convince the Court that Conrail's contractual arguments were either "frivolous or insubstantial."

Heightened concern about drugs has also produced questions regarding investigatory stops, a technique frequently used to combat drug trafficking. The question in *United States v. Sokolow* (104 L. Ed. 2d 1: 1989) was whether reasonable suspicion exists when an individual fits the characteristics of a drug courier "profile," a composite of factors based on law enforcement experience that correlate with involvement in drug trafficking. Sokolow was stopped as he entered a taxi at the Honolulu airport. When Sokolow was stopped, Drug Enforcement Agency agents knew, among other things, that Sokolow had paid more than $2,000 for two round-trip airline tickets from a large roll of $20 bills. He was also traveling under a name that did not match the name under which his telephone number was listed. His original destination had been Miami, a "source" city for illicit drugs. He had stayed in Miami only a short time despite a 20-hour one-way flight. Further, he had appeared nervous throughout the flight and had checked none of his luggage. Warrants were subsequently obtained after a drug-detection dog alerted officers to a shoulder bag Sokolow was carrying. A search of the shoulder bag yielded an amount of cocaine in excess of 1,000 grams. The court of appeals had reversed Sokolow's conviction, saying the stop was impermissible because there was no objective evidence of "ongoing criminal behavior" prior to the stop. The Supreme Court reversed the court of appeals, characterizing the lower court's standard as creating "unnecessary difficulty" by drawing an "unnecessarily sharp line between types of evidence." Rather, the Court recognized the probative significance of the "probabilistic" factors from the profile. While none of these factors was itself proof of illegal conduct, and may even be "quite consistent with innocent travel," when the factors are "taken together, they amount to reasonable suspicion." The factors observed have evidentiary value by themselves, and the fact that these factors were listed in the profile does not "detract from their evidentiary significance as seen by a trained agent." Finally, Sokolow contended that the agents were obligated to use the "least intrusive means to verify or dispel their suspicions." Sokolow argued that the agents should have "approached and spoken with him" rather than detaining him. The Court disagreed. The reasonableness of a stop "does not turn on the availability of less intrusive investigatory techniques." Such a rule would "unduly hamper the police's ability to make swift on-the-spot decisions, . . . and it would require courts to indulge in unrealistic second-guessing." Finally, the Supreme Court authorized warrantless seizure of nonresident alien property located outside the United States in *United States v. Verdugo-Urquidez* (108 L. Ed. 2d 222: 1990). This decision is particularly significant in light of the present "war on drugs" as it removes one potentially effective line of defense for foreign nationals prosecuted in the United States for drug trafficking. Verdugo-Urquidez, a Mexican resident, was taken into custody by Mexican officials in Mexico for various drug-related violations of American law. He was transported to a border station and turned over to American officers, who placed him under arrest. Several days later, U.S. Drug Enforcement Agency officers, working with Mexican authorities, searched two of Verdugo-Urquidez's residences in Mexico and seized a variety of documents. A six-justice majority ruled that the Fourth Amendment does not apply in this situation. Chief Justice Rehnquist said that the Fourth Amendment "functions differently" from other rights of the accused protections. The framers of the amendment chose to use the term *people* in the amendment as opposed to any *person* or an *accused*. This was meant to refer to a "class of persons who are part of a national community or who have otherwise developed sufficient connection with this country to be considered part of that community." The purpose of the Fourth Amendment was to "protect the people of the United States against arbitrary action by their own Government." It was not intended to restrain the federal government's "actions against aliens outside United States territory." Clearly, warrants are required to search overseas property of American citizens. Further, Rehnquist indicated that aliens with "substantial connections" to the United States are reached by the protections of the Fourth Amendment. Verdugo-Urquidez's involuntary presence on American soil, however, did not establish such a connection. He had no "previous significant voluntary connection" with the United States that "might place him among 'the people'" of the national community. Justices Brennan, Marshall, and Blackmun dissented. In Brennan's view, Verdugo-Urquidez had "sufficient connection" to the United States by virtue of the government's own action. He is a member of "our community" and is entitled to Fourth Amendment protection because the government is "attempting to hold him accountable under United States criminal laws." Verdugo-Urquidez, said Brennan, "has become, quite literally, one of the governed." On a related matter, the Supreme Court upheld the use of so-called sobriety check lanes against Fourth Amendment challenge in *Michigan Department of State Police v. Sitz* (110 L. Ed. 2d 412: 1990). Law enforcement officers briefly stop all drivers at such checkpoints in an attempt to detect signs of intoxication. Every state utilizes some kind of checkpoint method in the current effort to combat drunken driving. Chief Justice Rehnquist, speaking for a six-justice majority, said such stops are "seizures within the meaning of the Fourth Amendment." The question in *Sitz* was "whether such seizures are reasonable." The question was resolved by weighing the state's interest in "preventing drunk driving" against the "intrusion" on drivers as individuals. The Court began by characterizing the scope of the problem. "No one can seriously dispute the magnitude of the drunk driving problem or the state's interest in eradicating it." Rehnquist referred to both media accounts of "alcohol-related death and mutilation" and statistical data showing an annual death toll in excess if 25,000. At the same time, the "intrusion on motorists stopped briefly at sobriety checkpoints is slight." The Court said that these stops were similar to highway stops used to detect illegal aliens. Such stops as these do not involve "standardless and unconstrained discretion" on the part of law enforcement officers. Empirical data show that operation of the checkpoints produces arrests for alcohol impairment. While the check lanes may not be the best means available for enforcing drunk driving laws, the approach "can reasonably be said to advance" the state interest in preventing alcohol-impaired driving. Justices Brennan, Marshall, and Stevens dissented. They felt the Fourth Amendment precluded any stop without "some level of individualized suspicion." Justice Stevens doubted the utility of the checkpoints. The check lanes create the "disquieting" possibility that "anyone, no matter how innocent, may be stopped for police inspection." He referred to the check lanes as "publicity stunts" designed for their "attention-getting . . . shock value." The majority, said Stevens, was "driven by nothing more than symbolic state action." The Court, he said, is "transfixed by the wrong symbol—the illusory prospect of punishing countless intoxicated motorists—when it should keep its eyes on the road plainly marked by the Constitution."

3. The Fifth Amendment

Double Jeopardy

Price v. Georgia, **398 U.S. 323, 90 S. Ct. 1757, 26 L. Ed. 2d 300
(1970)** Involved the concept of "implicit acquittal" by which it can
be said that if a jury chooses to convict an individual on a lesser
included charge, the jury acquitted the individual on the greater
charge. Price was convicted of manslaughter, although the state had
charged him with murder. Price appealed his conviction on jury instruction grounds and had the conviction set aside by a Georgia appellate court. Price was then retried, with the indictment again
charging him with murder. The jury again convicted Price of manslaughter and Price appealed on double jeopardy grounds, claiming
impermissible jeopardy on the murder charge in the second trial. The
Supreme Court agreed with Price in a unanimous decision (Justice
Blackmun not participating). Chief Justice Burger wrote for the majority that the "first verdict, limited as it was to the lesser included
offense, required that the retrial be limited to that lesser offense."
The chief justice emphasized that the double jeopardy protection
"flows inescapably" from a concern about "risk of conviction," and
Price was "twice put in jeopardy." Price's jeopardy on the murder
charge "ended when the first jury was given a full opportunity to
return a verdict on that charge and instead reached a verdict on the
lesser charge." Burger concluded the opinion by suggesting that there
was no effective difference between a direct or explicit acquittal and
one "implied by a conviction on a lesser included offense when the
jury was given a full opportunity to return a verdict on the greater
charge." *See also* ASHE *v.* SWENSON (397 U.S. 436), p. 213; BREED *v.* JONES
(421 U.S. 519: 1975), p. 216; BULLINGTON *v.* MISSOURI (451 U.S. 430:
1981), p. 217; DOUBLE JEOPARDY, p. 403; FIFTH AMENDMENT, p. 201;
WALLER *v.* FLORIDA (397 U.S. 387: 1970), p. 212.

Significance *Price v. Georgia* (398 U.S. 323: 1970) raises and settles
the question of implicit acquittal, but it also addresses the more general question of the extent to which double jeopardy protection applies to a case in which a defendant successfully appeals a conviction.

Reprosecution typically does not constitute double jeopardy as such. The Court advanced a waiver rationale in *Green v. United States* (355 U.S. 184: 1957), saying that an appealing defendant is waiving double jeopardy protection by requesting that the conviction be reversed. Although the waiver argument is not wholly persuasive, and while some cases subsequent to *Green* have seemed to temper the waiver approach, defendants remain vulnerable to the reinstitution of charges following a successful appeal. The exception to the retrial rule applies to those cases where successful appeal has determined that the conviction was based on legally deficient evidence. The "implicit acquittal" principle of *Price* applies at this point. It limits the charge on reprosecution to no greater than the equivalent of the original conviction. Thus, if a jury opted to convict at a lesser included level at the initial trial, the retrial is limited to a charge no more serious than that lesser included offense. *Price* sets the limitation on the scope of reprosecution following a successful appeal. On a related matter, the Court ruled in *Ohio v. Johnson* (467 U.S. 493: 1984) that the double jeopardy clause did not preclude prosecution for offenses not included in a guilty plea to other charges stemming from the same indictment. Johnson was indicted for four offenses. Over the prosecution's objection, he pled guilty to two of the charges at his arraignment. The trial judge dismissed the remaining charges on the ground that prosecution would constitute double jeopardy. The Supreme Court reversed the trial judge, ruling that dismissal of the remaining and more serious charges did more than prevent cumulative punishment—it precluded a verdict on the charges. Johnson had not been "exposed to conviction" on the charges to which he did not plead, and the state is entitled to an opportunity to marshal its evidence on these charges. Acceptance of the plea to lesser included offenses does not have implications of implied acquittal. The overreaching of government is not involved, so double jeopardy does not apply. But a new trial is not always required. In *Morris v. Mathews* (475 U.S. 237: 1986), the Court held that the modification of a double jeopardy-barred conviction to a lesser included offense that was not barred by double jeopardy was an adequate remedy. Mathews and another person robbed a bank and fled to a farmhouse. Shots were fired inside the farmhouse, and Mathews then surrendered. His companion was found dead. The death was ruled a suicide by the coroner and Mathews was charged only with robbery. He pled guilty to that charge. Subsequently, Mathews admitted killing his companion, and the state indicted him for aggravated murder in connection with the robbery. He was convicted of the aggravated murder charge. An appeals court barred the conviction for aggravated murder on double jeopardy grounds. The Court said that under such circumstances the burden shifts to the defendant to demonstrate a reasonable probability that he would not have been convicted on the nonbarred offense "absent the presence of the jeopardy-barred offense."

An unusual convergence of double jeopardy, plea bargaining, and death penalty issues surfaced in *Ricketts v. Adamson* (483 U.S. 1: 1987). Adamson was indicted for first-degree murder for his part in the killing of a newspaper reporter. Shortly after his trial began, Adamson and the prosecutor agreed that Adamson could plead guilty to second-degree murder in exchange for testifying against other persons involved in the crime. The agreement specified not only the actual time Adamson would spend in prison, but also that the bargain was null and void if he refused to testify. Included as well was a specific provision that the original charge would automatically be reinstated if Adamson changed his mind. Adamson testified, he and the others were convicted, and the trial court accepted the sentence proposed for Adamson. The convictions of the others were eventually set on appeal, however, and remanded for trial. The prosecutor sought Adamson's testimony at the retrial, but Adamson refused, saying his obligation had ended when he was sentenced. The state then instituted new first-degree murder charges against Adamson and eventually secured a conviction. In a 5–4 decision, the Supreme Court ruled against Adamson. The Court was satisfied that the agreement covered any retrial and that Adamson was aware of the consequences of his breaching the agreement. Further, the Court said that double jeopardy need not be waived in the agreement. The agreement provided that any refusal to testify would automatically return the parties to the status quo ante, in which case Adamson would have had no double jeopardy defense to waive. The double jeopardy question examined in *Lockhart v. Nelson* (488 U.S. 33: 1988) was whether a state could seek resentencing following an appellate court decision that crucial evidence in the initial sentencing was inadmissible. Arkansas secured a supplemented sentence for Nelson as a habitual offender by demonstrating to a jury that he had four prior felony convictions. Nelson subsequently filed a habeas corpus petition claiming that one of the convictions used to support the recidivist sentencing had been pardoned. The district court found that the conviction in question had indeed been pardoned, and set aside the supplemental sentence. It also ruled that the state was prohibited on double jeopardy grounds from attempting to resentence Nelson as a habitual offender because the initial sentence had been based on insufficient evidence. The Supreme Court disagreed. Rather, the Court held that retrial is not barred when the evidence submitted by the state, erroneously or not, would have been "sufficient to sustain a guilty verdict." The trial court's judgment was founded on the proposition that appellate reversal for evidence insufficiency is the "functional equivalent" of an acquittal. The trial court erred here by admitting the conviction for which Nelson had been pardoned. Using that evidence, however, there clearly had been enough evidence to support the supplemental sentence. Permitting retrial in this case is "not the sort of governmental oppression at which the Double Jeopardy Clause is aimed." The decision not to bar resentencing "merely recreates" the situation that would have existed had the trial judge excluded the conviction in the first place. *Jones v. Thomas* (105 L. Ed. 2d 322: 1989) raised a multiple punishment issue. Thomas was convicted of attempted robbery and first-degree murder. The offenses arose out of the same incident. He was sentenced to terms of 15 years (for the attempted robbery) and life (for the murder). The terms were to run consecutively, beginning with the 15-year sentence. While a postconviction motion was pending in the trial court, the governor commuted Thomas's 15-year sentence for attempted robbery to time served. The state supreme court subsequently ruled that the state legislature had not intended separate punishments for felony murder and the underlying felony. The trial court vacated the attempted robbery conviction, left the murder conviction intact, but applied time served for the attempted robbery against the life sentence. Thomas contended that because he had completed the commuted attempted robbery sentence, he could not be confined for the longer murder sentence. The Supreme Court disagreed and ruled that the state court remedy sufficiently protected Thomas's rights against multiple punishment. The Double Jeopardy protection against such punishments was intended, said the Court, to "prevent a sentencing court from prescribing greater punishment than the legislature intended." The remedy chosen by the state court "fully vindicated" Thomas's rights because when resentencing had concluded, he stood convicted of felony murder "alone," and his "confinement under the single sentence imposed for that crime is not double jeopardy."

Ashe v. Swenson, **397 U.S. 436, 90 S. Ct. 1189, 25 L. Ed. 2d 469 (1970)** Considered whether the principle of collateral estoppel is contained within the double jeopardy protection in state criminal proceedings. Collateral estoppel is a legal principle that prohibits relitigation of an issue once a valid judgment has been made on that issue. Six persons were robbed while they were playing poker. Ashe was charged with armed robbery of each of the six players, i.e., six separate offenses. He was also charged with theft of the getaway car. Ashe was tried for robbing one of the victims and was acquitted. The jury found the evidence "insufficient" to convict. Several weeks later Ashe was tried for the robbery of another of the victims and was convicted.

With only Chief Justice Burger dissenting, the Supreme Court reversed Ashe's conviction. Five justices concurred in three different opinions. The majority felt the only issue in dispute in the first trial was the identification of Ashe as one of the robbers. The jury had resolved that question in the negative. Substituting one victim for another "had no bearing whatever upon the issue of whether the petitioner was one of the robbers." The majority found the fact issue of the two trials to be identical and suggested the "situation is constitutionally no different" than had the state attempted to reprosecute Ashe for the robbery of the first victim. The two offenses were the same. Chief Justice Burger's dissent focused on two points. First, Burger felt that collateral estoppel had been extended too far. If the double jeopardy protection is intended to prohibit harassment of an accused through repeated prosecution, use of collateral estoppel was "truly a case of expanding a sound basic principle beyond the bounds—or needs—of its rationale and legitimate objectives." Second, Burger disagreed that the fact question in the second case was the same as the first. Using the same evidence test, Burger concluded that the evidence required to convict was at least partially different in the second case. *See also* BREED v. JONES (421 U.S. 519: 1975), p. 216; BULLINGTON v. MISSOURI (451 U.S. 430: 1981), p. 396; COLLATERAL ESTOPPEL, p. 396; DOUBLE JEOPARDY, p. 403; FIFTH AMENDMENT, p. 201; PRICE v. GEORGIA (398 U.S. 323: 1970), p. 215; WALLER v. FLORIDA (397 U.S. 387: 1970), p. 212.

Significance   Ashe v. Swenson (397 U.S. 436: 1970) addressed the most troublesome double jeopardy question, that of "sameness." The double jeopardy protection prevents a second prosecution only if charges are brought for the same offense. Thus determination of sameness is fundamental. With a large number of acts defined as crime, it is likely that multiple prosecutions can arise out of overlapping offenses and single transactions. Prior to *Ashe*, one of two criteria was typically used in handling this problem. The first related to evidence required to convict on particular charges. If the "same evidence" was required for both, the offenses were deemed to be the same for purposes of double jeopardy. If, however, at least one element of each offense could not be proved with common evidence, the offenses were considered different. The same evidence approach created limits to the protection afforded because of the overlapping character of contemporary criminal codes. The same evidence criterion does, however, preclude prosecution for included offenses, offenses that are generally less serious than a connected greater offense but are so tightly related that one cannot convict on the greater charge without convicting on the lesser charge as well. In *Brown v. Ohio* (432 U.S. 161: 1977), for example, the Court held that prosecution for auto theft, a greater offense, following conviction for joyriding, a lesser included offense arising out of theft of the car, was prohibited based on the same evidence test. *Brown* also said that "same evidence" was the test to be applied in determining sameness. In some instances, the "same transaction" test is substituted for determining sameness of offense. This test measures offenses by actions. Though multiple charges arising out of a single incident may be brought in consolidated proceedings, the transaction test prevents multiple prosecutions for criminal conduct occurring in a single episode. The primary defect of the transaction test is that the definition of *transaction* remains vague. What are the actual parameters of a single transaction? Application of the collateral estoppel principle in *Ashe* provides some clarification of the same problem. *Ashe* forbids reprosecution in cases where a person has been acquitted on the basis of an ultimate fact issue present in the second case. Since the fact issue had been resolved in the defendant's favor previously, a second prosecution cannot constitutionally occur. The Court ruled in *Dowling v. United States* (107 L. Ed. 2d 708: 1990) that the doctrine of collateral estoppel did not prevent the admission of evidence relating to another alleged crime for which a defendant had been acquitted. Dowling was prosecuted in federal court for bank robbery. The prosecution sought to introduce evidence that Dowling had been involved in other crimes. Specifically, the prosecution attempted to obtain testimony from a woman into whose house Dowling had allegedly broken. In both the break-in and the robbery, the perpetrator had worn a ski mask and carried a small hand gun. The woman had unmasked Dowling during the break-in and was able to identify him. Notwithstanding that identification, Dowling had been acquitted on charges associated with the break-in. The prosecution for the bank robbery wished to have the woman describe Dowling to strengthen identification of him as the bank robber. The woman could also identify a second man from the break-in. This same man had been seen outside the bank in what was believed to be the intended getaway car, and the prosecutor wished to reinforce the link between Dowling and the second man. As the woman concluded her testimony, the jury was informed that Dowling had been acquitted on the charge involving the witness. The jury was also instructed of the limited purpose for which the testimony was introduced. The Supreme Court ruled that neither the doctrine of collateral estoppel nor considerations of due process precluded her testimony. Collateral estoppel prohibits relitigation of an "ultimate fact issue" that has already been resolved. The doctrine is not categorical in application, however. In this case, the prior acquittal did not "determine the ultimate fact issue" in the bank robbery because the prosecution was not required to prove that

Dowling had entered the witness's home. The Court was also of the view that the judge's limiting jury instructions kept the testimony from being "fundamentally unfair" because the jury could assess the "truthfulness and significance" of the witness's testimony. Justices Brennan, Marshall, and Stevens dissented, contending that the introduction of the testimony compelled Dowling once again to defend against a charge for which he had already been acquitted. The Court returned to the sameness issue in *Grady v. Corbin* (109 L. Ed. 2d 548: 1990). Under the sameness test established in *Blockberger v. United States* (284 U.S. 299: 1932), two offenses are not the same if they contain at least one different element. Corbin was responsible for an automobile accident in which a person died. Corbin was ticketed at the scene for drunk driving and driving on the wrong side of the road. Shortly thereafter, Corbin pleaded guilty to those charges. The prosecution failed to inform the trial court that the accident had resulted in a fatality before the court accepted Corbin's plea and imposed sentence. Two months later, Corbin was indicted on several charges stemming from the accident, including negligent homicide and third-degree reckless assault. Under the *Blockberger* test, the indictments covered charges that were not the same as those to which Corbin had earlier pleaded. The Supreme Court said that a subsequent prosecution must do more than "merely survive" *Blockberger* standards, however. The state had admitted in this case that it would attempt to establish the essential elements of the homicide and assault charges on the basis of Corbin's conduct that had led to the earlier convictions. The Court ruled that the state is precluded from establishing an "essential element" of a crime on the basis of the same conduct for which a defendant has been convicted. The Court made it clear this was not a "same evidence" test. Rather, the "critical inquiry is what conduct the State will prove, not the evidence the State will use to prove that conduct." Subsequent prosecutions for homicide and assault could have been pursued in this case if they did not rely on proving the conduct for which Corbin had already been convicted. The Court also pointed out that with "adequate preparation and foresight" on the part of the prosecution, the traffic offenses and the charges from the indictment could have been pursued in a single proceeding, thus "avoiding this double jeopardy question."

Self-Incrimination

Miranda v. Arizona, **384 U.S. 436, 86 S. Ct. 1602, 16 L. Ed. 2d 694 (1966)** Examined custodial interrogation practices. The *Miranda* decision was based on the relationship between the Fifth

Amendment's privilege against self-incrimination and the Sixth Amendment's right to counsel in the pretrial period. The groundwork for *Miranda* began two years earlier in *Escobedo v. Illinois* (378 U.S. 478: 1964). In a controversial 5–4 decision, the Court overturned the conviction of Escobedo, holding that when a police investigation begins to focus on a particular individual, and when interrogation turns from mere information gathering to eliciting a confession, the American legal system requires that the individual must be allowed to consult with legal counsel. *Miranda* and three companion cases allowed the Warren Court to develop this theme further and broaden its application. The Court was particularly concerned with the interrogation environment, believing it to be a closed process and inherently coercive. Chief Justice Warren said, "Even without employing brutality . . . the very fact of custodial interrogation exacts a heavy toll on individual liberty and trades on the weaknesses of individuals." He added, "It is obvious that such an interrogation environment is created for no other purpose than to subjugate the individual to the will of the examiner. This atmosphere carries its own badge of intimidation." The majority specified four warnings that must be administered at the time of arrest, prior to beginning interrogation. The "Miranda Rules" require that an arrested person (1) be told of his or her right to remain silent, (2) be told that anything he or she says can be used against the accused in court, (3) be told that he or she has a right to consult with an attorney prior to questioning and the failure to request counsel does not constitute waiver of the right, and (4) be told that counsel will be provided to the accused in the event that he or she cannot afford counsel. *Miranda* held that statements made by the accused without these warnings are inadmissible in a trial. *See also* BREWER *v.* WILLIAMS (430 U.S. 387: 1977), p. 223; ESTELLE *v.* SMITH (451 U.S. 454: 1981), p. 227; HARRIS *v.* NEW YORK (401 U.S. 222: 1971), p. 220; MICHIGAN *v.* TUCKER (417 U.S. 433: 1974), p. 222; NORTH CAROLINA *v.* BUTLER (441 U.S. 369: 1979), p. 225; SELF-INCRIMINATION, p. 448.

Significance   *Miranda v. Arizona* (384 U.S. 436: 1966) instituted extensive changes in constitutional policy involving rights of the accused. No single decision of the Warren Court has had more impact, except perhaps *Mapp v. Ohio* (367 U.S. 643: 1961). The Warren Court clearly assigned high priority to confronting inappropriate police practices. It recognized the utility of defense counsel as a means of discouraging misconduct. Basically it tried to give meaning to constitutional protections and to prevent them from becoming empty formalisms. Protection against self-incrimination, for example, could be achieved by extending the right to counsel to critical pretrial stages;

hence the linkage of the two provisions in *Miranda*. The decision intensified criticism of the Warren Court's approach to defining rights of the accused. The Court's detractors felt that *Miranda* made confessions virtually impossible to secure, thus handcuffing law enforcement authorities. Many felt the Court had preempted legislative prerogatives in setting law enforcement standards. The negative feeling toward *Miranda* was manifested in the Omnibus Crime Control Act of 1968. Provisions of this legislation softened some of the *Miranda* requirements, at least at the federal level. Federal judges, for example, were given greater latitude in determining the voluntariness of incriminating statements. It was left to later courts to determine the status of *Miranda* for state trials. Several recent decisions have narrowed the scope of its provisions.

One case in which the Court had occasion to examine the scope of the term *interrogation* was *Arizona v. Mauro* (481 U.S. 520: 1987). Mauro was taken into custody for allegedly killing his son. He was advised of his *Miranda* rights, and he indicated he did not wish to make a statement in the absence of his lawyer. At that point, all questioning stopped and Mauro was placed in a police captain's office, since no other detention area was available. Mauro's wife, who had herself been questioned in another room, insisted on seeing her husband. A meeting was allowed in the captain's office on the condition that an officer remain in the room. The police used a plainly visible recording device to tape Mauro's entire conversation with his wife. During the conversation, Mauro instructed his wife to answer no further questions in the absence of counsel. At the trial, the prosecutor used the recording to challenge Mauro's insanity defense, arguing that the tape demonstrated otherwise. The question in this case was whether the police actions in permitting and monitoring the meeting between Mauro and his wife were an interrogation or its functional equivalent. The Court concluded they were not. Interrogation includes any practice "reasonably likely to elicit an incriminating response." The purpose of *Miranda* warnings is not to prevent the government from capitalizing on the coercive nature of confinement to extract incriminating statements. Mauro was not subjected to compelling influences, psychological ploys, direct questioning, or any other practice of interrogation. The police had not initiated the meeting. Given various safety and security considerations, the Court considered the officer's presence at the meeting between Mauro and his wife to be legitimate. The Court also examined the situation from Mauro's perspective and concluded that it was unlikely he felt coerced to incriminate himself simply because he was allowed to speak with his wife. While the police might have been aware of the possibility that Mauro would say something incriminating during the meeting, an interrogation does not occur simply because the police may hope a suspect will confess. The Burger Court rejected opportunities to over-rule *Miranda,* however, and embarked on a case-by-case examination of the *Miranda* standards. The Rehnquist Court has essentially fol-lowed the same course. The Court considered in *Duckworth v. Eagan* (106 L. Ed. 2d 166: 1989), for example, whether the warnings man-dated by *Miranda* were adequately conveyed. Among other things, persons are to be advised of their right to counsel, and that counsel will be appointed if the suspect is indigent. Eagan was "Mirandized" at the time he was first questioned about a sexual assault and stabbing, although he was not placed under arrest. The warnings he received contained additional language on appointment of counsel for indi-gent persons, however. After being told that a lawyer could be pro-vided to persons who could not afford to hire one, Eagan was told that appointment would occur "if and when you go to court." He was further advised that he need not answer any questions in the absence of counsel. Eagan signed a waiver form and answered questions about the crime. Eagan was formally placed in custody 29 hours later, at which point he was again advised. He signed a second waiver form that contained a statement of rights. The form did not contain the "if and when you go to court" language. At this point, Eagan confessed to the crime. At his trial, Eagan sought to suppress statements made after both warnings. The question before the Court in this case was whether the additional language interfered with Eagan's securing "clear and unequivocal" warning of his rights prior to interrogation. The Supreme Court ruled 5–4 that Eagan's warnings were adequate notwithstanding the additional language. The Court said it has "never insisted that *Miranda* warnings be given in the exact form described in that decision." Indeed, *Miranda* itself refers to the adequacy of a "fully effective equivalent" in meeting the requirements of the ruling. The "prophylactic" *Miranda* warnings are not themselves constitutional rights, but instead are "measures to insure that the right against com-pulsory self-incrimination is protected." Eagan's initial warning "touched all of the bases required by *Miranda.*" The Court held in *Berkomer v. McCarty* (468 U.S. 420: 1984) that *Miranda* warnings are not required for ordinary traffic stops. The Court affirmed that rule in *Pennsylvania v. Bruder* (102 L. Ed. 2d 172: 1988). Bruder was stopped for erratic driving and was given field sobriety tests. While awaiting the results of the tests, Bruder was asked to recite the alpha-bet and to respond to some questions. When it was determined that he failed the sobriety tests, Bruder was arrested and properly advised of his rights. He sought to suppress all prearrest statements. The issue was whether Bruder's prearrest statements were elicited through cus-todial interrogation. In a 7–2 decision, the Supreme Court ruled that

Bruder had not been subjected to improper custodial interrogation. Persons "temporarily detained" by traffic stops are not "in custody for the purposes of *Miranda*." Such stops "typically are brief, unlike a prolonged stationhouse interrogation." Furthermore, traffic stops occur in "public view," and in an atmosphere less "dominated" by police than the kind of interrogation involved in *Miranda*. The generally "noncoercive" character of the ordinary traffic stop thus can be distinguished from those situations requiring the *Miranda* warnings. In *Miller v. Fenton* (474 U.S. 104: 1985), the Court held that the voluntariness of a confession cannot be presumed. Rather, it is a question meriting independent consideration in a federal court review. Thus the provisions of the U.S. Code that presume state court findings to be correct in habeas corpus proceedings do not restrict fresh federal inquiry as they do in search issues. Police-initiated conversations that produce incriminating statements have been a particularly problematic aspect of *Miranda*. In *Edwards v. Arizona* (451 U.S. 477: 1981), the Court refused to allow admission of a confession obtained the day following a defendant's request for counsel. Even the rereading of the *Miranda* warnings was insufficient to overcome the failure to have counsel present. Once the right to assistance of counsel is invoked, no subsequent conversation may occur except on the defendant's initiative. The reasoning in *Edwards* was applied in *Michigan v. Jackson* (475 U.S. 625: 1986). Following his arraignment on a murder charge, Jackson requested that counsel be appointed. Before he could meet with his lawyer, officers administered *Miranda* warnings to Jackson and interrogated him. The interrogation yielded a confession. The Court said that when the officers initiated the interview after the defendant requested counsel "at arraignment or similar proceeding," any subsequent waiver of the right to counsel for that police-initiated interrogation is invalid. The Supreme Court held in *Edwards v. Arizona* (451 U.S. 477: 1981) that an interrogation must end when the detained person requests to consult with a lawyer. Following that point, incriminating statements may be admissible only if the suspect starts a conversation. *Arizona v. Roberson* (460 U.S. 675: 1988) raised the issue of whether the *Edwards* rule reaches separate investigations of wholly independent offenses. Roberson was arrested for burglary and advised of his rights. He indicated that he wished to consult counsel before responding to any questions. Three days later, while Roberson was still detained and awaiting contact with a lawyer, a different officer who was unaware that Roberson had requested counsel again advised Roberson of his rights and began questioning him about another burglary. The interrogation on the second offense produced an incriminating statement. The Supreme Court held that *Edwards* extended to such situations. The *Edwards* rule, said the Court, "benefits the accused and the State alike." It protects the suspect against "inherently compelling pressures of custodial interrogation" by "creating a presumption" that a waiver of counsel is defective. At the same time, the rule provides "clear and unequivocal" guidelines for conducting custodial interrogations. Given these benefits, the Court saw no reason to create an exception to *Edwards* for the interrogation relating to a separate offense. The "eagerness" of officers to question a suspect is comparable for the officers engaged in separate investigations and those involved in a single inquiry. If the suspect is unable to "cope with" custodial interrogation, additional questioning without counsel will "exacerbate whatever compulsion to speak" the suspect may feel. Simply giving "fresh sets" of warnings will "not necessarily reassure" a suspect who is yet to receive requested counsel. Neither did the Court regard the second officer's ignorance of the earlier request for counsel to be relevant. The *Edwards* rule "focuses on the state of mind of the suspect, not the police." Moreover, the officer could have discovered that Roberson had requested counsel simply by examining the arresting officer's report. As part of standard procedure, a videotape recording was made as Inocencio Muniz was booked for drunk driving. Muniz was asked a number of questions, including his name, address, and age. In addition, he was asked to calculate the date of his sixth birthday. The sobriety tests Muniz failed in the field were administered again and also taped. During the course of these tests, Muniz said a number of things. He was not given his *Miranda* warnings until the booking process was about to end. The question in *Pennsylvania v. Muniz* (110 L. Ed. 2d 528: 1990) was whether the tape could be used as evidence against Muniz. The Court's decision in this case hinged on whether the statements were testimonial and produced by actual police interrogation. The Court ruled that Muniz's statements were admissible even though the "slurred nature of his speech was incriminating." The Court viewed the absence of the "physical ability to articulate words in a clear manner" to be nontestimonial. Revealing the "physical manner" of the way Muniz spoke the Court saw as analogous to requiring him to reveal the physical properties of his voice for a voice print. Second, the Court allowed use of Muniz's responses to questions about his name, height, weight, age, and so on. These were "routine" booking questions and were exempt from *Miranda* because they sought only basic biographical information needed to complete booking. Third, the Court allowed use of the tape showing the repeated sobriety tests and the statements made during them. Like slurred speech, test performances were nontestimonial. Further, the statements made by Muniz were not elicited by the officer conducting the tests. The situation did not constitute an interrogation, thus Muniz's statements were voluntarily offered. The Court did rule, however, that the response to the question about the date of Muniz's sixth birthday should have been suppressed. Like the remainder of the tape, it came before the *Miranda* warnings and was incriminating. Unlike the rest, it was incriminating because of the content of his answer. Here, the question was not whether Muniz's impairment could be fairly "characterized as an aspect of his physiology," but rather whether Muniz's response to the question "gave rise to the inference whether such an impairment was testimonial in nature."

Harris v. New York, 401 U.S. 222, 91 S. Ct. 643, 28 L. Ed. 2d 1 (1971) Considered whether statements made by a defendant in violation of *Miranda* could be used to impeach that defendant's own testimony at his or her trial. *Miranda* established that criminal defendants must be informed of their right against self-incrimination and to assistance of counsel. While Harris was testifying at his own trial, he was asked during cross-examination whether he had made any statements immediately following his arrest. When he claimed he could not recall making any statements, the statements he in fact made were introduced into evidence for the purpose of impeaching Harris's credibility. The jury instruction attempted to differentiate between use of statements for impeachment purposes and their use as evidence of guilt. The jury was instructed it could not do the latter. Harris was subsequently convicted. The Supreme Court rejected his appeal in a 5–4 decision. The majority said that *Miranda* is not an absolute prohibition against use of statements taken without proper warnings. *Miranda* bars the prosecution from "making its case with statements" taken in violation of *Miranda*. But "it does not follow from *Miranda* that evidence inadmissible against an accused in the prosecution's case in chief is barred for all purposes." Use of such evidence, however, must satisfy conditions of trustworthiness. Crucial to the outcome in *Harris* is the use of statements in an adversary process: specifically, impeachment of a witness through cross-examination. The "impeachment process here undoubtedly provided valuable aid to the jury in assessing petitioner's credibility." The majority felt that information was of more value than guarding against the "speculative possibility" that police misconduct would be encouraged. The majority emphasized the need to maintain the integrity of the trial itself. A defendant can testify in his or her own defense but does not have "the right to commit perjury." Once the defendant takes the witness stand, the prosecution can "utilize the traditional truth-testing devices of the adversary process." Chief Justice Burger concluded the opinion by saying, "The shield provided by *Miranda* cannot be perverted into a license to use perjury by way of defense, free from the risk of confrontation with prior inconsistent utterances." The dissenters—Justices Douglas, Black, Brennan, and Marshall—argued that tainted statements should not be used under any circumstances. They felt the decision would "seriously undermine" the maintenance of constitutional protections against police misconduct. *See also* BREWER v. WILLIAMS (430 U.S. 387: 1977), p. 223; FIFTH AMENDMENT, p. 201; *MICHIGAN v. TUCKER* (417 U.S. 433: 1974), p. 222; *MIRANDA v. ARIZONA* (384 U.S. 436: 1966), p. 219; *NORTH CAROLINA v. BUTLER* (441 U.S. 369: 1979), p. 225; SELF-INCRIMINATION, p. 448.

Significance   *Harris v. New York* (401 U.S. 222: 1971) seriously qualified *Miranda*. The Court allowed *Miranda*-defective statements and confessions to be utilized to impeach a defendant, as opposed to being used in making the case in chief. *Harris* reflected the Burger Court's reluctance to embrace the *Miranda* holding fully as well as its general unwillingness to disturb the dynamics of the adversary process. The basic thrust of *Harris* is that a jury ought to be given every opportunity to assess a defendant and the defense being advanced. The underlying theme of *Harris* was reiterated in *Oregon v. Hass* (420 U.S. 714: 1975) by a 6–2 margin. The *Harris-Hass* rule does not apply, however, where statements are obtained involuntarily. In *Mincey v. Arizona* (437 U.S. 385: 1978), the Court ruled that interrogation of a defendant hospitalized in critical condition produced involuntary and untrustworthy responses. They could not be used even for impeachment purposes. The Court has also held that postwarning silence cannot be used to impeach a defendant. In *Doyle v. Ohio* (426 U.S. 610: 1976), two defendants offered exculpatory explanations at their trial, explanations not previously shared with police officers or prosecutors. They were cross-examined as to why they had withheld their stories until the trial. A six-justice majority concluded that "silence in the wake of these [*Miranda*] warnings may be nothing more than the arrestee's exercise of these *Miranda* rights." On the other hand, silence occurring previous to receiving *Miranda* warnings may be used for impeachment purposes on the grounds that the silence was not "induced by the assurances contained in the *Miranda* warnings."

Michigan v. Jackson (475 U.S. 625: 1986) held that essentially any waiver of right to counsel stemming from a police-initiated conversation was invalid. The Court ruled in *Michigan v. Harvey* (108 L. Ed. 2d 293: 1990) that while the statements were properly suppressed from the prosecution case, the statements could be used to impeach the accused's testimony. The Court's reasoning was virtually identical to that found in *Harris*. The prosecution, said the Court, "must not be allowed to build its case . . . with evidence acquired in contravention of constitutional guarantees." Using such statements for impeachment purposes, however, "is a different matter." The Court said it has "consistently rejected" arguments that would allow an accused to turn the illegal method by which government evidence was obtained "to his own advantage, and provide himself with a shield against contradiction of his untruths." The Court ruled that the same rules apply in these Fifth and Sixth Amendment situations. The statements are inadmissible in the prosecutor's case in chief in both instances. At the same time, impeachment of a defendant's conflicting testimony should be allowed as well. While a defendant may "sometimes later regret" the decision to make a statement, the Sixth Amendment "does not disable a criminal defendant from exercising his free will." The cases establishing "prophylactic rules that render some otherwise valid waivers of constitutional rights invalid" when they are the product of police-initiated interrogation should not be "perverted into a license to use perjury by way of a defense, free from the risk of confrontation with prior inconsistent utterances." The question in *James v. Illinois* (107 L. Ed. 2d 676: 1990) was whether this principle extended to the impeachment of any other defense witness. James was arrested on a charge of involvement in a shooting as he sat under a hair dryer at his mother's beauty salon. James indicated at the time of arrest that he was attempting to change his appearance. He also described the color and style of his hair prior to alteration. His statements were subsequently suppressed as the product of an improper arrest. At James's murder trial, several witnesses identified him. Each witness described the style and color of James's hair at the time of the shooting. These descriptions corresponded to James's own representation in the suppressed statement. James did not testify on his own behalf, but called a witness whose testimony differed as to James's hair. The witness testified that James's hair before the shooting was the same as it appeared when James emerged from the hair dryer. After determining that James's statements about his hair had been obtained voluntarily, the prosecution was allowed to enter the statement to impeach the credibility of the defense witness. The Supreme Court ruled that James's statements could not be used to impeach the witness. Justice Brennan began for the majority by reiterating the reason for the defendant impeachment exception to the exclusionary rule—furthering the "truthseeking function" of the criminal trial. Expanding the exception to all defense witnesses, on the other hand, creates "different incentives affecting the behavior of both defendants and law enforcement officers." The defendant exception discourages perjured testimony because the defendant does not want to

have the otherwise inadmissible statements used. The threat of a perjury prosecution creates a sufficient deterrent for the witness who is
not also the defendant. The exception adds little to the likelihood of
obtaining truthful testimony from other witnesses. More important,
said the Court, the exception would have a "chilling effect" on the
calling of certain defense witnesses. Defense could "reasonably fear"
that a "hostile" or even "friendly" but inattentive defense witness
would make some statement "in sufficient tension" with tainted evidence to allow introduction of that evidence for impeachment purposes. The defendant exception was intended to keep defendants
from being able to "pervert" the exclusion of illegally obtained evidence as a "shield for perjury." In the Court's view, it is no more
appropriate for the state to "brandish" illegally obtained evidence as
a "sword with which to dissuade defendants from presenting a meaningful defense through other witnesses." The Court also feared that
expansion of the impeachment exception would "significantly weaken
the exclusionary rule's deterrent effect on police misconduct." The
rule's deterrent effect works, notwithstanding the defendant exception, because police believe it "unlikely" that a defendant will open the
door to the use of illegal evidence for impeachment purposes. Extending the exception to all witnesses, on the other hand, "vastly"
increases the number of occasions during which illegal evidence could
be used. Further, illegally obtained evidence would have even greater
value to the prosecution because of the chilling effect. Prosecutorial
access to impeachment evidence would deter more than perjury. It
would also "deter defendants from calling witnesses in the first place."
This encourages police misconduct because law enforcement officials
"would recognize that obtaining evidence through illegal means stacks
the deck heavily in the prosecutor's favor." In *Wainwright v. Greenfield*
(88 L. Ed. 2d 623: 1986), the Court ruled that a suspect's silence after
receiving the *Miranda* warnings could not be used as evidence to
counter his insanity defense. A unanimous Court said the source of
the unfairness is the assurance contained in the *Miranda* warnings
that silence will carry no penalty. It is fundamentally unfair to promise a person that silence will not be used against him or her and then
breach that promise by using silence to overcome a defendant's plea
of insanity. In *Oregon v. Elstad* (470 U.S. 298: 1985) the Court opined
that a voluntary admission coming prior to *Miranda* warnings does
not necessarily require suppression of a confession coming later. At
the time of his arrest, Elstad incriminated himself before receiving
any warnings. He made statements voluntarily, in the presence of his
mother, and in an environment that could be characterized as noncoercive. He was subsequently taken to the sheriff's office and advised
of his rights. Elstad waived his rights and confessed again. While the

initial statements were unquestionably admissible, Elstad later argued that his sheriff's office confession was tainted by the statements made prior to his receiving any warnings. The Supreme Court disagreed, saying that as long as the initial statements were voluntary, the later confession need not be suppressed. A defendant who responds to "unwarned yet uncoercive questioning is not disabled from waiving his warnings." In circumstances such as these, "thorough administration of *Miranda* warnings serves to cure the condition that rendered the unwarned statements inadmissible."

North Carolina v. Butler, **441 U.S. 369, 99 S. Ct. 1755, 60 L. Ed. 2d 286 (1979)** Considered whether the waiver of a constitutional right need be explicit. Butler was arrested and informed of his *Miranda* rights. He was given an "Advice of Rights" form, which he read and said he understood. He refused, however, to sign the waiver provision at the bottom of the form, although he indicated he was "willing to talk." Butler subsequently tried to have statements made during the ensuing conversation suppressed. The case revolved around a determination of whether Butler had actually waived his rights. The Supreme Court decided that Butler's statements could be admitted. The majority, in an opinion written by Justice Stewart joined by Chief Justice Burger and Justices White, Blackmun, and Rehnquist, held that while explicit waiver is usually strong proof of the validity of a waiver, it is not "inevitably either necessary or sufficient to establish waiver." The Court said further, "The question is not one of form, but rather whether the defendant in fact knowingly and voluntarily waived the rights delineated in *Miranda.*" The burden of demonstrating the adequacy of a waiver rests with the prosecution, and the prosecution's "burden is great." However, "in at least some cases, waiver can be clearly inferred from the actions and words of the person interrogated." Waivers must be evaluated in terms of the facts and circumstances of each case. The Court's judgment was that Butler made a knowing and voluntary waiver even though it was not explicit. The majority clearly rejected the establishment of an "inflexible *per se* rule" requiring explicit waiver. The dissenters—Justices Brennan, Marshall, and Stevens—argued that an affirmative or explicit waiver is required to satisfy *Miranda.* The dissenting justices claimed that *Miranda* recognized that custodial interrogation is "inherently coercive," and that ambiguity must be "interpreted against the interrogator." They would have required a "simple prophylactic rule requiring the police to obtain express waiver." *See also BREWER v. WILLIAMS* (430 U.S. 387: 1977), p. 223; FIFTH AMENDMENT, p. 201; *HARRIS v. NEW YORK* (410 U.S. 222: 1971), p. 220; *MICHIGAN v. TUCKER* (417 U.S. 433:

1974), p. 222; *MIRANDA v. ARIZONA* (384 U.S. 436: 1966), p. 219; SELF-INCRIMINATION, p. 448.

Significance   *North Carolina v. Butler* (441 U.S. 369: 1979) specifies what must be done by a defendant to waive the associated rights of assistance of counsel and protection against self-incrimination. The *Miranda* protections may be waived, but the waiver must be voluntary, knowing, and intelligent. It may not be the product of coercion, trick, threat, persuasion, or inducement. While the waiver need not be written or explicit, it cannot be presumed from silence under any circumstances. The burden rests with the prosecution to demonstrate that a waiver was freely, knowingly, and intelligently made. Determinations of the adequacy of a waiver are to be based on the "totality of the circumstances" of a particular case and may include such matters as the background and overall conduct of the defendant. *Butler* provides some latitude by not requiring firm rules relative to explicit waiver. At the same time it clarifies and maintains the general protections afforded by *Miranda*. The latter was intended to draw a clear and bright line obviating the need for a case-by-case determination of voluntariness. *Butler* brings the Court full circle. The dissent recognizes that *Butler* implicitly, if not explicitly, overruled part of *Miranda's* clear holding. The governing role of a valid waiver is reflected in *Moran v. Burbine* (475 U.S. 412: 1986). Burbine was arrested for breaking and entering. The police subsequently came to believe that he was involved in a murder in another community. Officers from the second community were notified, and they came to question Burbine about the murder. In the meantime, and unknown to Burbine, his sister was arranging for counsel on the breaking and entering charge. Neither Burbine's sister nor the public defender she obtained knew anything about the murder charge. Counsel contacted the police, indicating that she was ready to represent Burbine if the police wished to question him. She was told he would not be questioned further until the next day. She was not told that police from the second community were present and ready to begin their questioning of Burbine. He was given *Miranda* warnings before each of the three interview sessions. He signed waivers prior to each and proceeded to sign admissions to the murder. At no time was Burbine aware of his sister's arrangement of counsel or the attorney's telephone call. Yet in a 6–3 decision, the Court allowed use of the confession. It said the police followed "with precision" the *Miranda* procedure for obtaining the waivers. The failure to inform Burbine of the attorney's call did not deprive him of information essential to his ability to make a knowing and voluntary waiver. Events taking place outside his presence and unknown to him "can have no bearing on the capacity to comprehend and knowingly relinquish a constitutional right." As long as it could be shown that his waiver was uncoerced and that he knew he did not have to speak and could request counsel, the waiver was valid. The Court said *Miranda* would not be extended to require reversal of conviction if police are "less than forthright" in dealing with an attorney or if they fail to inform the suspect of the attorney's unilateral efforts to contact him or her. The purpose of *Miranda* is to "dissipate the compulsion inherent in custodial interrogation" and thus protect the *suspect's* Fifth Amendment rights. A rule that focuses on how police must treat an *attorney*—conduct that has no relevance to the matter of compulsion of the defendant—would "ignore both *Miranda's* mission and its only source of legitimacy."

The Rehnquist Court returned to the issues surrounding waiver of *Miranda* three times during the 1986–87 term. In *Colorado v. Spring* (479 U.S. 564: 1987), Spring was arrested on a stolen weapons charge. He was advised of his *Miranda* rights, and he signed a statement that he understood and waived those rights. Authorities proceeded to ask Spring about the weapons charge but also about a murder, even though they had not told Spring they intended to do so. The interrogation produced a disclosure that Spring had shot someone, but there was no confession as such. At a subsequent interview, where Spring was again advised of his rights, he admitted participation in the murder. The Court held that admission of Spring's statements was proper. Inquiry into whether a waiver is coerced, said Justice Powell, has two distinct dimensions. First, the relinquishment must be voluntary, "the product of free and deliberate choice." Second, the waiver must have been made with full awareness of the right being abandoned and the consequences of the decision to abandon it. Spring's waiver was found to be voluntary. There was no evidence of coercion. Neither did the contention that the police failed to supply him with certain information relate to any traditional indicia of coercion. There was no doubt that the waiver was knowingly and intelligently made. Spring knew he could remain silent. The Constitution, wrote Powell, does not require that a suspect "know and understand every possible consequence of his Fifth Amendment waiver." The Court also rejected Spring's contention that failure to inform him of all the potential subjects of interrogation constituted illegal trickery or deception. Powell said it is difficult to see how mere silence on the subject matter of interrogation could cause a suspect to misunderstand the nature of his right to refuse to answer questions. The additional information could affect only the wisdom of the *Miranda* waiver, not its essentially voluntary and knowing nature. In *Colorado v. Connelly* (479 U.S. 157: 1986), the Court ruled that a defendant diagnosed as a schizophrenic is not categorically unable to waive his

Miranda rights. Connelly approached a Denver police officer and said he had killed someone. He was immediately advised as per *Miranda*, but he replied he understood his rights and wished to discuss the murder. A detective was summoned, and on his arrival Connelly was once again advised of his *Miranda* rights. He was taken to police headquarters, where he told his story in detail. The following morning, Connelly became disoriented and said he had been ordered by the voice of God to confess. Subsequent psychiatric examination revealed that Connelly suffered from a psychosis that interfered with his capacity to make free and rational choices. A psychiatrist said that his psychosis had motivated his confession. It was also the psychiatrist's view, however, that Connelly's condition had not impaired his ability to understand his *Miranda* rights. The Supreme Court allowed the use of both the initial statements and the confession. Speaking for the majority, Chief Justice Rehnquist said that coercive police conduct was required to reach a finding that *Miranda* had been violated. Despite the significance of an individual's mental condition as a factor in the voluntariness calculus, the condition, "by itself and apart from its relation to official coercion," should never dispose of an inquiry into voluntariness. The purpose of suppression was to deter future violations, and the Court did not see that end served by excluding Connelly's statement in this case. Only if "we were to establish a brand new constitutional right—the right to confess only when totally rational and properly motivated—could Connelly's claim be supported." Coercive police conduct was seen as a necessary predicate to finding that a confession was not voluntary. In addition, mental illness will not invariably preclude a defendant from understanding and waiving his or her *Miranda* rights. The third decision came in *Connecticut v. Barrett* (479 U.S. 523: 1987). Barrett was arrested on suspicion of sexual assault and was advised on three separate occasions of his *Miranda* rights. Each time, Barrett signed a form acknowledging that he had been so advised, and proceeded to talk about the incident. He refused, however, to sign a written statement in the absence of counsel. Barrett orally confessed to the assault. One of the police officers present at the time of the confession made written notes of Barrett's statements, and these were admitted into evidence. The Court permitted the use of the confession. The Court said Barrett had made clear his willingness to talk. There was no evidence to suggest that he was threatened, tricked, or cajoled into waiving his right to remain silent. Nothing in the rationale that underlies *Miranda* requires police to ignore the tenor or sense of a defendant's response to *Miranda*. That Barrett desired counsel prior to making a written statement had no bearing, since no written statement was taken. Barrett's limited requests for counsel were accompanied by affirmative announcements of his willingness to talk. That the police took the opportunity provided by Barrett to take his oral statement is "quite consistent" with the Fifth Amendment. *Miranda* gives the defendant a right to "choose between speech and silence, and Barrett chose to speak." *Miranda* clearly governs the custodial interrogation where a suspect is aware that questions are posed by the police. The question raised in *Illinois v. Perkins* (110 L. Ed. 2d 243: 1990) was whether *Miranda* applies to statements made by a suspect in custody on other matters to an undercover officer posing as a prisoner. With only Justice Marshall dissenting, the Court ruled that an officer can pose as a fellow inmate to elicit statements without a *Miranda* warning. The warning "mandated by *Miranda* was meant," said Justice Kennedy, to serve the privilege against self-incrimination during "incommunicado interrogation of individuals in a police-dominated atmosphere." On the other hand, conversations between suspects and undercover officers "do not implicate the concerns underlying *Miranda*." The "essential ingredients" of a "police-dominated atmosphere and compulsion are not present" when a suspect "speaks freely" to an officer "he believes to be a fellow inmate." When an individual believes he is in the company of cellmates and not the police, the "coercive atmosphere is lacking." The Court rejected the argument that *Miranda* warnings "are required whenever a suspect is in custody in a technical sense and converses with someone who also happens to be a government agent." *Miranda* forbids the use of coercion, not "mere strategic deception by taking advantage of a suspect's misplaced trust in one he supposes to be a fellow prisoner." "Ploys to mislead" a prisoner into a "false sense of security that do not rise to the level of compulsion or coercion to speak are not within *Miranda's* concerns." *Miranda* was not meant, Kennedy concluded, "to prevent suspects from boasting about their criminal activities in front of persons they believe to be their cellmates." As a result, Perkins spoke "at his own peril."

Carter v. Kentucky, 450 U.S. 288, 101 S. Ct. 1112, 67 L. Ed. 2d 241 (1981) Involved a defendant who chose not to testify in his own defense. Carter requested a specific jury instruction indicating he was not obligated to testify and that his failure to testify should not prejudice him in any way. The trial judge refused the request, and Carter was convicted. The Supreme Court reversed the conviction, with only Justice Rehnquist dissenting. The majority found that the Fifth Amendment does more than simply preclude adverse comment on the defendant's silence. The "defendant must pay no court-imposed price for the exercise of his constitutional privilege not to testify."

And that penalty "may be as severe when there is no adverse comment" and the jury "is left to roam at large with only its untutored instincts to guide it." A defendant is entitled to request special mention of his choice not to testify so as to "remove from the jury's deliberations any influence of unspoken adverse inferences." The Court noted the impact of the jury instruction and concluded that a trial judge "has an affirmative constitutional obligation to use that tool when a defendant seeks its enforcement." While those instructions may not prevent jurors from speculating about a defendant's silence, the "unique power of the jury instruction . . . [can] reduce that speculation to a minimum." Justice Rehnquist argued in dissent that the instruction requested by Carter was a matter to be determined at the state level rather than by construction of the Fifth Amendment. Rehnquist felt Carter was not constitutionally entitled to such special instruction. *See also* FIFTH AMENDMENT, p. 201; *MIRANDA v. ARIZONA* (384 U.S. 436: 1966), p. 219; SELF-INCRIMINATION, p. 448.

Significance   *Carter v. Kentucky* (450 U.S. 288: 1981) is a milestone in the evolution of self-incrimination standards. An important related case is *Twining v. New Jersey* (211 U.S. 78: 1908), in which the Court refused to examine a New Jersey law permitting a jury instruction that an unfavorable inference could be drawn from the defendant's unwillingness to take the stand in his or her own defense. The Court held in *Twining* that the Fifth Amendment privilege against self-incrimination did not extend to the states, thus no specific practice allegedly abridging it could be considered. Essentially the same position was taken 40 years later in *Adamson v. California* (332 U.S. 46: 1947), where prosecutorial comment on a defendant's failure to testify was permitted. When the Supreme Court overturned *Twining* and *Adamson* relative to state applicability of the self-incrimination protection in *Malloy v. Hogan* (378 U.S. 1: 1964), the comment practice was a primary target. It was declared unconstitutional a year later in *Griffin v. California* (380 U.S. 609: 1965). *Carter* extends the "no comment" rule one last step.

   Baltimore City Department of Social Services v. Bouknight (107 L. Ed. 2d 992: 1990) considered whether the privilege against self-incrimination applied to a woman who was ordered to produce her child to juvenile authorities. The Baltimore City Department of Social Services sought to remove the child from Bouknight's custody. The child had been removed once before on grounds of child abuse and was returned to her custody only subject to extensive conditions contained in a protective order. Bouknight was ordered to produce the child, but refused. She was held in civil contempt. The state court of appeals ruled that the order was unconstitutional on self-incrimination grounds. It held that the production order compelled Bouknight to acknowledge control over the child in a situation where she could have "reasonable apprehension that she would be prosecuted." The Supreme Court reversed the state court, however. Justice O'Connor wrote for the majority and addressed the scope of the privilege. It is generally reserved for testimonial communication, but she acknowledged that compliance with the production order might constitute a "limited testimonial assertion" for purposes of the privilege. The mere possibility of testimonial assertions, however, "does not, in all contexts, justify involving the privilege to resist production." O'Connor did indicate that if the production order is complied with, parents such as Bouknight could assert self-incrimination protection if the government sought to prosecute on the basis of information derived from production. The Court ruled that Bouknight may not invoke the privilege in this case for two reasons. First, her prior abusive conduct had required that she submit herself to assistance and supervision by juvenile authorities as a condition of custody. As a result, she cannot invoke the privilege to prevent enforcement of those conditions. Second, the production of the child was not ordered in furtherance of the state's prosecutorial function. Rather, production of the child was required as part of a "noncriminal regulatory regime." The state has a legitimate interest in the well-being of children. When a person has control over items—such as children—that are the object of government's noncriminal regulatory control, "the ability to invoke the privilege is reduced." Viewing the use of custodial orders as part of a general, noncriminal regulatory scheme was key to rejecting Bouknight's contention that parents subjected to such orders were part of a "selective group inherently suspect of criminal activities." Justices Marshall and Brennan viewed the regulatory approach used here as closely connected to the enforcement of criminal child abuse laws, which creates a substantial need for utilization of the self-incrimination privilege.

4. The Sixth Amendment

Confrontation

Pointer v. Texas, **380 U.S. 400, 85 S. Ct. 1065, 13 L. Ed. 2d 923
(1965)**   Considered the applicability to the states of the Confrontation Clause of the Sixth Amendment, which requires that the accused "be confronted with witnesses against him." Pointer was tried
for robbery. His chief accuser provided a detailed account of the
crime at a preliminary hearing, an occasion at which Pointer was
unrepresented by defense counsel. At the trial the prosecution used
transcripts of the testimony of the witness from the preliminary hearing because the witness had moved to another state. Pointer was convicted. A unanimous Supreme Court reversed the conviction, saying
that the right to cross-examine a witness was a central aspect of confrontation. Inclusion of the confrontation protection in the Sixth
Amendment reflected the framers' belief that "confrontation was a
fundamental right essential to a fair trial." As for the practice in Texas
of allowing use of a transcript, the Court said the confrontation protection would have been satisfied had the statements been made at a
"full-fledged hearing" where Pointer had been represented by counsel with "a complete and adequate opportunity to cross-examine."
Absent that condition, what occurred was an unconstitutional denial
of the Sixth Amendment right of confrontation. *See also CHAMBERS v.
MISSISSIPPI* (410 U.S. 284: 1973), p. 248; CONFRONTATION CLAUSE, p.
397; SIXTH AMENDMENT, p. 241.

Significance   *Pointer v. Texas* (380 U.S. 400: 1965) applied the confrontation right to state trial proceedings for the first time. The Supreme Court held specifically that the right to confront and cross-
examine witnesses is a fundamental right essential to a fair trial and is
obligatory on state courts by virtue of the Fourteenth Amendment.
Pointer is one of a series of cases in which the Warren Court extended
to defendants in state courts rights of accused persons long protected
in federal courts. The right to confront historically has meant that
witness and defendant must be present in the courtroom for the
various stages of the judicial process. Though that expectation

generally holds, it is not inflexible. A defendant may waive the right to presence and choose not to attend any or all of the proceedings. A defendant's courtroom behavior may also become sufficiently disruptive to justify his or her removal from the courtroom as a prerequisite to continuing, as in *Illinois v. Allen* (397 U.S. 337: 1970). The capability to cross-examine, however, remains the heart of the confrontation protection. Soon after *Pointer,* the Court reinforced the decision in *Bruton v. United States* (391 U.S. 123: 1968). Bruton was tried in a federal court. A postal inspector gave testimony that described an oral confession by Bruton's codefendant. The confession implicated both the codefendant and Bruton. The trial judge instructed the jury that the confession was inadmissible hearsay and must be disregarded in deciding Bruton's guilt. The Supreme Court held the instruction was insufficient protection. The use of the codefendant's confession "added substantial, perhaps even critical, weight to the Government's case in a form not subject to cross-examination, since Evans [the codefendant] did not take the stand." While conceding that some situations might be remedied by jury instructions, the Court found that remedy insufficient here. The introduction of the confession "posed a substantial threat" to Bruton's capability to confront. "In the context of a joint trial we cannot accept limiting instructions as an adequate substitute for the petitioner's constitutional right of cross-examination. The effect is the same as if there had been no instruction at all."

The Court extended the *Bruton* doctrine to cases where the defendant's own admissible confession corroborates that of the codefendant in *Cruz v. New York* (481 U.S. 186: 1987). Prior to *Cruz,* the governing rule was that when a defendant had entered his own confession, the introduction of a codefendant's confession would seldom, if ever, be of the "devastating" character required by *Bruton* to prove a Confrontation Clause violation. In *Cruz,* however, the Court rejected the prior rule, saying that devastation is rendered untenable by the infinite variability of inculpatory statements and their likely effects on juries. To the contrary, interlocking bears an inverse relationship to devastation, and a corroborating confession from a codefendant significantly harms the defendant's position. For that reason, the Court extended the *Bruton* rule to confessions of nontestifying codefendants despite the use of the defendant's own confession. In the case of *Richardson v. Marsh* (481 U.S. 200: 1987), the Court said that the *Bruton* rule need not be extended to joint trials where the confession of a nontestifying codefendant is edited to omit any reference to the defendant. *United States v. Owens* (484 U.S. 554: 1988) involved the testimony of a witness whose memory loss precluded his fully explaining the basis of his previous and out-of-court identification of the defendant. The witness, a federal prison counselor, was the victim of a brutal assault. He suffered a fractured skull that resulted in extensive memory impairment, and was hospitalized for a lengthy period after the attack. During the hospital visit of an investigating agent, the victim described the incident, named the attacker, and identified his photograph. At the defendant's trial, the witness recalled identifying the accused, but admitted on cross-examination that he could not remember seeing his assailant or whether anyone visiting him in the hospital had suggested the accused had assaulted him. Defense counsel unsuccessfully sought to refresh the witness's memory with hospital records, one of which indicated that he attributed the assault to someone other than the accused. The defendant was convicted nonetheless. The Supreme Court held that the Confrontation Clause had not been violated. The Confrontation Clause guarantees only an "opportunity for effective cross-examination." It is not a guarantee that cross-examination will be successful. Here, the defendant had a "full and fair" opportunity to point out the witness's impaired memory as well as other "facts tending to discredit his testimony." That the out-of-court identification constitutes hearsay was seen as immaterial because the requirements of the confrontation clause are "satisfied when a hearsay defendant is present at trial, takes an oath, is subject to unrestricted cross-examination, and the jury has an opportunity to observe his demeanor."

Coy v. Iowa, **487 U.S. 1012, 108 S. Ct. 2798, 101 L. Ed. 2d 857 (1988)** Examined the issue of whether placing a screen between the defendant charged with child molestation and the child victims violated the Confrontation Clause. Under provisions of a state law, while the victims testified, a screen was used that blocked Coy from their view, although he was able to both see and hear them. The trial court rejected Coy's contention that the procedure violated his right to confront witnesses against him. Coy was convicted and was unsuccessful on appeal within the state courts. The Supreme Court struck down the procedure in a 6–2 decision. The Court said that it "never doubted" that the confrontation protection "guarantees the defendant a face-to-face meeting" with witnesses. The protection has been essential to fairness "over the centuries" because a witness may "feel quite differently" when testifying while looking at the person he or she can harm by "distorting or mistaking the facts." The face-to-face confrontation, like the right to cross-examine, "ensures the integrity of the fact-finding process." The state, said the Court, cannot deny the "profound effect" the presence of the defendant may have on a witness, since it is the "same phenomenon used to establish the potential trauma that allegedly justified the extraordinary procedure" used in this case. That face-to-face presence "may unfortunately upset the truthful rape victim or abused child," the Court said, but it may also "undo the false accuser, or reveal the child to be coached by a malevolent adult." Constitutional protections simply "have costs," the Court observed. The Court then turned to the matter of whether the confrontation right had been violated here, and its conclusion was that it had. The state argued that the confrontation interest was "outweighed by the necessity of protecting victims of sexual abuse." The state claimed that such necessity was established by the statute, which created a "legislatively imposed presumption of trauma." The Court ruled that this was not enough. "Something more" than the "generalized finding" underlying the law is required when an exception to a constitutional protection is not "firmly rooted in our jurisprudence." The Court said the exception created by the law "could hardly be viewed as firmly rooted." Since the state made no "individual findings" that the witnesses in this case "needed special protection," the judgment in this case could not be "sustained by any conceivable exception." *See also* CONFRONTATION CLAUSE, p. 397; *POINTER v. TEXAS* (380 U.S. 400: 1965), p. 247.

Significance   As reflected in *Coy v. Iowa* (487 U.S. 1012: 1988), maintenance of the right to confront may exact a high price. This has been especially true in cases where children are the victims of criminal conduct. Another example is *Pennsylvania v. Ritchie* (480 U.S. 39: 1987). Ritchie was prosecuted for several sex offenses against his minor daughter. He sought to obtain records on the daughter from a state child welfare agency in hope of finding information helpful to his defense. The agency refused to comply with a subpoena, citing a state statute intended to protect the confidentiality of such records. The law limited access to specific persons or agencies, including courts with appropriate jurisdiction. The trial judge in Ritchie's case refused to order disclosure. The Supreme Court did not agree that there was a confrontation violation, but ruled that Ritchie had a Due Process Clause right to have the records of the child welfare agency submitted to the trial court for review by the judge. Release of any germane material to the defendant would follow. The Court found the state's interest in protecting the records to be considerable, but the interest of ensuring Ritchie a fair trial was also substantial. Ritchie's due process right to discover any exculpatory evidence did not require full disclosure. Rather, the interests of both the state and Ritchie, the Court ruled, could be protected by submission of the records to the trial court for in camera review. The Court ruled in *Kentucky v. Stincer* (482 U.S.

730: 1987) that a defendant charged with child molestation is not entitled to attend a pretrial hearing on the competency of child witnesses to testify. Stincer argued that the competency hearing was a stage of trial and was therefore subject to the requirements of the Confrontation Clause. The Court replied that since the functional purpose of the clause was to promote reliability by ensuring an opportunity for cross-examination, a more useful inquiry was whether exclusion of Stincer interfered with that opportunity. The Court saw no such interference. Once witness competency was determined, the witnesses were subject to full and complete cross-examination in the presence of the defendant. The kinds of questions asked at the competency hearing were directed at determining the capacity of two children to recollect and communicate facts truthfully. These are matters unrelated to the basic issues of the trial. The Court found no indication that Stincer's presence at the competency proceeding "would have been useful in ensuring a more reliable determination as to whether the witnesses were competent to testify."

Coy held that physical courtroom confrontation is an irreducible minimum of the confrontation protection. Exceptions would be considered only in furtherance of important public policy. *Maryland v. Craig* (111 L. Ed. 2d 666: 1990) clarified *Coy* by holding that states could protect child abuse victims by allowing them to testify on closed-circuit television. Justice O'Connor said for a five-justice majority that neither *Coy* nor any other previous ruling established that a defendant has an "absolute right to a face-to-face meeting" with witnesses. While the Confrontation Clause "reflects a preference for face-to-face confrontation at trial, . . . we cannot say that such confrontation is an indispensable element of the Sixth Amendment guarantee." O'Connor rejected a "literal reading" of the clause and used hearsay exceptions as illustrative of cases where "competing interests, if closely examined, may warrant dispensing with confrontation at trial." The "central concern" of the clause is to "insure the reliability of evidence . . . by subjecting it to rigorous testing in the context of an adversary proceeding." Maryland's procedure of using closed-circuit television does prevent the child witness from seeing the defendant, but it "preserves all the other elements of the confrontation right." The child witness must be competent and testify under oath; the judge, jury, and defendant can view the witness's demeanor as he or she testifies; and the defendant "retains full opportunity for contemporaneous cross-examination." The presence of these other elements "adequately insures that the testimony is both reliable and subject to rigorous adversarial testing in a manner functionally equivalent to that accorded live, in-person testimony." As a result, O'Connor said the Court was "confident" that use of the television procedure, "where necessary to further an important state interest, does not impinge upon the truth-seeking or symbolic purposes of the confrontation clause." The"critical inquiry" in *Craig* then became whether use of the television procedure is needed to further an important state interest. The Court concluded that protection of minor victims of sex crimes from "further trauma and embarrassment is a compelling one." Further, the Court determined that the interest in the "physical and psychological well-being of child abuse victims may be sufficiently important to outweigh, at least in some cases, a defendant's right to face his or her accusers in court." The Court did not require use of closed-circuit television, but rather permitted it in those cases where a trial court hears evidence and determines that the technique is "necessary to protect the welfare of the particular child witness who seeks to testify." In *Coy*, the Iowa legislature had made that judgment in advance for all child witnesses. Justice Scalia, in dissent, said that the Court had seldom "failed so conspicuously to sustain a categorical guarantee of the Constitution against the tide of prevailing current opinion." He saw the protection as absolute, and said the Court had "no authority" to "speculate" that where confrontation "causes significant emotional distress in a child witness," it might "disserve" the "truth-seeking goal" of the clause. For "good or bad," said Scalia, the "Sixth Amendment requires confrontation, and we are not at liberty to ignore it." In *Idaho v. Wright* (111 L. Ed. 2d 638: 1990), the Court said that states may not utilize hearsay exceptions that permit doctors or other adults to testify about their conversations with abuse victims. At issue in this case was the testimony of a pediatrician who represented statements made to him by a 3-year-old girl. The Court concluded that the statements could not be admitted because they "lacked the particularized guarantees of trustworthiness necessary to satisfy the requirement of the Confrontation Clause." The state had urged that trustworthiness should be determined by considering the "totality of circumstances," including other evidence that "corroborates the truth of the statement." The Court rejected this argument. To be admissible, said the Court, hearsay evidence "must possess indicia of reliability by virtue of its inherent trustworthiness, not by reference to other evidence at trial. . . . Corroboration of a child's allegation of sexual abuse by medical evidence of abuse, for example, sheds no light on the reliability of the child's allegations regarding the identity of the abuser." In these situations, the Court concluded, there is "very real danger that a jury will rely on partial corroboration to mistakenly infer the trustworthiness of the entire statement."

Compulsory Process

Washington v. Texas, **388 U.S. 14, 87 S. Ct. 1920, 18 L. Ed. 2d 1019 (1967)**   Examined whether the compulsory process provision of the Sixth Amendment, which gives the accused the right to obtain witnesses in his or her favor, applies to the states through the Fourteenth Amendment, and whether a state may prohibit "principals, accomplices, or accessories" in the same crime from being witnesses for each other. Defendant Washington, charged with murder, wished to use Charles Fuller as a defense witness. Fuller was a coparticipant with Washington in the alleged crime. Washington was denied use of Fuller as a witness by Texas statute. Fuller could testify for the prosecution under Texas law, however. The Supreme Court unanimously reversed Washington's conviction. The Court held that the right of compulsory process for the defense "stands on no lesser footing than other Sixth Amendment rights" previously held applicable to the states. The Court considered it fundamental because it is the "right to present a defense." Thus the Court subordinated the trial court's interest in deterring perjury to the defendant's right to present a defense. The Court was unconvinced that codefendants would perjure themselves on behalf of other codefendants anyway. If a witness is convicted and awaiting sentence, or simply awaiting trial, "common sense would suggest that he often has a greater interest in lying in favor of the prosecution rather than against it." The Court concluded that to think that "criminals will lie to save their fellows but not to obtain favors from the prosecution for themselves is indeed to clothe the criminal class with more nobility than one might expect to find in the public at large." *See also* BLACKSTONE'S COMMENTARIES, p. 11; COMPULSORY PROCESS, p. 397; SIXTH AMENDMENT, p. 241.

Significance   *Washington v. Texas* (388 U.S. 14: 1967) extended to state actions through the Fourteenth Amendment the expectation that a defendant in a criminal case can present, through his or her own witnesses and evidence, an alternate version of the facts. The ability to subpoena witnesses can be of paramount importance to a defense against criminal charges. In *Washington,* the Court opined, Texas arbitrarily denied a defendant the right to have the material testimony of a witness, thus denying him the right to compulsory process. The compulsory process provision of the Sixth Amendment has not frequently been before the Supreme Court. The Burger Court has rendered two decisions in this regard, both of which found for the defendant in appeals focusing on violation of the compulsory process protection. *Webb v. Texas* (409 U.S. 95: 1972) involved judicial intimidation of a defense witness. The witness, serving a sentence on a prior criminal conviction, was admonished by the trial judge about the "dangers of perjury," how a perjury conviction would mean substantial supplement of the sentence being served, and how perjury would impair his chances of parole. The witness decided not to testify, and Webb argued that his only witness had been coerced into not testifying by the trial judge. The Supreme Court agreed. It cited the judge's "threatening" remarks as effectively driving the witness from the stand and denying Webb due process. In *Cool v. United States* (409 U.S. 100: 1972), the Court again ruled for the defendant because the defense was impaired by an improper jury instruction. Defendant Cool relied on the testimony of a codefendant. The witness, while admitting his own guilt, testified that Cool had nothing to do with the crime. The trial judge gave the jury "a lengthy 'accomplice instruction' to be used in evaluating Vogles' [the codefendant's] testimony." The judge suggested that the testimony was "open to suspicion" and that unless the jury believed the testimony "beyond a reasonable doubt," it should be discarded. The Supreme Court concluded "the clear implication of the instruction was that the jury should disregard Vogles' testimony." An instruction of that kind "places an improper burden on the defense." Thus *Washington, Webb,* and *Cool* establish a firm expectation that the defense will be able to present a full and undeterred case.

Similarly, the Court held in *Rock v. Arkansas* (483 U.S. 44: 1987) that hypnosis-enhanced testimony could not be categorically inadmissible. Rock was charged with shooting her husband. She twice underwent hypnosis to refresh her memory on details of the incident. The trial court ruled that hypnotically refreshed testimony could not be permitted and limited Rock's testimony to repeating statements she made prior to hypnosis. The Court said the state rule that excluded all hypnotically refreshed testimony impermissibly interfered with Rock's right to testify on her own behalf. While the right to present relevant testimony is not without limitation, the restrictions "may not be arbitrary or disproportionate to the purposes they are designed to serve." The Court concluded that the Arkansas rule operated to the detriment of any defendant who undergoes hypnosis without regard to the reasons for it, the circumstances under which it took place, or any independent verification of the information it produced. While hypnosis may be unreliable in some situations, it has been found effective in obtaining certain kinds of information. In addition, hypnotically refreshed testimony is subject to verification by a variety of means, and any inaccuracies produced by the process can be reduced by the use of procedural safeguards. The issue in *Taylor v. Illinois* (480 U.S. 400: 1988) was whether the Compulsory Process Clause permitted the defense to use surprise witnesses. Prior to Taylor's trial, prosecution filed a discovery motion to obtain a list of defense witnesses. Taylor's response, as well as an amended answer, failed to list a particular witness. After the trial had begun, the defense attorney sought to amend the discovery answer orally to include the previously undisclosed witness. Defense counsel indicated that he had been unable to locate the witness earlier, thus he had not included his name on the list. Subsequently, the witness disclosed, among other things, that defense counsel had come to his home prior to the trial. The trial judge refused to allow the witness to testify on the grounds that the defense attorney had violated discovery rules. The judge also had his own doubts about the veracity of the witness's testimony. The Supreme Court ruled that disallowing the testimony of the undisclosed witness as a sanction for the discovery violation did not abridge the defendant's compulsory process rights. The Court described these rights as affording the defendant the fundamental right to present witnesses in his defense. While noting that violations of the right may occur by imposition of discovery sanctions that preclude testimony by the witness, the right is not an "absolute bar to preclusion." In part this is because there is a "significant difference" between the right to compulsory process and other Sixth Amendment rights. Most Sixth Amendment protections "arise automatically" when the criminal process begins, whereas the compulsory process protection depends on the defendant's initiative. The "very nature" of the right requires that its "effective use be preceded by deliberate planning and affirmative conduct." Such limitations are a product of the same principle upon which the defendant's right to present exculpatory evidence is based. The adversary process "could not function effectively" without adherence to rules of procedure that govern "orderly presentation of facts and arguments." The trial process would be a "shambles" if either party had the absolute right to "control the time and content of his witnesses' testimony." Discovery, like cross-examination, "minimizes the risk" of a judgment based on "incomplete, misleading, or even deliberately fabricated testimony." The state's interest in protecting against an "eleventh hour" defense is "merely one component of the broader public interest in a full and truthful disclosure of critical facts." The Court further concluded that the defense attorney's conduct was deliberate and aimed at gaining "tactical advantage." Such willful misconduct warranted protection of the integrity of the judicial process and justified the sanction of precluding the witness from testifying.

Jury Trials

Williams v. Florida, **399 U.S. 78, 90 S. Ct. 1893, 26 L. Ed. 2d 446 (1970)** Considered whether a jury of fewer than 12 persons satisfied the constitutional requirement of *Duncan v. Louisiana* (391 U.S. 145: 1968) that no state could deny trial by jury in a criminal case. The Court found that Florida's trial of Williams with a jury of 6 persons met the requirement. Justice White concentrated on three principles in the majority opinion. First, while the jury is deeply rooted in our legal history, he said he found nothing from historical evidence to suggest the framers intended that exactly 12 persons should always serve on a jury, or that the number 12 was an "indispensable component" of the Sixth Amendment. Second, juries should be large enough to promote group deliberation, free from "outside attempts at intimidation." The Court found nothing to lead it to believe that this goal was "in any meaningful sense less likely to be achieved when the jury numbers six than when it numbers twelve." Third, juries must "provide a fair possibility for obtaining a representative cross section of the community." The Court found the difference between 12 and 6 to be "negligible" in this regard. As long as selection processes prevent arbitrary or discriminatory exclusions, the Court felt "the concern that the cross section will be significantly diminished if the jury is decreased in size from 12 to six seems an unrealistic one." Justice Marshall dissented, arguing that the Fourteenth Amendment requires a 12-member jury in cases where a defendant such as Williams could be sent to prison for the remainder of his life upon conviction. Justice Blackmun did not participate in the decision. *See also* APODACA *v.* OREGON (406 U.S. 404: 1972), p. 257; JURY, p. 431; SIXTH AMENDMENT, p. 241.

Significance *Williams v. Florida* (399 U.S. 78: 1970) represented an unexpected departure from English common law tradition. The tradition clearly acknowledged a jury of 12 persons. When *Duncan v. Louisiana* (391 U.S. 145: 1968) established the fundamental character of the jury trial at the state level, it presumed state juries would have 12 jurors, as do federal juries. The rationale offered by the Court in *Williams* has been subjected to serious criticism, particularly as it relates to the deliberative and representational aspects of 12- versus 6-person juries. The Court did establish that 6 was the constitutionally acceptable minimum. In *Ballew v. Georgia* (435 U.S. 223: 1978) the Court considered a conviction by a 5-member jury in a state obscenity case. A unanimous Court, including all five justices who voted in the *Williams* majority eight years earlier, found a 5-member jury to be constitutionally defective. The Court's opinion used as its rationale the reasons offered by critics of the Williams decision. The Court found that "effective group deliberation" and the ability to represent a cross section of the community were seriously threatened by a 5-member jury. Critics say the difference between 6 and 5 appears to be arbitrary. The *Williams* decision provided the states with considerable latitude in utilizing juries in criminal cases.

Jury trials are guaranteed to any defendant charged with a "serious" offense. *Blanton v. City of North Las Vegas* (103 L. Ed. 2d 550: 1989) considered whether the right to a jury trial extends to a first-offense driving-while-intoxicated charge for which the maximum detention is six months. The Court ruled unanimously that the penalty faced by first-offense defendants was not sufficiently severe to constitute a "serious" offense for jury trial purposes. The "most relevant criterion" for determining the seriousness of an offense is the "maximum authorized penalty fixed by the legislature." When an offense carries a maximum sentence of less than six months, it is "presumed to be petty" unless it can be shown by the defendant that additional penalties, when viewed "in conjunction with the maximum authorized period of incarceration, are so severe that they clearly reflect a legislative determination that the offense in question is a 'serious' one." Applying this standard to Blanton's first-offense driving-while-intoxicated charge, the Court saw no evidence that the state legislature saw the offense as "serious." The Court said it was immaterial that other penalties, such as suspension of the driver's license, community service, or fines, could be imposed concurrent with incarceration. Incarceration is the key factor because, while other penalties "may engender a significant infringement of personal freedom," they cannot "approximate in severity the loss of liberty that a prison term entails." Because incarceration is an "intrinsically different" kind of penalty, it is the "most powerful indication of whether an offense is 'serious.'" The Federal Magistrates Act was enacted in 1968 to provide some relief for judges of federal district courts. The act allowed district judges to delegate a number of functions to U.S. magistrates. The question presented in *Gomez v. United States* (104 L. Ed. 2d 923: 1989) was whether federal judges could delegate to magistrates the responsibility of presiding over the selection of felony trial juries. It was the unanimous view of the Court that the act did not authorize magistrates to preside over jury selection in federal felony cases absent the consent of the accused. The act assigns certain duties to magistrates as well as "such additional duties as are not inconsistent with the Constitution and laws of the United States." Jury selection was not among the duties assigned, and the issue was whether it was one of the "additional" duties that could be delegated. The Court agreed that "without reference to its statutory context," the provision could be interpreted to include anything not explicitly prohibited. The "settled policy" governing construction of a statute, however, is to avoid an interpretation that "engenders constitutional issues" if possible. Inquiry into the purpose of the statute revealed that a magistrate's range of duties was limited with regard to criminal cases. Magistrates could conduct bench trials only in misdemeanor cases and only with consent of the parties. Involvement in felony cases was confined to certain "specific pretrial and post-trial functions" subject to at least one level of review by a judge. Furthermore, the Court viewed the absence of specific reference in the act to felony trial jury selection as significant. The conduct of *voir dire* in a felony case is a "critical stage" in the process, and Congress could not have intended the "additional duties" language to convey that responsibility by implication.

Assistance of Counsel

United States v. Monsanto, **109 S. Ct. 2657, 105 L. Ed. 2d 512 (1989)** Upheld forfeiture provisions under federal law, including seizure of those assets intended to secure privately retained defense counsel. Under provisions of the Racketeer Influenced and Corrupt Organization Act (RICO) and the Continuing Criminal Enterprise Act (CCE), the federal government may seize assets that are the proceeds of criminal activity. Congress expanded these forfeiture provisions in the Comprehensive Forfeiture Act of 1984, which focused on proceeds from organized crime activities and narcotics trafficking. The issues in *Monsanto* were whether forfeiture covers those assets intended to pay for defense counsel and, if so, whether such compelled forfeiture interferes with the defendant's Sixth Amendment right to counsel. When Monsanto was indicted for various crimes, including RICO and CCE violations, the government obtained a restraining order freezing his assets as a preliminary step in the forfeiture process. Monsanto was unable to secure private counsel because attorneys feared forfeiture of their fees. Under "relation back" terms of the 1984 law, proceeds from criminal activity belong to the government from the time the crime is committed. In addition, the forfeiture applies not only to proceeds still in the hands of the defendant, but also to proceeds that had been paid to third parties subsequent to the crime. The trial judge appointed a publicly paid lawyer as Monsanto's counsel, recognizing that the restraining order had left Monsanto virtually indigent. The court of appeals heard the case *en banc* and ruled that attorney's fees were exempt from forfeiture. The

United States sought review. By a vote of 5–4, the Supreme Court ruled that assets intended to cover attorneys' fees are not exempt from seizure, and that such seizure did not unconstitutionally interfere with the right to counsel. Justice White spoke for the Court. He said that language in the Forfeiture Act is "plain and unambiguous." Congress could not have chosen "stronger words to express its intent that forfeiture be mandatory" under circumstances presented in these appeals. Neither does the statute contain any language that "even hints" that assets used for attorneys' fees are not included in seizable property. By enacting the Forfeiture Act, said White, Congress "decided to give force to the old adage that 'crime does not pay.'" There is no evidence, he continued, that Congress "intended to modify that nostrum to read, 'crime does not pay, except for attorney's fees.'" He noted that if the Court were mistaken as to congressional intent on this issue, "that body can amend at statute, to otherwise provide." On the constitutional issue of assistance of counsel, the Court said that "nothing in [the act] prevents defendant from hiring the attorney of his choice," or disqualifies any attorney from serving as a defendant's counsel. A defendant with nonforfeitable assets remains free to retain "any attorney of his choosing." There will be cases like this, however, in which a defendant is unable to retain an attorney of choice. "Impecunious" defendants, said the Court, do not have the right to "choose their counsel." Neither do they have a "cognizable complaint" as long as they are "adequately represented by attorneys appointed by the court." Compulsory forfeiture of assets, even if such forfeiture renders a defendant unable to retain counsel privately, is not unconstitutional because defendants are not entitled to "spend another person's money for services rendered by an attorney." This proposition holds even if that money is the "only way that a defendant will be able to retain the attorney of his choice." The Court said that there is a "compelling" public interest in "stripping criminals . . . of their undeserved economic power," and this interest "overrides any Sixth Amendment interest in permitting criminals to use assets adjudged forfeitable to pay for their defense." Justices Blackmun, Brennan, Marshall, and Stevens dissented. They viewed the Sixth Amendment as a bar to congressional interference with the right to counsel. Justice Blackmun said that to consider attorney fees as part of forfeitable assets is "unseemly and unjust." The decision, said Blackmun, loses sight of the "distinct role of the right to counsel in protecting the integrity of the judicial process." Indeed, if Congress had set out to "undermine the adversarial system as we know it," it could not have "found a better engine of destruction" than to seize assets intended to pay for defense counsel. *See also* ASSISTANCE OF COUNSEL, p. 399.

Significance   *United States v. Monsanto* (105 L. Ed. 2d 512: 1989) was one of two asset seizure cases decided by the Court during the 1988 term. The second case was *Caplin & Drysdale, Chartered v. United States* (105 L. Ed. 2d 528: 1989). The fact situation differed, but the outcome was identical to *Monsanto*. A law firm's (Caplin & Drysdale) client (Christopher Reckmeyer) was indicted for various narcotics offenses and a CCE violation. The defendant owed the law firm in excess of $26,000 in fees before the indictment, and had made a payment (with two $5,000 checks) on the day prior to his being indicted. Also on the day prior to the indictments, the government obtained a court order restraining Reckmeyer from transferring any assets relating to the indictment charges. When the law firm attempted to deposit Reckmeyer's checks, they were returned unpaid on the basis of the restraining order. Reckmeyer eventually pleaded guilty, was sentenced, and had virtually all his assets seized. Caplin & Drysdale filed a claim for the two $5,000 checks returned unpaid at the outset, plus additional fees amounting to almost $200,000. As in *Monsanto,* the Court ruled that the assets intended to compensate private counsel were subject to forfeiture. The decision upheld forfeiture of assets even though such action deprived the defendant of the capacity to select private counsel himself. Defendant choice of counsel was also an issue in *Wheat v. United States* (486 U.S. 153: 1988). The Sixth Amendment generally entitles a defendant to select his or her counsel, but the right does not extend to a selection that creates a conflict of interest with the counsel's other clients. In *Wheat,* the Court reviewed a case in which the trial court, on motion by the prosecution, refused to allow a defendant to be represented by the attorney of his codefendants. Two days prior to his trial for participation in an extensive drug distribution conspiracy, Wheat sought to substitute the counsel of his two codefendants for his original attorney. Wheat and his codefendants were all willing to waive the right to conflict-free counsel. The trial court refused to allow the substitution on the grounds that the conflicts were "irreconcilable and unwaivable" because of the likelihood that Wheat would have to testify at the trial of the second codefendant, and the third codefendant would have to testify at Wheat's trial. The Supreme Court upheld the trial court's denial of the substitution of counsel. The Court noted that the Sixth Amendment right to choose one's own counsel is "circumscribed in several important respects." In cases where there is multiple representation, the trial court "has a duty" to take measures that are "appropriate to protect criminal defendants against counsel's conflicts of interest, including the issuance of separate representation orders." Such determinations are made more difficult, the Court pointed out, because they often occur at the pretrial stage, when "relationships between parties are unclear, and the likelihood and dimensions of nascent conflicts of interest are hard to predict." Simply securing waivers from codefendants may not necessarily address the problem, since the trial courts have an "independent interest in assuring compliance with ethical standards and the appearance of fairness." As a result, trial courts must be allowed "substantial latitude" to assess each case in light of its own facts and circumstances. Although the courts must recognize the Sixth Amendment's "presumption" in favor of a defendant's choice of an attorney, the presumption may be overridden not only by a showing of actual conflict, but also by a demonstration of "serious potential for conflict." When, as in this case, the motion for substitution comes too close to the trial, it cannot be concluded that the trial court "abused its discretion" as it was presented with "complex litigation that was likely to engender conflicts of interest" by the multiple representation.

Argersinger v. Hamlin, 407 U.S. 25, 92 S. Ct. 2006, 32 L. Ed. 2d 530 (1972)   Extended to misdemeanors the *Gideon* doctrine that an indigent defendant must be provided with a lawyer. *Gideon v. Wainwright* (372 U.S. 335: 1963) required that all indigent felony defendants be provided counsel at state expense. Argersinger was convicted on an offense punishable by up to six months imprisonment. He was indigent and unrepresented by counsel. In a unanimous decision, the Supreme Court found his trial and conviction to be constitutionally defective. The opinion of the Court stresses these points: (1) The Court found nothing historically to indicate Sixth Amendment rights should be retractable in cases involving petty offenses. (2) The nature of the legal issues of a case should be the criterion for assessing necessity of counsel. Cases where lesser terms of imprisonment result may not be any less complex than cases where lengthy sentences may occur. (3) Given the assembly-line character of misdemeanor proceedings, assistance of counsel may be especially important. The basic holding of *Argersinger* is that absent a "knowing and intelligent waiver," no defendant may receive jail or prison time unless the defendant was represented by counsel at his or her trial. Several members of the Court wrote concurring opinions addressing the decision's implementation problems, but the basic holding was unanimous. *See also GIDEON V. WAINWRIGHT* (372 U.S. 335: 1963), p. 264; *POWELL v. ALABAMA* (287 U.S. 45: 1932), p. 263; *UNITED STATES v. WADE* (388 U.S. 218: 1967), p. 167.

Significance   *Argersinger v. Hamlin* (407 U.S. 25: 1972) reveals stress stemming from implementation considerations. On the one hand, the

Court wished to extend *Gideon* and did so with fairly strong language. On the other hand, the Court was faced with implementation of policy where the court system is most congested and where pressures for "assembly-line justice" are most acute. *Argersinger* was a compromise. It required counsel in misdemeanor cases, recognizing that the legal needs of defendants in these cases may be equal to or greater than those of defendants in felony cases. It also provided trial judges with the choice of not appointing counsel at all, although in refusing to do so the trial judge must forfeit imprisonment as a sentence option. Despite the problems in implementation, *Argersinger* has fundamentally altered the process of justice in misdemeanor courts, often called "city courts," "municipal courts," or "justice of the peace" courts. It has also produced important legislation at the state and local levels. Many cities, for example, now appoint or contract with private counsel to provide legal assistance to persons who desire to try misdemeanor charges. Some states have decriminalized many traffic offenses in order to avoid the consequences of *Argersinger*. *Argersinger* was refined in *Scott v. Illinois* (440 U.S. 367: 1979), in which the Supreme Court held that a state court does not have to appoint counsel where imprisonment is authorized for a particular offense but not actually imposed. Together, *Argersinger* and *Scott* require greater caution by state and local governments in criminal proceedings. Many local judges are loath to imprison for misdemeanor convictions where counsel is not present, unless the defendant was made aware of his or her right to counsel before tendering a guilty plea. The *Scott* emphasis on actual incarceration was reinforced in *Lassiter v. Department of Social Services* (452 U.S. 18: 1981), in which the Court held that counsel need not be provided to an indigent parent at a hearing that could terminate that person's status as a parent. The Court said an indigent litigant was entitled to counsel only when the litigant is threatened with deprivation of physical liberty. On a related matter, the Court held in *Ake v. Oklahoma* (470 U.S. 68: 1985) that an indigent defendant seeking to utilize the insanity defense is entitled to court-appointed psychiatric assistance. Justice Marshall wrote that a trial or sentencing proceeding is fundamentally unfair if the state proceeds against an indigent without ensuring that he or she has access to advice that is "integral to the building of an effective defense." The impact of *Ake* is limited in that the great majority of states already provide such aid to indigent defendants.

Perry v. Leake (488 U.S. 272: 1989) considered whether a defendant could be barred from conversing with his attorney during a 15-minute recess in proceedings. The recess occurred after the witness had testified on direct examination, but before cross-examination had taken place. When a defendant becomes a witness, rules that serve the "truth-seeking" function of trials are applicable to him as well as to witnesses generally. A judge must be able to determine if cross-examination is "more likely to elicit truthful responses" if it occurs without allowing a witness to consult with counsel (or any third party). The Court was concerned with more than "unethical coaching" taking place. Effective cross-examination, said the Court, "often depends" on the ability to "punch holes" in testimony "at just the right time, in just the right way." Consultation with counsel after direct examination, but before cross-examination, gives a witness an "opportunity to regroup and regain a poise and sense of strategy that the unaided witness would not possess." It is "simply an empirical predicate" of the adversary system that cross-examination of a witness uncounseled after direct examination is "more likely to lead to the discovery of truth than is cross-examination of a witness who is given time to pause and consult with his attorney." The Court concluded that a trial judge's "unquestioned power" to refuse to declare a recess is akin to limiting consultation. The judge "must have the power to maintain the status quo" during a recess. There is "virtual certainty," said the Court, that a conversation between counsel and witness during a short recess would "relate to the ongoing testimony." In a short recess it is "not inappropriate to presume that nothing but the testimony will be discussed." Under these circumstances, a defendant is not constitutionally entitled to advice. A federal statute authorized federal courts to request attorneys to represent indigent civil litigants. A federal district judge ordered a lawyer to represent three indigent prison inmates in a civil rights action against state prison officials. The attorney sought to be excused on several grounds, one of which was that the court did not have the authority to compel his representation of the litigants. The Supreme Court ruled in *Mallard v. United States District Court for the Southern District of Iowa* (490 U.S. 296: 1989) that the statute does not authorize compulsory appointment. The decision hinged on interpretation of the statute. Interpretation of the provision "must begin," said the Court, with the language of the law, and the operative term *request*. In "everyday speech" the closest synonyms to the word are *ask* or *entreat*. The verbs *require* and *demand* are "not usually interchangeable with it." The Court found no reason to conclude that Congress did not intend the word *request* to "bear its most common meaning." The Court also pointed to adjoining subsections of the same law, where the Congress expressly required certain conduct. It was clear to the Court that the choice of the word "'request' bespeaks an intent not to authorize mandatory appointment of counsel." Justice Brennan concluded the majority opinion by saying the ruling was not intended to "question, let alone denigrate, lawyers' ethical obligation to assist those who are too poor to afford counsel." Neither did the Court intend that requests made under the law be "lightly declined because they give rise to no ethical claim." To the contrary, the Court emphasized the great need for attorneys to volunteer time. The language of the statute, however, was not seen as allowing "coercive appointments" of counsel. *Mallard* involved involuntary appointment of private counsel. *Federal Trade Commission v. Superior Court Trial Lawyers Association* (107 L. Ed. 2d 851: 1990) involved compensation for appointed counsel. The case examined whether a boycott by attorneys who frequently acted as appointed counsel for indigent criminal defendants constituted illegal price-fixing. This case was not decided on Sixth Amendment grounds, but bears directly on the provision of counsel to indigent defendants. The Federal Trade Commission (FTC) had found the boycott to be a restraint of trade in violation of federal antitrust laws, and attempted to enforce its finding. The attorneys, who were seeking increases in the rate of compensation for the court-appointed cases, countered that the boycott was meant to communicate a political message and was, therefore, expression protected by the First Amendment. The Supreme Court disagreed in a 6–3 decision. Justice Stevens said for the majority that reasonable lawyers may "differ about the wisdom" of enforcing the FTC ruling. The Court acknowledged that the boycott may have served a "worthwhile and unpopular" cause. Increasing rates of compensation for the presumably "unreasonably low" pre-boycott levels produced "better legal representation for indigent defendants." Those considerations, however, were not seen as controlling the case. Neither did the Court see assessing the "social utility or political wisdom of price-fixing agreements" as part of its task. Controlling was that the boycott constituted a "horizontal arrangement among competitors" that was "unquestionably" a "naked restraint of price and output" in violation of antitrust law. The "social justifications" asserted for the restraint of trade "do not make it any less unlawful." The Court also distinguished First Amendment-protected boycotts from the boycott involved here. The FTC order did not preclude lawyers from publicizing their concerns or seeking favorable response from government officials. Moreover, the lawyers' boycott was undertaken for the economic advantage of the participants. No matter how "altruistic the motives," the lawyers' objective was increased compensation, which made it an economic boycott. Boycotts undertaken to advance the cause of civil rights, on the other hand, sought "no such special advantage for themselves." Neither did the Court support the creation of a new exception to antitrust liability rules for economic boycotts also having an expressive component. Such an exception "exaggerates the significance of the expressive content" of the lawyers' boycott, since any "concerted refusal" to do business with a customer or supplier "has such a component." An exception whenever an economic boycott has an "expressive component" would create a "gaping hole in the fabric" of antitrust law.

Critical Stages for Assistance of Counsel

United States v. Wade, **388 U.S. 218, 87 S. Ct. 1926, 18 L. Ed. 2d 1149 (1967)** Considered whether counsel must be present at a post-indictment lineup session. Once the Supreme Court determined in *Gideon v. Wainwright* (372 U.S. 335: 1963) that assistance of counsel was a fundamental ingredient of due process at the trial stage of any felony prosecution, it followed that assistance of counsel at other stages in the criminal process would have to be evaluated. *Wade* represents a number of cases that define the stages critical enough to require assistance of counsel. The Court vacated Wade's conviction and ordered a new trial, saying that postindictment process was "peculiarly riddled with innumerable dangers and variable factors which might seriously, even crucially, derogate from a fair trial." Denial of counsel at this stage was seen as critical. There exists "grave potential for prejudice, intentional or not, in the pre-trial lineup." The presence of counsel "can often avert prejudice and assure a meaningful confrontation at trial." The Court's conclusion was that there was "little doubt" that the lineup was a "critical stage," a stage at which Wade was entitled to aid of counsel. *See also* ARGERSINGER *v.* HAMLIN (407 U.S. 25: 1972), p. 266; GIDEON *v.* WAINWRIGHT (372 U.S. 335: 1963), p. 264; POWELL *v.* ALABAMA (287 U.S. 45: 1932), p. 263.

Significance United States v. Wade (388 U.S. 218: 1967) settled the question of whether earlier or later stages in criminal proceedings other than trial similarly required assistance of counsel. The Warren Court approached the issue by defining the concept of "critical stages." A critical stage is one at which advice of counsel may be essential to protecting a defendant's rights and at which the outcome of the criminal process as a whole is substantially affected. Within five years of *Gideon,* pretrial steps or proceedings such as custodial interrogation prior to charging, postcharge investigations, and preliminary hearings and identifications such as the lineup in *Wade* were found to be critical stages requiring assistance of counsel. These rulings came in *Miranda v. Arizona* (384 U.S. 436: 1966), *Massiah v. United States* (377 U.S. 201: 1964), and *White v. Maryland* (373 U.S. 59: 1963), respectively. Even before *Gideon,* counsel provisions had been extended to arraignments in *Hamilton v. Alabama* (368 U.S. 52: 1961). Expansion of the concept of critical stage also occurred with respect to posttrial proceedings. In *Douglas v. California* (372 U.S. 353: 1963), the Court held that counsel was required for those appeals that are a matter of right. To the present point in the development of critical stage doctrine, counsel is not required for second or discretionary appeals. In *Pennsylvania v. Finley* (481 U.S. 551: 1987), the Court ruled that a state law providing assistance of counsel for collateral postconviction proceedings need not require all the procedural protections established for trials and first appeals. It said the right to appointed counsel extends to the first right of appeal, and no further. An attorney is not required for an indigent simply because an affluent defendant may retain one. The state's obligation is not to duplicate the legal arsenal that may be privately retained in a continuing effort to reverse a conviction. The state needs only to assure that the indigent defendant has an adequate opportunity to present his or her claims fully in the context of the state's appellate process. This does not include collateral postconviction review.

Counsel is required for juvenile proceedings, however, as in *In re Gault* (378 U.S. 1: 1967), and at the sentencing stage of adult criminal proceedings. In *Mempa v. Rhay* (389 U.S. 128: 1967), the Court said that an individual is entitled to counsel in a proceeding where probation is revoked and a sentence is to be imposed. These cases demonstrate the exceptionally high priority assigned by the Supreme Court to making legal counsel available to all persons at most stages of the criminal charge process. They reflect the Court's recognition that other constitutional protections are best preserved through assistance of counsel. Similarly, the Court ruled in *Murray v. Giarratano* (106 L. Ed. 2d 1: 1989) that Sixth Amendment counsel protection did not require states to provide assigned counsel to indigent death-row inmates as they pursue postconviction review. Currently, states are required under the Sixth Amendment to provide counsel for an appeal of right, but have discretion over whether counsel is provided for additional proceedings. Giarratano claimed that those on death row are entitled to personal counsel assigned to assist them in seeking, for example, habeas corpus relief. The state did provide death-row prisoners with access to a law library, access to a "unit" attorney, and assignment of counsel after the formal filing of a petition. An indigent is entitled as a "matter of right" to counsel for an initial appeal from the "judgment and sentence of the trial court." The right to counsel at the various stages of the criminal process, on the other hand, does not "carry over to a discretionary appeal." The analysis from *Finley* "requires the conclusion" that no different rules should extend to capital cases. State collateral proceedings are not constitutionally required as an "adjunct" to the state criminal proceedings, and "serve a different and more limited purpose than either the trial or appeal." Furthermore, the "additional safeguards" stemming from the trial stage of a capital case are "sufficient to assure the reliability of the process by which the death penalty is imposed." Under a rule established in *Anders v. California* (386 U.S. 738: 1967), court-appointed counsel wishing to withdraw from a frivolous appeal must submit a withdrawal motion accompanied by a brief that refers to "anything in the record that might arguably support the appeal." A Wisconsin court rule embraced this requirement, but further required that the brief include discussion of "why the issue lacks merit." The case of *McCoy v. Court of Appeals of Wisconsin* (486 U.S. 429: 1988) examined the Wisconsin variation on the *Anders* procedure. McCoy's court-appointed counsel concluded that appeal of McCoy's conviction would be frivolous, but was unwilling to include in his withdrawal brief the additional discussion required by Wisconsin. Counsel unsuccessfully challenged the requirement in the state courts on the grounds that it was incompatible with *Anders* and that it compels counsel to violate a client's right to assistance of counsel. In a 5–3 decision, the Court ruled the discussion requirement to be constitutional. In the Court's view, the rule "merely goes one step further than the minimal requirements stated in *Anders*." It serves the "same objectives" of *Anders* of assuring an appellate court that a review has been "diligently and thoroughly" researched, and it allows the reviewing court to "determine whether counsel's frivolous conclusion is correct." An additional protection against mistaken conclusions exists because counsel may "discover previously unrecognized aspects of the law" in preparing the statement. The Court pointed out that it is "settled" that counsel can advise a court that an appeal is frivolous "without impairing" the constitutional rights of the client. Explaining the basis for a conclusion does not "burden the right to effective representation or to due process" any more than simply stating the conclusion, as *Anders* requires. Further, the Wisconsin rule does not diminish counsel's "obligations as an advocate, since his duty to his client is fulfilled once he has conducted a zealous review of the record." *Penson v. Ohio* (102 L. Ed. 2d 300: 1988) examined the consequences of deviating from *Anders*. Penson's appointed counsel filed a motion with the appellate court indicating that he had reviewed the record and concluded the appeal was meritless. The court granted his motion requesting withdrawal even though no supporting *Anders* brief had been filed. In addition, the court indicated that it would perform its own review of the record. Penson requested a new attorney. The appeals court noted "several arguable claims," and commented that the withdrawn counsel's conclusion of the meritlessness of the appeal was "highly questionable." The court refused to appoint new counsel, but reversed one of Penson's convictions as plain error. At the same time, the court concluded that Penson was not injured by counsel's failure to examine the record more conscientiously because the court had independently done so. In addition, the court noted that it had also reviewed arguments submitted on behalf of Penson's codefendants. The Supreme Court reversed, finding that Penson had been deprived of his right to adequate representation on appeal. The appellate court erred in failing to require submission of the supporting brief as per *Anders*. Absence of such a brief deprived the court of an adequate basis for determining whether a careful enough review of the record had been conducted by counsel. Further, the lower court should not have ruled on the motion to withdraw prior to making its own examination of the record. More critical was the failure to provide Penson with a new attorney once determining that several "arguable" claims existed. Once the court found potentially meritorious claims, a "constitutional imperative" existed to appoint counsel. Denial of counsel left Penson "completely without representation during the appellate court's actual decisional process." This the Court found "quite different" from a situation in which it is claimed that "counsel's performance was ineffective." Accordingly, the Court concluded that what happened to Penson must be presumed to be prejudicial.

Plea Bargaining

Bordenkircher v. Hayes, **434 U.S. 357, 98 S. Ct. 663, 54 L. Ed. 2d 604 (1978)** Weighed the question of how far a prosecutor should go in putting a criminal defendant under pressure to plead guilty. After defendant Hayes refused to plead to a particular felony indictment, the prosecutor carried out his threat to have the defendant reindicted under Kentucky's habitual offender statute. The statute allowed the possibility of a mandatory life sentence. Threat of this action was conveyed by the prosecutor during the course of plea negotiations. A jury subsequently convicted Hayes of the original charge and made an additional finding that he was eligible for a life term under the recidivist statute. Hayes appealed, claiming violation of due process. The Supreme Court decided against Hayes 5–4. The majority's decision took two lines of argument. First, the Court acknowledged the breadth of prosecutorial discretion in the charging process. The majority found little difference between charging initially and offering to drop the recidivist part of the subsequent charge. Second, the Court said the plea-bargaining process should be afforded substantial operating margin. The bargaining process should entertain the whole range of options available to the defendant. In this case, Hayes was informed of what the prosecutor would do if he did not plead guilty, and since he was properly chargeable under the recidivist statute, the prosecutor had not acted improperly. The Court concluded that the prosecutor "openly presented the defendant with the unpleasant alternatives of foregoing trial or facing charges on which he was plainly subject to prosecution." This was not viewed as a deprivation of due process. And, "in the 'give and take' of plea bargaining, there is no such element of punishment or retaliation so long as the accused is free to accept or reject the prosecutor's offer." The four dissenters— Justices Brennan, Marshall, Blackmun, and Powell—viewed the prosecutorial conduct as creating a "strong inference of vindictiveness." While expressing general deference to prosecutorial discretion, the minority thought the prosecutor had intended to discourage and penalize Hayes for pursuing his constitutional right to a trial. Justice Powell concluded by saying, "Implementation of a strategy calculated solely to deter the exercise of constitutional rights is not a constitutionally permissible exercise of discretion." *See also* BOYKIN *v.* ALABAMA (397 U.S. 238: 1969), p. 270; BRADY *v.* UNITED STATES (397 U.S. 742: 1970), p. 272; SANTOBELLO *v.* NEW YORK (404 U.S. 257: 1971), p. 273.

Significance   Bordenkircher v. Hayes (434 U.S. 357: 1978) extended substantial latitude to the prosecutor in plea-bargaining situations. The Court majority was unwilling to view the prosecutor's conveyed incentives to plead guilty as either punitive or malicious threats. Thus *Bordenkircher* defined the plea-bargaining setting itself as one permitting broad prosecutorial discretion. *Bordenkircher* clarified the opinion of the Court in *Blackledge v. Perry* (417 U.S. 21: 1974), and freed the plea-bargaining process from the limitations of *Blackledge*. Perry was convicted of a misdemeanor. He pursued his statutory right to a retrial and was subsequently charged with a felony for the same conduct that was originally charged as a misdemeanor. The Court disallowed the substitute charge on the grounds that the recharging was motivated by vindictiveness. An actual retaliatory motive need not be shown. The Court's perception of vindictiveness sufficient to "deter a defendant's exercise of the right to appeal" was the crucial factor in *Blackledge*. Some observers felt the thrust of *Blackledge* might carry over to the plea process. *Bordenkircher* resolved the doubt otherwise and enhanced the leverage a prosecutor may bring to bear in plea negotiations. The Supreme Court established a presumption of vindictiveness in *North Carolina v. Pearce* (395 U.S. 711: 1969) in situations where a person is resentenced more severely following successful appeal. The objective of *Pearce* was to lessen the possibility of resentencing being used as retaliation for appeal. In *Alabama v. Smith* (104 L. Ed. 2d 865: 1989), the Court considered whether the *Pearce* presumption extends to a case where a defendant sentenced on the basis of a subsequently vacated guilty plea is sentenced more harshly after a jury trial on the charges. The Court decided the presumption did not apply to Smith and allowed the enhanced sentence following the trial. *Pearce* was not designed, said the Court, to "prevent imposition of an increased sentence on retrial for some valid reason associated with the need for flexibility and discretion in the sentencing process." Rather, the presumption is to be used when there is a "reasonable likelihood" that an increase in sentence is the "product of actual vindictiveness" on the part of the sentencing judge. Where no such likelihood exists, the defendant must demonstrate actual vindictiveness in the absence of the presumption. In cases such as Smith's, considerably more information is typically available to the sentencing judge than after a guilty plea. Further, leniency that may have come in response to the plea is no longer a consideration. Thus there often exists "enough justification for a heavier sentence." These two factors, concluded the Court, make it much less likely that a judge who imposes a heavier sentence is "motivated by vindictiveness."

Independent Counsel

Morrison v. Olson, **487 U.S. 654, 108 S. Ct. 2597, 101 L. Ed. 2d 529 (1988)** Upheld the federal independent prosecutor statute. The authorization for appointment of independent counsel is found in the Ethics in Government Act, which requires the attorney general to conduct preliminary investigations of particular high-level executive officers alleged to have engaged in criminal misconduct. If there is cause to believe "further investigation is warranted," the attorney general is obligated to refer the case to the U.S. Court of Appeals for the District of Columbia. The federal appellate court then appoints independent counsel. Once appointed, counsel may be removed by the attorney general only for "good cause," a decision subject to judicial review. The dispute in *Morrison v. Olson* began in 1982 as Congress sought certain documents from the Environmental Protection Agency concerning the "superfund" toxic waste law. On advice of Justice Department counsel, the documents were withheld. Olson, an assistant attorney general in the Office of Legal Counsel, testified before the House Judiciary Committee, which was investigating the matter. The committee issued a report sometime later suggesting, among other things, that Olson had given false testimony during the inquiry. The committee chair requested independent counsel to look into the actions of Olson and two other officials of the Office of Legal Counsel. Morrison was appointed following the preliminary investigation of the attorney general. As part of the inquiry into whether a conspiracy to obstruct the Judiciary Committee investigation had occurred, subpoenas were issued by a grand jury to obtain both testimony and documents from Olson and the others. They, in turn, sought to quash the subpoenas, asserting that Morrison had no authority to proceed because the independent counsel law was unconstitutional. The law was upheld by a federal district court, but the court of appeals found for Olson. The court of appeals ruled that the law violated the separation of powers principle by encroaching on executive prerogatives. With only Justice Scalia dissenting (Justice Kennedy not participating), the Supreme Court reversed. Chief Justice Rehnquist offered the Court's rationale. He began with consideration of the Appointments Clause of Article II. Under that clause, the president shall nominate various "principal officers" of the government, but Congress has the authority to appoint "inferior" officers. While the line between principal and inferior officers is "far from clear," the independent counsel "clearly falls on the 'inferior officer' side of that line." Rehnquist offered several reasons in support of this conclusion. First, Morrison was subject to removal by the attorney general, an indication that she was "inferior in rank and authority." Second, the special prosecutor is empowered to "perform only certain, limited duties." While counsel has the authority to exercise "all investigative and prosecutorial functions and powers" of the Justice Department, counsel has no authority to "formulate policy" or to have administrative duties "outside those necessary to operate her office." Third, the office is "limited in jurisdiction" and has "limited tenure." Rehnquist then moved to the contention that the clause did not permit "interbranch" appointments. That is, Congress cannot place the authority to appoint an inferior officer outside the Executive Branch. In the Court's view, Congress possesses "significant discretion" to empower courts to make such appointments. Such power is not unlimited. Congress could not, for example, vest the courts with power to appoint officers where "incongruity" exists between the "functions normally performed by the courts and the performance of their duty to appoint." The Court concluded that there is no "inherent incongruity" about a court "having the power to appoint prosecutorial officers." When Congress created the office of independent counsel, it was concerned with conflicts of interest that could occur when the Executive Branch was called upon to investigate its own officials. If it was necessary to remove the appointing authority from the Executive, the "most logical place to put it was the Judicial Branch." Neither did the Court find that the law was incompatible with Article III provisions assigning the courts their judicial functions. The court's role in the independent counsel process is "passive," with the court having no supervisory power over the special prosecutor's performance. Particularly, the court is not entitled to approve or disapprove the content of any report or finding of either the attorney general or special counsel. Finally, the Court ruled that the law did not improperly encroach on executive power. While the independent counsel cannot be removed at will, the Court did not find this factor decisive. The executive retains "sufficient control" over independent counsel to support the conclusion that Congress had not "unduly" interfered with the president's executive power. Important to its finding was the Court's observation that the law did not represent an attempt by Congress to "increase its own powers at the expense of the Executive Branch."

Significance   *Morrison v. Olson* (101 L. Ed. 2d 529: 1988) is not a Sixth Amendment case. Rather, it rests squarely on separation of powers considerations. It warrants mention in this volume nonetheless because of its direct relationship to federal criminal justice processes and current attempts to implement more demanding ethics standards for government officials. The Court's ruling in *Morrison* represented a short-term loss for the Reagan administration and a number of former administration officials. The administration had strongly argued that the law was unconstitutional. Convictions of former Reagan advisers Lyn Nofziger and Michael Deaver in cases prosecuted by independent counsel became more secure in the wake of *Morrison*. The decision also applied to the ongoing investigation of the Iran-contra affair. What *Morrison v. Olson* means over the longer term is not clear. While the holding says that Congress can establish processes for investigations within the Executive Branch, the Court did not give Congress unlimited authority to designate areas subject to investigation by independent counsel. The exact dimensions of congressional authority and the limits that apply will be defined over the next several years.

5. *The Eighth Amendment*

Preventive Detention

Schall v. Martin, **467 U.S. 253, 104 S. Ct. 2403, 81 L. Ed. 2d 207
(1984)** Upheld the preventive detention of juveniles. *Schall v.
Martin* examined a state statute that authorized pretrial detention of
a juvenile as long as it could be shown that there was "serious risk" of
the juvenile committing additional crimes if released. Martin brought
suit claiming the statute was unconstitutional on due process and
equal protection grounds. A U.S. district court found the law in violation of the Due Process Clause and ordered the release of all juveniles detained under the statute. The Supreme Court reversed the
district court in a 6–3 decision. The opinion of the Court was delivered by Justice Rehnquist. He said the question before the Court was
whether or not preventive detention of juveniles is compatible with
"fundamental fairness." To address this issue properly, the Court felt
that answers to two inquiries were necessary: (1) Is a legitimate state
interest served by preventive detention? and (2) Are the procedural
safeguards adequate to authorize the pretrial detention? The Court
determined that crime prevention is a "weighty social objective," and
a state's legitimate and compelling interest in protecting its citizenry
from crime "cannot be doubted." That interest "persists undiluted in
the juvenile context." The harm caused by crime is not dependent
upon the age of the perpetrator, and the harm to society may be even
greater given the high rate of recidivism among juveniles. In addition,
the juvenile's liberty interest may be subordinated to the state's
"parens patriae interest in preserving and promoting the welfare of
the child." Rehnquist argued that society has a legitimate interest in
protecting a juvenile from the consequences of his or her criminal
activity. This includes the potential injury that may occur when a
victim resists and "the downward spiral of criminal activity into which
peer pressure may lead the child" persists. The Court saw the state
interest as substantial and legitimate, a view "confirmed by the wide-
spread use and judicial acceptance of preventive detention for juveniles." Rehnquist observed that "mere invocation of a legitimate
purpose" will not justify particular restrictions and conditions of

confinement amounting to punishment. The Court found the statute in question to have nonpunitive objectives, however. The detention specified was "strictly limited in time," and it entitled the juvenile to an expedited fact-finding hearing. The Court then addressed the procedural issue of whether there was "sufficient protection against erroneous and unnecessary deprivation of liberty." The Court found that the statute provided "far more pre-detention protection" than required for probable cause determinations for adults. While the initial appearance is informal, full notice is given and stenographic records are kept. The juvenile is accompanied by a parent or guardian and is informed of his or her constitutional rights, including the rights to remain silent and to be represented by counsel. Finally, the Court rejected the contention that the statute's standard for detention, serious risk of additional criminal conduct, was "fatally vague." Prediction of future criminal conduct is a judgment based on "a host of variables which cannot be readily codified." Nonetheless, the decision on detention is based on "as much information as can reasonably be obtained at the initial appearance," and is not impermissibly vague. Justices Marshall, Brennan, and Stevens dissented. They saw the statute as a violation of due process because it allowed punishment before final adjudication of guilt. They felt the crime prevention interest was insufficient justification for the infringement of the detainee's rights. *See also* BAIL, p. 387; DUE PROCESS CLAUSE, p. 405.

Significance   The Court's decision in *Schall v. Martin* (467 U.S. 253: 1984) was its first treatment of preventive detention. Prior to *Schall*, the Court had allowed preventive detention statutes to stand without review, silently agreeing with their view of pretrial release. While bail should have the effect of ensuring an appearance at subsequent proceedings, those persons released also constitute a continuing threat to society. The policy of preventive detention is aimed at confining defendants who present a serious threat of additional criminal conduct. Although such a policy may be effective as a crime prevention strategy, it also runs counter to the presumption of innocence. For many, it constitutes imposition of punishment before adjudication of guilt. Congress enacted the Bail Reform Act of 1984, which authorized federal judges to order pretrial detention of persons accused of serious crimes if appearance could not reasonably be assured, and if the person was deemed sufficiently dangerous to others. The preventive detention provisions of the act were upheld by the Supreme Court in *United States v. Salerno* (481 U.S. 739: 1987). The Court rejected the contention that the act was defective because it authorized punishment before trial. The history of the act "clearly indicates that the Congress chose detention as a potential solution to the pressing societal problem of crimes committed by persons on release." Preventing danger to the community is a legitimate regulatory goal. Further, the incidents of detention are not excessive in relation to that goal. The Court then said unequivocally that the Due Process Clause does not prohibit pretrial detention as a regulatory measure. The government's regulatory interest in public safety can, under certain circumstances, outweigh an individual's liberty interest. The Court said the act narrowly focuses on the acute problem of crime by arrestees in a situation where the governmental interest is overwhelming. In addition, the act contains extensive procedural safeguards that both limit the circumstances under which detention may be sought for the most serious crimes and further the accuracy of the likelihood-of-dangerousness determination. Finally, the Court said the act did not violate the Excessive Bail Clause. It simply permits bail to be set at an infinite amount for reasons not related to the risk of flight. Nothing in the clause, said the Court, limits the government's interest in setting bail solely for the prevention of flight. Where Congress has mandated detention on the basis of some other compelling interest—here, public safety—the Eighth Amendment does not require release on bail. In *United States v. Montalvo-Murillo* (109 L. Ed. 2d 720: 1990), the Court considered whether failure to provide a timely detention hearing under the Bail Reform Act of 1984 required release of a person who would otherwise be detained. The act provides that a detention hearing should occur "immediately" unless either side has "good cause" to obtain a continuance. Continuance on motion by the defendant is limited to 5 days, and a government-initiated continuance may not exceed 3 days. For several reasons, Montalvo's detention did not occur until 13 days after his arrest. Because the statutory time limit had elapsed, the trial Court ruled that release was required. The Supreme Court disagreed. While the time limits of the act must be followed "with care and precision," the act "is silent" on the issue of remedy for violation. Nothing in the act "can be read to require, or even suggest, that a timing error must result in release of a person who should otherwise be detained." Furthermore, said Justice Kennedy, the act has been upheld as an "appropriate regulatory device to assure the safety of persons in the community and to protect against the risk of flight." Automatic release "contravenes the object of the statute." The end of "exact compliance" with the letter of the act "cannot justify the means of exposing the public to an increased likelihood of violent crimes by persons on bail, an evil the statute aims to prevent." The safety of society, Kennedy continued, does not "become forfeit to the accident of noncompliance with statutory time limits where the Government is ready and able to come forward with the requisite showing to meet the burden of proof required by the statute." He concluded by saying there is "no reason to bestow upon the defendant a windfall and to visit upon the Government and the citizens a severe penalty by mandatory release of possibly dangerous defendants every time some deviation from [the act] occurs." No remedy was established by the act, and the Court said it could not and should not "invent a remedy to satisfy some perceived need to coerce the courts and the Government into complying with the statutory time limits."

Mandatory Death Penalty

Woodson v. North Carolina, **428 U.S. 280, 96 S. Ct. 2978, 49 L. Ed. 2d 944 (1976)** Examined the adequacy of the mandatory death sentence. Several states responded to *Furman v. Georgia* (408 U.S. 238: 1972) with revisions in their capital punishment statutes, making the death penalty mandatory for certain offenses. A five-justice Supreme Court majority held that the mandatory approach was "unduly harsh and unworkably rigid." The five said allowing some discretion in sentencing was more compatible with "evolving standards of social decency," a frequently mentioned criterion in cruel and unusual punishment cases. The fact that juries possessing discretion infrequently impose capital punishment suggests that capital punishment is viewed as "inappropriate" in a large number of cases. A second defect cited by the majority was that mandatory sentences did not remedy *Furman* flaws. The mandatory approach "papers over" the problem of jury discretion. There are no standards by which to determine "which murderer shall live and which shall die." Neither does the mandatory approach allow a review of arbitrary death sentences. The third flaw in the mandatory approach was said to be its undifferentiating character. The statutes did not allow for the consideration of factors particular to the crime and the defendant. They precluded consideration of "compassion or mitigating factors." The statutes treated all convicted persons "as members of a faceless, undifferentiated mass to be subjected to the blind infliction of the death penalty." The four dissenters, through Justice Rehnquist, were troubled by the majority's process focus. Rehnquist felt the Court should confine itself to a simple determination of whether a punishment is cruel. The Court had already concluded in *Gregg v. Georgia* (428 U.S. 153: 1976) that capital punishment was not a cruel and unusual punishment per se. To invalidate the statute on procedural grounds was therefore inappropriate. *See also* COKER *v.* GEORGIA (433 U.S. 584: 1977), p. 298; EIGHTH AMENDMENT, p. 289; *FURMAN v. GEORGIA* (408 U.S. 238: 1972), p. 294; *GREGG v. GEORGIA* (428 U.S. 153: 1976), p. 295.

Significance   *Woodson v. North Carolina* (428 U.S. 280: 1976) gave the Court an opportunity to choose between two alternative approaches to capital punishment. *Woodson* clearly reflected the Court's preference for retaining some discretion with sentencers in capital cases. To implement capital punishment reasonably, the sentencer must evaluate the specific details of a particular case against criteria defined by state legislatures. The mandatory approach precludes consideration of the factors that make a case unique. The Court has since underscored the inadequacy of the mandatory approach. In striking down a Louisiana statute that called for capital punishment for the deliberate killing of a fire fighter or police officer, the Court said, "It is incorrect to suppose that no mitigating circumstances can exist when the victim is a peace officer." The Court maintained this position in *Sumner v. Shuman* (483 U.S. 66: 1987). Under Nevada law, a prisoner serving a life term without the possibility of parole could receive an automatic death sentence upon conviction of first-degree murder. The Court ruled that even under this circumstance, there could be no exception to the ban on mandatory capital punishment. Neither can the scope of sentencer consideration be improperly restricted. In *Lockett v. Ohio* (438 U.S. 586: 1978), the Court held that limiting a sentencer to a narrow range of possible mitigating circumstances was unsatisfactory. In *Eddings v. Oklahoma* (455 U.S. 104: 1982), the Court remanded the case of a 16-year-old boy sentenced to death by a trial judge who determined that, as a matter of state law, he could not consider as a mitigating circumstance the youth's "unhappy upbringing and emotional disturbance." And in *Skipper v. South Carolina* (476 U.S. 1: 1986), the Court held that a state could not exclude introduction of certain testimony representing the defendant's record of good behavior while in jail from the jury making a determination of his sentence in a capital case. Using a rationale similar to that in *Lockett* and *Eddings,* the Court said the defendant's capacity to make a good adjustment to prison life reflected an aspect of his character relevant to the jury's sentencing decision. *Woodson* struck a middle ground between complete sentencer discretion and the complete mandating of the sentence of death.

The Court reviewed three additional cases during the 1989 term that involved mandatory actions for sentencing juries. Pennsylvania requires the death penalty if a jury unanimously finds aggravation in the absence of mitigation, or aggravation that outweighs mitigation. The Court upheld this method in *Blystone v. Pennsylvania* (108 L. Ed. 2d 255: 1990). The Court distinguished this approach from those in cases like *Woodson* by pointing out that the sentence was not automatically imposed upon conviction, but only after a consideration of aggravating and mitigating factors. An aggravating factor "serves the purpose of limiting the class of death-eligible defendants" while the mitigating factor satisfies the requirement that a capital sentencing jury be able to "consider and give full effect to all relevant mitigating evidence." North Carolina had a death penalty law similar to Pennsylvania's, but it required that jurors unanimously find a mitigating circumstance to exist. It also required a jury to find unanimously, beyond a reasonable doubt, that aggravating factors are sufficiently substantial to warrant the death penalty when considered along with any mitigating factors. The Court struck down these provisions in *McKoy v. North Carolina* (108 L. Ed. 2d 369: 1990) because the unanimity requirement precluded giving full effect to mitigating factors. Although the law allowed a jury to choose a penalty other than death in the absence of mitigation, it was required to make its choice based only on mitigating circumstances for which there is unanimity. As a result, "one juror can prevent the others from giving effect to evidence they feel calls for a lesser sentence." Further, even if all the jurors agree there are *some* mitigating factors, "they cannot give effect to evidence supporting any of those circumstances unless they agree unanimously on the *same* circumstances." California's death penalty statute also provided that a jury "shall impose" the death sentence in the presence of aggravating factors that outweigh any mitigating factors. In addition, the California law contained a list of specific factors a capital jury must consider before determining sentence. The last of these factors, factor (k), was a residual or "catch-all" factor that directed jurors to consider "any other circumstance which extenuates the gravity of the crime even though it is not a legal excuse for the crime." The Supreme Court upheld both provisions in *Boyde v. California* (108 L. Ed. 2d 316: 1990). The mandatory nature of the "shall impose" direction was seen as identical to the Pennsylvania law upheld in *Blystone*. It was the Court's judgment that the language did not foreclose "individual assessment" of Boyde's sentence or interfere with jury consideration of all mitigating evidence. Further, the Court rejected Boyde's contention that a jury "must have freedom to decline to impose the death penalty even if the jury decides that the aggravating circumstances 'outweigh' the mitigating circumstances." Rather, states are "free to structure and shape consideration of mitigating evidence 'in an effort to achieve a more rational and equitable administration of the death penalty.'" The Court also allowed the language in factor (k). Boyde had contended that the factor precluded the jury from considering non–crime-related factors such as defendant background and character. The Court concluded that there was no "reasonable likelihood" that the jurors interpreted the factor, either in isolation or together with the other factors, as limiting full consideration of all mitigating evidence.

Death Penalty

McCleskey v. Kemp, **481 U.S. 278, 107 S. Ct. 1756, 95 L. Ed. 2d 262 (1987)**   Rejected statistical data representing racial bias in the implementation of Georgia's death penalty law as insufficient to establish a constitutional violation. Following his death sentence and subsequent unsuccessful appeals in state courts, McCleskey sought habeas corpus relief in the federal courts. He claimed that Georgia's death penalty process was administered in a racially discriminatory manner. McCleskey supported his claim by submitting statistical data developed by Professor David C. Baldus and others (the Baldus Study) based on more than 2,000 Georgia murder cases tried in the 1970s. The study revealed that blacks whose victims were white had the greatest possibility of receiving the death sentence. In a 5–4 decision, the Court ruled that the Baldus Study did not sufficiently demonstrate unconstitutional discrimination. Justice Powell wrote the opinion of the Court. In order for McCleskey to prevail, he said, it was necessary to demonstrate that the decision makers in this specific case had acted with discriminatory purpose. The Baldus Study data offered in support of McCleskey's claim were insufficient to support such an inference. The statistics submitted must be viewed in the context of McCleskey's challenge, one that aimed at the heart of the state's criminal justice system. Implementation of murder laws necessarily requires discretionary judgments. Because discretion is essential to the criminal justice process, the Court demands exceptionally clear proof before inferring that discretion has been abused. Similarly, the Court rejected McCleskey's claim that the Baldus Study showed that Georgia had violated the Equal Protection Clause by adopting and retaining a death penalty law that allegedly discriminated in its operation. Here McCleskey was required to show that Georgia's legislature had enacted or maintained the law because of an anticipated racially discriminatory effect. The Baldus Study did not prove such intent. The Court also rejected McCleskey's Eighth Amendment arguments. The statistics did not show that Georgia's death penalty law was arbitrary or capricious in application, because they did not prove that race governs capital punishment decisions generally or was a factor in McCleskey's case. The likelihood of prejudice allegedly shown did not produce an unacceptable risk of racial prejudice. The inherent lack of predictability of jury decisions does not justify their condemnation.

All the Baldus Study data show is "a discrepancy that appears to correlate with race, but this discrepancy does not constitute a major systemic defect." Any technique for determining guilt or sentence has its weaknesses and the potential for misuse. Despite such imperfections, the Constitution's requirements are satisfied when these techniques have been surrounded with safeguards to make them as fair as possible. The Constitution does not require that Georgia or any other state "eliminate any demonstrable disparity that correlates with a potentially irrelevant factor in order to operate a criminal justice system that includes capital punishment." A four-justice minority of Brennan, Marshall, Blackmun, and Stevens found the statistical evidence compelling. Brennan pointed out that because of the finality of the death sentence, the Court has required a uniquely high degree of rationality in the processes of imposing it. A process in which race likely plays a disproportionate role does not meet this standard. To the dissenters, the Baldus Study raised the probability that race influenced McCleskey's sentence, and such a perversion of justice is "intolerable by any imaginable standard."

Significance   *McCleskey v. Kemp* (481 U.S. 278: 1987) was one of the most important capital punishment decisions since the Court conditionally upheld the death penalty in *Gregg v. Georgia* (428 U.S. 153: 1976). In the years following *Gregg,* the Court focused on relatively narrow procedural questions and basically refined the general approach elucidated in *Gregg.* The Court's rejection of the race discrimination issues possibly represents the last broad-based challenge to the death penalty the Rehnquist Court will entertain. It seems clear from *McCleskey* that the Court feels the capital punishment procedures now in place are generally free of constitutional defect. It is also apparent that future changes in policies governing death sentences will emanate from state legislatures and state courts rather than the Supreme Court. The *McCleskey* decision also had the short-term effect of avoiding the turmoil that would have occurred if McCleskey had won. Such a ruling would have halted the capital punishment process all across the country until the case of every death-row prisoner had been reviewed to determine the role of racial discrimination in his or her sentence.

Pulley v. Harris, 465 U.S. 37, 104 S. Ct. 871, 79 L. Ed. 2d 29 (1984)   Held that a state need not conduct a comparative proportionality review in capital cases. While such comparative reviews are performed in a number of states, the Court ruled in *Pulley v. Harris* that the Eighth Amendment did not mandate such reviews. Harris was convicted of a capital crime and sentenced to death. He appealed to the California Supreme Court on the grounds that appellate review did not require a comparison of his sentence with sentences imposed in similar capital cases. Failing with the state courts, Harris sought habeas corpus review in the federal courts. The U.S. Court of Appeals eventually ruled that the proportionality relief Harris sought was constitutionally required. In a 7–2 decision, the Supreme Court disagreed. The opinion of the Court was written by Justice White. He stated that traditionally the concept of proportionality had been used in conjunction with "an abstract evaluation of the appropriateness of a sentence for a particular crime." This involved comparing the gravity of the offense and the severity of the penalty to determine if the punishment was disproportionate or excessive. In this case, however, the defendant sought review of a different sort. Harris asked the Court to consider whether his sentence was unacceptable because it was disproportionate to the punishment imposed on others convicted of the same crime. Harris argued that when the states redrafted their capital punishment laws after *Furman v. Georgia* (408 U.S. 238: 1972), most states required such a comparative review. The Court upheld some of the state capital punishment revisions, many of which did indeed require proportionality review. Finding proportionality review constitutional does not mean that it is indispensable, however. To endorse these rewritten statutes as a whole is not to hold that anything different is unacceptable. *Gregg v. Georgia* (428 U.S. 153: 1976) is an example of the Court upholding a revised death penalty statute that included proportionality review. While such review as found in *Gregg* was considered an "additional safeguard against arbitrary or capricious sentencing," the Court did not see it as so crucial that without the review the same statute would not have passed constitutional muster. The Court concluded that there was no basis for saying that a proportionality review is required in every case. The Court also said that even if a death penalty sentencing process was "so lacking in other checks on arbitrariness" that it could not pass scrutiny without a comparative proportionality review, the California statute was not of that sort. Rather, it provided a sufficiently deliberative and structured consideration of the sentencing process as to be beyond challenge. Justices Brennan and Marshall dissented. They said that while it is no panacea, proportionality review "often serves to identify the most extreme examples of disproportionality among similarly situated defendants." In their opinion, such review serves to eliminate a portion of the "irrationality that currently infects imposition of the death penalty." *See also* CRUEL AND UNUSUAL PUNISHMENT, p. 401; *FURMAN v. GEORGIA* (408 U.S. 238: 1972), p. 294; *GREGG v. GEORGIA* (428 U.S. 153: 1976), p. 295.

Significance　　The holding in *Pulley v. Harris* (465 U.S. 37: 1984) was that state courts are not required to perform a comparative proportionality review of death sentences. Following *Furman v. Georgia* (408 U.S. 238: 1972), 36 states undertook extensive revision of their capital punishment statutes. The Court subjected these revisions to careful scrutiny during the next decade and found procedural defects in some of them. Since 1983, however, the Court has seemed to be satisfied that the principal process questions have been adequately addressed. In *Pulley,* the Court acknowledged that comparative proportionality reviews may be a useful component of a capital punishment policy, but it refused to mandate the step. Similar deference to state sentencing procedures was shown in *Spaziano v. Florida* (468 U.S. 447: 1984), in which the Court upheld a death sentence imposed by a judge following a jury's recommendation of a life sentence. The Court said that a defendant is not entitled to jury determination of sentence. Neither is a jury's recommendation so final as to preclude override by the trial judge. The Court ruled in *Booth v. Maryland* (482 U.S. 496: 1987) that use of victim impact statements (VIS) at the sentencing stage of a capital murder trial violated the Eighth Amendment. The VIS, required by state law, were based on interviews with the victim's family. They contained descriptions of the impact of the crime on the family, characterizations of the victim, and family opinions of the crime and the defendant. The Court said the information contained in the VIS may be "wholly unrelated to the blameworthiness" of the defendant. Rather, the VIS may cause the sentencing decision to turn on such factors as the degree to which the victim's family is willing and able to articulate its grief, or the relative worth of the victim's character. Use of family members' emotionally charged opinions could "serve no other purpose than to inflame the jury and divert it from deciding the case on the relevant evidence concerning the crime and the defendant." Similarly, the Court held in *South Carolina v. Gathers* (104 L. Ed. 2d 876: 1989) that evidence about the character of the victim cannot be used in the sentencing phase of a capital case when that evidence does not directly bear on the crime itself. Gathers was convicted of murder. At the end of his argument to the jury during the sentencing stage of Gathers's murder trial, the prosecutor read from some of the religious materials the victim was carrying at the time of the murder. The prosecutor characterized the victim based on inferences drawn from the fact that he was carrying the religious materials and other items such as a voter registration card. The Court said that capital cases have "consistently recognized" that the death penalty be "tailored" to a defendant's "personal responsibility and moral guilt." Under the circumstances of this case, the Court said that the content of the various materials the victim

happened to be carrying when he was attacked was "purely fortu-
itous," and could not "provide any information relevant to the defendant's moral culpability."

Aubrey Adams was convicted of capital murder and sentenced to
death. During the selection of the jury, the judge told prospective
jurors that their role was only advisory on sentence, and that he would
make the ultimate sentence decision. As the selection process continued, remarks to the effect that he was solely responsible for the sentence decision were repeated many times by the judge. Adams
unsuccessfully appealed, but did not target the remarks about the
jury's sentencing role. Later, the Supreme Court ruled in *Caldwell v.
Mississippi* (472 U.S. 320: 1985) that the jury could not be led to
underestimate its serious responsibility in capital cases. Based on
Caldwell, Adams again sought review of his case. He pressed the limited character of judicial override of jury recommendations; that
override could take place only if facts were "so clear and convincing
that virtually no reasonable person could differ." In *Dugger v. Adams*
(103 L. Ed. 2d 435: 1989), the Supreme Court ruled that Adams was
barred from raising the matter on habeas corpus review. The Court
said that *Caldwell* did not provide an avenue for review in the absence
of asserting claims on direct review or in the absence of an excuse for
failing to do so. Further, the Court ruled that *Caldwell* required a
showing that the remarks or instructions were "objectionable under
state law," an issue the Florida courts had not examined. Thus even
though the judge's statements may have been improper, Adams's
failure to follow procedures of state law foreclosed federal habeas
corpus review. The Court ruled in *Whitmore v. Arkansas* (109 L. Ed. 2d
135: 1990) that third parties do not have standing to challenge the
death sentence of others. Whitmore, himself a death-row inmate,
sought to challenge the sentence imposed on convicted mass murderer Ronald Eugene Simmons. Arkansas law did not make review of
death sentences automatic, and Simmons had voluntarily elected to
forgo any appeal of his sentence. Whitmore argued that the Eighth
Amendment requires appellate review. He also contended that because Simmons's sentence was not reviewed by the Arkansas Supreme
Court, the basis for comparison that court uses would be affected,
thereby making his crime more deserving of the death penalty. In a
7–2 decision, the Court ruled Whitmore's injury was "too speculative"
to warrant review. It is "nothing more than conjecture that the addition of Simmons's crimes to a comparative review 'data base' would
lead the Arkansas Supreme Court to set aside the death sentence for
Whitmore." The majority also refused to establish a death penalty
exception to the standing doctrine. The Court said that the "case or
controversy" requirement of Article III is "not merely a 'rule of

practice,' but rather is imposed directly by the Constitution." It is "not for this Court to employ untethered notions of what might be good public policy to expand our jurisdiction." The impact of *Whitmore* will be minimal in that almost every state requires the kind of comparative appellate review Whitmore sought in this case.

Penry v. Lynaugh, **109 S. Ct. 2934, 106 L. Ed. 2d 256 (1989)**   Ruled that capital punishment of convicted murderers who are mentally retarded is not necessarily cruel and unusual punishment. At the same time, the Court reversed Penry's sentence in this case because the jury had not been properly instructed with respect to how it might give effect to his retardation and other mitigating factors. Under Texas law, a defendant convicted of capital murder is sentenced to death if a jury unanimously answers in the affirmative regarding three "special issues": (1) that the murder was committed deliberately and with the expectation that death would occur, (2) that the defendant would continue to pose a threat to society in the future, and (3) that the murder was an "unreasonable" response to victim provocation. Penry submitted various evidence in mitigation, including his IQ (between 50 and 63), his learning age (estimated as that of a 6- to 7-year-old child), his social maturity (estimated as that of a 9-year-old), and evidence that he had been severely abused as a child. Penry asked for jury instructions that defined the key terms in the three special issues in relation to the mitigating evidence he introduced. The trial court refused to provide those instructions, and the jury found in the affirmative on each of the special issues. Penry was then sentenced to death. Justice O'Connor, joined by Justices Brennan, Marshall, Stevens, and Blackmun, decided that Penry's death sentence must be vacated. An established principle for capital cases is that the punishment must relate directly to the defendant's "personal culpability," said O'Connor. Failure to elaborate on or further define the key terms in the special issues to give effect to the defendant's mitigating evidence "compels the conclusion" that the jury was not fully enabled to give a "reasoned moral response" to the evidence submitted at the sentencing stage of the trial. The jury was required to find that the murder had been committed "deliberately." Penry requested special instructions that defined the term *deliberately* in a manner that would direct jurors to consider Penry's mitigating evidence as pertaining to moral culpability. Without the special instructions, a juror who was persuaded by the mitigating evidence that the death penalty should not be imposed would be unable to give effect to that judgment if the juror also believed the crime to have been committed deliberately. Penry's retardation and history of childhood abuse also furnished a "two-edged sword" with respect to the special issue of future dangerousness. On the one hand, those factors may diminish his "blameworthiness"; on the other, Penry's "inability to learn from his mistakes" because of his retardation and his history of abuse also indicate there is a "probability that he will be dangerous in the future." The same kind of defect existed on the final special issue of victim provocation. The Court did not find sufficient the broad instruction that the jury could simply decline to impose the death penalty on Penry. Such an instruction is too unfocused and gives the sentencing jury impermissibly "unbridled discretion." Chief Justice Rehnquist and Justices White, Scalia, and Kennedy joined O'Connor to hold that the Eighth Amendment does not categorically preclude execution of mentally retarded murderers. The Court agreed that "profoundly retarded" people lack the "capacity to appreciate the wrongfulness" of their conduct and cannot be sentenced to death. The profoundly retarded person is "unlikely" to face the prospect of the death penalty, however, because he or she is rarely found competent to stand trial or can advance an "insanity defense" based on "mental defect." Persons such as Penry do not fit that category. The jury found him competent to be tried and rejected his insanity defense, "reflecting the conclusion that he knew his conduct was wrong" and that he was "capable of conforming it to the requirements of law." The Court was unconvinced that there existed any "national consensus" against executing mentally retarded capital murderers. Indeed, only one state had enacted a prohibition of the practice. The Court agreed that retardation may diminish culpability and warrants consideration as a mitigating factor. Nonetheless, the Court concluded that not all retarded persons, by virtue of that "retardation alone," and separate from any individual consideration of personal responsibility, "inevitably lack the cognitive, volitional, and moral capacity to act with the degree of culpability associated with the death penalty." In other words, the Court found "insufficient basis" for a "categorical" Cruel and Unusual Punishment Clause ban on the death penalty for the retarded murderer. *See also* CRUEL AND UNUSUAL PUNISHMENT, p. 401.

Significance   *Penry v. Lynaugh* (106 L. Ed. 2d 256: 1989) reflects the Rehnquist Court's reluctance to proscribe state capital punishment laws further with categorical restrictions. Mental retardation as such does not preclude imposition of the death sentence, but retardation is a mitigating factor that must be given full effect in the sentencing decision. Sentencers are required to make some very fine distinctions. The key process for doing so is the weighing of aggravating and mitigating factors. So long as these factors are given full consideration, the Rehnquist Court seems satisfied that these distinctions can be made by juries in capital cases. Two cases further illustrate. In 1982, the Court ruled in *Enmund v. Florida* (458 U.S. 782) that a defendant could not be sentenced to death unless it could be shown that he or she killed, attempted to kill, or intended to kill. The ruling suggested that aiders and abetters could not be subjected to the death penalty. In *Tison v. Arizona* (481 U.S. 137: 1987), the Court rejected the *Enmund* framework, saying it dealt with two distinct subsets of felony murder: one in which a person is a minor actor and neither intended to kill nor was found to have any culpable mental state, and the other where the felony murderer actually killed, attempted to kill, or intended to kill. The *Tison* case was in neither of these categories. The Tison brothers aided in their father's prison escape and were with him when he killed four persons taken captive. Though the brothers claimed surprise at the killings, neither attempted to aid the victims and both continued their participation in the escape. They were subsequently captured, tried, convicted, and sentenced to death. The issue before the Court in *Tison* was whether the death penalty is precluded for a case between the polar extremes described in *Enmund,* a case in which a defendant's participation is major and the defendant's mental state is one of reckless indifference to the value of human life. The Court said capital punishment was not inappropriate in this intermediate category. *Enmund's* narrow focus on intent to kill was a "highly unsatisfactory means of definitively distinguishing the most culpable and dangerous murderers." Some nonintentional murderers may be among the most dangerous and inhumane of all, such as the person who tortures another without caring whether the victim lives or dies, or the robber who shoots someone in the course of a robbery, utterly indifferent to the fact that killing may be an unintended consequence of the desire to rob. The Court ruled accordingly that "reckless disregard for human life implicit in engaging in criminal activities known to carry a grave risk of death represents a highly culpable mental state." This mental state may be taken into account in making a capital sentencing judgment when that conduct causes its natural, though not inevitable, lethal result.

In *Mills v. Maryland* (486 U.S. 367: 1988), the Court considered whether the Maryland capital punishment law deprived a defendant of full consideration of mitigating factors. Under the law, the death sentence was required if jurors found an aggravating circumstance in the absence of a mitigating circumstance. Mills contended that the law as applied required jurors to agree unanimously on a particular mitigating circumstance. A death sentence using this approach, argued Mills, was unconstitutional because it could require capital punishment where unanimity did not exist on a particular mitigating factor even though all jurors believed some mitigating circumstance(s) existed. The Court agreed and vacated Mills's death sentence on the ground the unanimity issue interfered with the full consideration of possible mitigation. The Court saw a "substantial probability that reasonable jurors" may have thought they were "precluded from considering" mitigating evidence unless all the jury members agreed on the existence of a particular factor. Given the finality of the death sentence, the Court said that review of such cases requires "greater certainty that the jury's conclusions rested on proper grounds" than the finding of guilt itself. The Court acknowledged that there was no "extrinsic evidence" of what the jury thought in this case, but said the verdict form and jury instructions created "at least a substantial risk that the jury was misinformed."

Barclay v. Florida, 463 U.S. 939, 103 S. Ct. 3418, 77 L. Ed. 2d 1134 (1983)   Addressed the issue of aggravating factors that must be present for the death penalty to be imposed. The clear command in *Gregg v. Georgia* (428 U.S. 153: 1976) was that sentencers must be guided when considering the death penalty. Contemporary capital punishment statutes therefore contain lists of both aggravating and mitigating circumstances that must be evaluated when making the sentence judgment. Barclay was convicted of first-degree murder, a crime apparently racially inspired. The trial judge set aside the jury recommendation of life imprisonment and ordered the death penalty. The judge made his own determination that several statutory aggravating circumstances were present. He also defined the defendant's extensive criminal record as an aggravating factor. The judge discussed what he believed to be the racial motive for the crime and "compared it with his own experience in the Army in World War II, when he saw Nazi concentration camps and their victims." Barclay contended his death sentence was invalid because the judge considered his criminal record as an aggravating circumstance in the absence of statutory authorization and because the judge improperly mentioned "racial hatred" and "his own experiences" in the sentencing opinion. The Supreme Court agreed with Barclay regarding the judge's use of the criminal record, but affirmed the death sentence nonetheless in a 6–3 decision. Through Justice Rehnquist, the Court was emphatic that sentencers are not permitted to redefine sentencing guidelines or add factors to the statutory list of aggravating circumstances. While the Eighth Amendment does not preclude the use of other evidence, Florida law prohibited consideration of nonstatutory factors in this case. The more crucial question was whether the inappropriate consideration of Barclay's prior criminal record contaminated the findings of statutory aggravating circumstances and disturbed the overall balance of aggravating and mitigating factors. The Court ruled that the other findings were independent of and undisturbed by the reference to Barclay's criminal record. The Court allowed the trial judge to take account of the racial motive of the crime. Barclay's professed desire to "start a race war" was relevant to several statutory aggravating factors, and the judge's discussion of it was "neither irrational nor arbitrary." Comparison to Nazi concentration camps was seen as an appropriate way of weighing the "heinous, atrocious and cruel" aggravating circumstance. The purpose of statutory standards is to remove arbitrariness, but they do not make sentencing determinations "mechanical and rigid." Justice Rehnquist said it is "fitting for the moral, factual, and legal judgment to play a meaningful role in sentencing." The statutory standards themselves must be reasonable, and they must provide genuine guidance for identifying those offenders for whom capital punishment is appropriate. *See also GREGG v. GEORGIA* (428 U.S. 158: 1976), p. 295; EIGHTH AMENDMENT, p. 289; *WOODSON v. NORTH CAROLINA* (428 U.S. 280: 1976), p. 297.

Significance   *Barclay v. Florida* (463 U.S. 939: 1983) gave notice to sentencers that they cannot depart from statutory guidelines in determining aggravating circumstances for imposing the death penalty. This is not to say that the Supreme Court will ignore statutory language it deems vague and ambiguous. It struck down such language in *Godfrey v. Georgia* (446 U.S. 420: 1980). In *Zant v. Stephens* (462 U.S. 862: 1983) the Court underscored the jury's independence in determining aggravating circumstances where statutes are clear. In *Zant* a jury had found three statutory aggravating factors and imposed the death penalty. One of the factors was later found defective for reason of vagueness, but the Court held the remaining two factors properly fulfilled the requirements for such a penalty. In *California v. Ramos* (463 U.S. 992: 1983) the Court permitted an instruction that told the jury at the penalty stage of the trial that sentence of life imprisonment without the possibility of parole could be commuted to a sentence that included potential parole. This information was viewed by the Court as providing data that focused the jury's attention on "probable future dangerousness," a service that helped the jury "individualize" its deliberation. The Court examined the issue of sympathy as a factor in the penalty phase of a capital murder trial in the case of *California v. Brown* (479 U.S. 538: 1987). Just prior to the jury's deliberation of sentence, its members were instructed by the court to consider the aggravating and mitigating factors of the crime. The judge said the jury "should not be swayed by mere sentiment, conjecture, sympathy, passion, prejudice, public opinion, or public feeling." The Supreme

Court ruled that this instruction did not violate the Eighth Amendment. The Court felt it unlikely that jurors would focus on the term *sympathy* to the exclusion of the other terms accompanying it. The instruction referred to "mere" sympathy, and even a juror focusing on the word *sympathy* would likely interpret the phrase as an admonition to ignore emotional responses not derived from the evidence offered during the penalty proceeding. An instruction, said Chief Justice Rehnquist, that prohibits jurors from basing their judgments on factors not present or irrelevant to issues of the trial cannot violate the Constitution.

Capital punishment statutes require the proof of at least one aggravating circumstance before the death penalty can be imposed. A number of states consider an aggravating circumstance to be a murder that is "especially heinous, atrocious, or cruel." The issue in *Maynard v. Cartwright* (486 U.S. 356: 1988) was whether such an aggravating factor is unconstitutionally vague. The Supreme Court unanimously held that it was. The notion that factual circumstances "in themselves" may characterize a murder as "especially heinous, atrocious, or cruel" is an approach that gives the sentencer impermissible discretion in the death penalty decision. Subsequently, the Court held in *Clemons v. Mississippi* (108 L. Ed. 2d 725: 1990) that a state supreme court could eliminate a defective "especially heinous" aggravating factor and then reweigh the remaining factors. Prior conviction for a violent crime, including prior conviction in another state, is often used as such an aggravating circumstance. *Johnson v. Mississippi* (486 U.S. 578: 1988) reviewed a death sentence where an aggravating out-of-state conviction was subsequently reversed. Johnson was convicted of murder in Mississippi and sentenced to death. The sentencing jury found three aggravating circumstances to exist, one of which was a prior felony conviction. This factor was supported exclusively by a New York conviction for second-degree assault with intent to commit rape. After his death sentence was affirmed by the Mississippi Supreme Court, Johnson's New York conviction was vacated by the New York Court of Appeals. The Mississippi Supreme Court refused to set aside Johnson's death sentence, however, arguing, at least in part, that Mississippi's capital sentencing process would be rendered "capricious and standardless" if a postsentence decision from another state could invalidate a Mississippi death sentence. The U.S. Supreme Court unanimously held that reexamination of Johnson's sentence was required. The reversal of Johnson's New York conviction "deprives the prosecutor's sole piece of evidence as to the aggravating circumstance of any relevance to the sentencing decision." Extending such relief "reduces the risk that a capital sentence will be imposed arbitrarily." *Lowenfield v. Phelps* (484 U.S. 231: 1988) raised an additional procedural issue. The question was whether a death sentence based on but one aggravating circumstance was proper when that circumstance of aggravation was identical to an element of the crime for which the defendant was convicted. Lowenfeld had been convicted of three counts of first-degree murder, an element of which was his intent to "kill or inflict great bodily harm upon more than one person." At the sentencing phase of the trial, the only aggravating circumstance found by the jury was that he "knowingly created a risk of death or great bodily harm to more than one person." Lowenfeld asserted that the overlap allowed the jury to "merely . . . repeat one of its findings in the guilt phase," and thus not to "narrow further" in the sentencing stage the "class of death-eligible murderers." The Court rejected this contention. A constitutional scheme must "genuinely narrow" the class of persons eligible for the death penalty and must "reasonably justify" use of the comparatively more severe punishment. The narrowing function may be provided in two ways: by narrow legislative definition or, where broadly defined offenses are narrowed by jurors, by identifying aggravating circumstances. Use of aggravating circumstances is not an "end in itself," but a means of channeling jury discretion. This function can be performed by a jury finding at "either the sentencing phase of the trial or the guilt phase." In this case, the state law narrowed the definition of capital offenses, and the jury performed the narrowing function when it convicted the defendant at the guilt phase. That the jury was required to find an aggravating circumstance in addition is "no part" of the required "narrowing process," and that the aggravating circumstance duplicated one of the elements of the crime does not make the sentence "constitutionally infirm." Finally, the Court clarified several other capital punishment issues in two cases from Arizona. In *Walton v. Arizona* (111 L. Ed. 2d 511: 1990), the Court reiterated that the Sixth Amendment does not require that a jury determine the presence or absence of aggravating or mitigating circumstances. These circumstances serve as "standards to guide" the sentencing decision. A judge's finding that aggravating circumstances exist "does not itself convict" a defendant, and the failure to find a condition of aggravation does not result in acquittal. The Court also rejected the argument that placing the burden of proving mitigating circumstances on the defendant was unconstitutional. As long as a state's method of "allocating the burdens of proof" does not lessen the state's obligation to prove guilt or the existence of aggravating circumstances, a defendant's rights are not violated by "placing on him the burden of proving mitigating circumstances sufficiently substantial to call for leniency." Finally, Walton contended that Arizona's "especially heinous, cruel, or depraved" aggravating circumstance was unconstitutionally vague. The Court had previously invalidated this factor, but only in cases where jury sentencing or unclear jury instructions were involved. The Court said the "logic of those cases has no place in the context of sentencing by a trial judge." Here, the Arizona Supreme Court had sufficiently narrowed the definition of the "especially heinous" factor, and the Court "presume[d]" that Arizona trial judges were "applying the narrower definition." The "especially heinous" aggravating factor was also an issue in *Lewis v. Jeffers* (111 L. Ed. 2d 606: 1990), but was resolved on the same basis as *Walton*. In addition, the Court said that habeas corpus review does not allow a federal court to examine whether a state court misapplied a satisfactorily narrowed aggravating circumstance. Federal habeas corpus review "does not lie for errors of state law." Rather, review is limited to determining whether a state court finding was "so arbitrary or capricious as to constitute an independent due process or Eighth Amendment violation."

Death Penalty: Juveniles

Thompson v. Oklahoma, **487 U.S. 815, 109 S. Ct. 2687, 101 L. Ed. 2d 702 (1988)**   Ruled that a person may not be executed for a crime committed before he or she reaches 16 years of age. The Court split 5–3 in the *Thompson* case (Justice Kennedy not participating), although only four justices joined the plurality opinion. Justice O'Connor supplied the decisive fifth vote, but preferred to offer her own rationale for the decision. Chief Justice Rehnquist and Justices Scalia and White dissented. The Court said that the "contours" of the cruel and unusual punishment protection are determined by judges who are to be guided by the "evolving standards of decency that mark the progress of a maturing society." Measures of these "evolving standards" are present in recent legislative determinations on the issue as well as jury decisions in particular cases. The Court began by reviewing numerous examples in which the law recognizes differences that "must be accommodated in determining the rights and duties of children as compared with those of adults." The Court found "near unanimity" in all states and the District of Columbia "in treating a person under 16 as a minor for several important purposes." "Most relevant" of these policies was the designation by every state for juvenile court jurisdiction at "no less than 16." The Court then examined the statutes authorizing capital punishment and found that of the 18 states that established a minimum age, all required the defendant to have "attained at least the age of 16 at the time of the capital offense." The Court concluded from this that it was offensive to "civilized standards of decency" to execute a juvenile. It was pointed out that this conclusion was also held by "respected professional organizations" such as the American Bar Association and other nations that "share our Anglo-American heritage." The Court then turned to the second "societal factor" to be used in assessing the "acceptability of capital punishment to the American sensibility." This factor is jury behavior. Department of Justice data on homicide for the years 1982–86 revealed that about 1,400 persons were sentenced to death from the group of more than 82,000 arrested for homicide. Only 5 of that number (including Thompson) were under 16 at the time of the offense. This led the Court to the "unambiguous conclusion" that the death penalty for a 15-year-old is now "generally abhorrent to the conscience of the community." The statistics also suggested, said the Court, that the 5 young offenders received sentences that were "cruel and unusual in the same way that being struck by lightning is cruel and unusual." In addition to the judgments of legislatures and juries, the Court said that it needed to consider the juvenile's comparative culpability and then determine whether the death sentence for a juvenile "measurably contributes to the social purposes" of retribution and deterrence served by the penalty. It was so clear to the Court that less culpability attaches to a crime committed by a juvenile that "extended explanation" was not deemed necessary. "Inexperience, less education, and less intelligence make the teenager less able to evaluate the consequences of his or her conduct" and at the same time more likely to be "motivated by mere emotion or peer pressure" than an adult. The reasons juveniles are not "trusted with the privileges and responsibilities of an adult also explain why their irresponsible conduct is not as morally reprehensible as that of an adult." Given the lesser culpability, retribution serves no purpose in the context of juveniles and is "simply inapplicable" to the execution of a juvenile. Similarly, deterrence is an "unacceptable" rationale in the case of a juvenile. Juveniles constitute such a small proportion of those receiving the death penalty that excluding them from the class eligible for that penalty will not "diminish the deterrent value of capital punishment." Since the Court was unpersuaded that use of the death penalty with juveniles made any "measurable contribution to the goals that capital punishment is intended to achieve," it is, therefore, "nothing more than the purposeless and needless imposition of pain and suffering." *See also* CRUEL AND UNUSUAL PUNISHMENT, p. 401.

Significance   The Court returned to the issue of capital punishment for juveniles in the companion cases of *Stanford v. Kentucky* and *Wilkins v. Missouri* (106 L. Ed. 2d 306: 1989). *Thompson v. Oklahoma* (487 U.S. 815: 1988) held that the Eighth Amendment does not permit execution of a person who committed a capital crime before reaching the age of 16. Stanford and Wilkins were both convicted of murder and both were over the age of 16 at the time of the crimes; Stanford was 17 years and 4 months of age, and Wilkins was 16 years and 6 months old. The Court ruled in these cases, by 5—4 vote, that imposition of the death penalty on Stanford and Wilkins did not constitute cruel and unusual punishment. Justice Scalia wrote for the majority. His opinion closely paralleled the dissenters' reasoning in *Thompson*. Whether the execution of juveniles violates the Cruel and Unusual Punishment Clause requires determination of whether such action is contrary to "evolving standards of decency that mark the progress of a maturing society." In assessing these "evolving standards," the Court must look to "conceptions of modern American society" as reflected by "objective evidence," as opposed to "its own subjective conceptions." The "most reliable" reflection of "national consensus" is the actions of state legislatures and the Congress. The Court concluded that a "settled" consensus does not exist to prohibit execution of 16-year-olds, as only 15 of the states that permit capital punishment so limit its use. The number of states restricting the death penalty decreases to 12 when the age is elevated to 17 years. This finding, said Scalia, does not "establish the degree of national agreement" necessary to "label" a punishment cruel and unusual. Neither does the jury conduct in cases involving 16- or 17-year-old defendants reveal a "categorical aversion" to the penalty. Scalia then turned to two other arguments advanced in the challenge to the juvenile death penalty. He rejected the relevance of 18 as the minimum legal age for such activities as "drinking alcoholic beverages and voting" to the capital punishment question. Such laws, he said, "operate in gross," and do not require individualized tests for application. The death sentence, by contrast, is highly selective, and "individualized consideration is a constitutional requirement." Scalia then addressed measures other than legislative actions and jury behavior purporting to be indicia of national consensus. Scalia said that public opinion data and the positions of interest groups and professional associations are "too uncertain a foundation for constitutional law." He characterized "socioscientific or ethicoscientific" evidence or arguments—such as arguments that the death sentence does not deter 16- or 17-year-olds because they have a "less highly developed fear of death"—as similarly inadequate. Similarly, it is argued that the death penalty fails to achieve retribution when a juvenile is involved because, being less "mature and responsible," juveniles are "less morally blameworthy." Scalia said the "audience for such arguments is not this Court but the citizenry." Though part of the five-justice majority, O'Connor did not fully subscribe to this portion of Scalia's opinion.

Sentencing Guidelines

Mistretta v. United States, **488 U.S. 361, 108 S. Ct. 1860, 102 L. Ed. 2d 714 (1989)** Considered the constitutionality of sentencing guidelines. Troubled by the "serious disparities" produced under the federal indeterminate criminal sentencing system, Congress passed the Sentencing Reform Act of 1984. Among other things, the act created the U.S. Sentencing Commission as an independent entity within the judicial branch. The commission was empowered to promulgate binding Sentencing Guidelines creating a range of determinate sentences for all federal crimes. Mistretta pled guilty to conspiracy to distribute cocaine and was sentenced under the guidelines. Mistretta claimed that Congress had delegated excessive authority to the Sentencing Commission, and that the commission was established in violation of the separation of powers principle. With only Justice Scalia dissenting, the Supreme Court upheld the guidelines. The Court first addressed Mistretta's claim that the commission possessed "excessive legislative discretion," producing a violation of the nondelegation doctrine. The Court said that the determination of whether delegation is excessive is "driven by a practical understanding" that, given the complexity of problems facing Congress, it "cannot do its job absent an ability to delegate power under broad general directions." The Court ruled that delegation is not forbidden so long as Congress sets forth an "intelligible principle" by which the body given power to act must conform. In establishing the Sentencing Commission, Congress offered three broad goals it wanted criminal sentencing to achieve. In addition, Congress mandated the technique of a guideline system to be used to regulate sentencing. Further, Congress directed the commission to consider a number of specific factors as it developed categories of both offenses and offender characteristics. Congress also forbade consideration of factors such as race, sex, national origin, creed, and socioeconomic status, or factors that might serve as their proxy. In short, the Court concluded that the act set forth "more than merely an 'intelligible principle.'" While the commission "enjoys significant discretion in formulating guidelines," the Court had "no doubt" the criteria supplied by Congress were "wholly adequate for carrying out the general policy and purpose of the Act." The Court then turned to the separation of powers claims. The Court embraced Madison's "flexible understanding" of separation of powers. There is a "degree of overlapping responsibility" among the three branches, and the greatest security against accumulation of excessive authority in a single branch "lies not in a hermetic division" among the branches, but in a "carefully crafted system of checked and balanced power within each branch." The separation of powers issues in this case divided into three parts. The first was the location of the Sentencing Commission within the Judicial Branch. Placement of the commission, an independent body that does not exercise judicial power as such, in the Judicial Branch made it a "peculiar institution," but separation of powers is not violated, said the Court, by "mere anomaly." Congress's decision to create an independent rule-making body under the Judicial Branch is not unconstitutional unless Congress vested in the commission "powers that are more appropriately performed by other branches or that undermine the integrity of the Judiciary." While judicial rule making falls into a kind of "twilight area," it has not been regarded historically as a function that cannot be performed by an entity within the Judicial Branch. Furthermore, location of the commission within the Judicial Branch "simply acknowledges the role that the Judiciary has always played, and continues to play, in sentencing." The second separation of powers question stemmed from the composition of the Sentencing Commission. In particular, it was argued that the requirement that three commission members be federal judges undermined the integrity of the Judicial Branch by diminishing its independence and impartiality (or appearance of impartiality). The Court disagreed. Inclusion on the commission of three federal judges who serve voluntarily "does not of itself" threaten the integrity of the judiciary. Neither does participation by judges on the commission undermine public confidence in judicial impartiality. Judicial participation in the promulgation of guidelines "does not affect their or other judges' ability impartially to adjudicate sentencing issues." In addition, the commission is "devoted exclusively" to producing rules to "rationalize a process" that is "performed exclusively" by the Judicial Branch. This is an "essentially neutral endeavor" and one in which participation of judges is "peculiarly appropriate." Third, the Court considered the presidential control issue—the matter of selection and removal of commission members. The Court dismissed as "fanciful" the contention that the president's power to appoint federal judges to the commission gives the executive inappropriate influence over the Judicial Branch or interferes with its performance of its functions. Presidential appointment power for positions that may be attractive to judges does not, in itself, corrupt the integrity of the judiciary. The Court could not "imagine" that federal judges would "comport their actions to the wishes of a President for the purpose of receiving an appointment to the Sentencing Commission." The Court also felt the removal power posed a "similarly negligible threat to judicial independence." The act cannot, emphasized the Court, "diminish the status of Article III judges, as judges." The Court concluded by saying that in creating the commission, an "unusual hybrid in structure and authority," Congress neither excessively delegated legislative power nor "upset the constitutionally mandated balance of powers among the Coordinate Branches." The Constitution does not prohibit Congress from delegating to an "expert body located within the Judicial Branch the intricate task of formulating sentencing guidelines consistent with such significant statutory direction as is present here." Nor, said the Court, does the checks and balances system prohibit Congress from "calling upon the accumulated wisdom and experience" of the Judicial Branch in "creating policy on a matter uniquely within the ken of judges."

Significance   The Supreme Court approved in *Mistretta v. United States* (488 U.S. 361: 1989) the process Congress had chosen through which to formulate judicial sentencing guidelines. Guidelines are an approach to reducing disparities in criminal sentences. Guidelines provide direction to judges as they make sentencing decisions and act to confine judicial discretion. Most guidelines provide sets of sentence ranges that vary by seriousness of the offense and prior criminal record of the offender. In most jurisdictions, guidelines are not binding. Rather, judges may impose a greater or lesser sentence than is suggested by the guidelines, but must offer written rationale for departing from the guidelines. Sentencing guidelines have been adopted in a number of states as well as for the federal courts. Guidelines may be mandated either legislatively, as in the Sentencing Reform Act, or by state supreme courts as they exercise their supervisory function in state judicial systems. *Mistretta* makes clear that procedures for developing these guidelines are generally immune to challenge on delegation or separation of powers grounds.

6. Equal Protection and Privacy

Racial Discrimination

The New Equal Protection

Right of Privacy

RACIAL DISCRIMINATION

Job Discrimination

Washington v. Davis, 426 U.S. 229, 96 S. Ct. 2040, 48 L. Ed. 2d 597 (1976)   Required demonstration of intent in order to prove employment discrimination. *Washington v. Davis* considered the question of whether statutory standards prohibiting racial discrimination in employment under Title VII of the Civil Rights Act of 1964 are the same as for adjudicating claims of invidious racial discrimination. The Court held that the latter required a showing not only of impact, but of intent as well. *Washington v. Davis* involved a written personnel test that was administered to all prospective federal employees, including those who, like Davis, sought positions with the Washington, D.C., police force. The test, called Test 21, was ostensibly used to measure verbal aptitude. Four times more black than white applicants failed the test. Davis claimed that the test was not reasonably related to an individual's performance as a police officer and that it discriminated against black applicants. In a 7–2 decision, the Supreme Court upheld use of the test. The Court's opinion was written by Justice White, who took exception to the understanding of the court of appeals that litigants proceeding under Title VII "need not concern themselves with the employer's possibly discriminatory purpose but instead focus on the racially differential impact." Justice White declared that this "is not the constitutional rule." The Court has "never held that the constitutional standard is identical to the standards applicable under Title VII, and declines to do so today." A law "neutral on its face and serving ends otherwise within the power of the government to pursue" is not invalid because it may affect a greater proportion of one race than another. While disproportionate impact is not irrelevant, it is not the sole touchstone of impermissible discrimination. Justice White termed "untenable" the proposition that the Constitution could keep government from seeking modestly to upgrade the communicative abilities of its employees. The Court was unconvinced that the test was a purposeful device used to discriminate. Such evidence as the affirmative effort of the police department to recruit black

189

officers, the changing racial composition of the recruit classes and the force in general, and the relationship of the test to the training program addressed the issue of intent. In this case the evidence "negated any inference that the Department discriminated on the basis of race." The Court concluded that to apply the Title VII approach to constitutional adjudication involves a more probing judicial review of "seemingly reasonable acts of administrators than is appropriate under the Constitution." The Court also observed that if all legislation designed to serve neutral ends is invalidated because in practice it benefits or burdens one race more than another, the results would be extremely far-reaching. Justices Brennan and Marshall dissented, arguing that once discriminatory impact is demonstrated, the employer must prove how the challenged practice has a demonstrable relationship to successful performance of the job for which it is used. *See also* CIVIL RIGHTS CASES (109 U.S. 3: 1883), p. 313; EQUAL PROTECTION CLAUSE, p. 321; *VILLAGE OF ARLINGTON HEIGHTS v. METROPOLITAN HOUSING DEVELOPMENT CORPORATION* (429 U.S. 252; 1977), p. 335.

Significance   *Washington v. Davis* (426 U.S. 229: 1976) held that discriminatory intent must be shown to establish a constitutional violation. *Davis* distinguished situations in which constitutional provisions such as equal protection are involved from those based upon federal civil rights statutes. While certain practices may be found in violation of federal law, such as Title VII, those practices may not be constitutional violations. The disproportionate impact standard set forth in *Griggs v. Duke Power Company* (401 U.S. 424: 1971) still applied to situations arising under Title VII. In *Griggs,* the Court refused to permit an employer to use a high school diploma and scores on an intelligence test as qualifying conditions for employment. Unanimously, the Court held that once a plaintiff shows unequal or disproportionate impact, the employer must demonstrate a relationship between the challenged practice and job performance. The intent element surfaced in a Title VI suit brought by black and Hispanic police officers laid off when financial problems beset New York City. Title VI bars racial or ethnic discrimination by recipients of federal monies. In a fragmented decision, the Court held in *Guardians Association v. Civil Service Commission of the City of New York* (463 U.S. 582: 1983) that without a showing of discriminatory intent, compensatory relief such as back pay and retroactive seniority was not available through Title VI. In *Watson v. Fort Worth Bank & Trust* (487 U.S. 977: 1988) the Court held that measures of "disparate impact" as distinct from demonstration of "disparate treatment" could be used in examining subjective employment criteria in job discrimination challenges. Watson, a black bank teller, was denied promotion four times. She brought suit in federal court and established a prima facie case of discrimination. The court, however, found that the bank had sufficiently justified its reasons for each denial. In so finding, the court refused to consider certain statistical evidence offered by Watson addressing the bank's subjective evaluations and the effects of its decisions on blacks as a class. The Supreme Court reversed on that point. In finding for Watson, the Supreme Court extended for the first time the disparate impact test of *Griggs* to subjective employment decisions. Previously, *Griggs* had applied only to standardized tests or criteria. In other words, the *Watson* decision altered the evidentiary standards that apply in cases flowing from Title VII of the Civil Rights Act of 1964, and applied the disparate impact test to the discretionary judgments of supervisors. The Court basically agreed with Watson's contentions that subjective criteria are as likely as objective tests to have discriminatory effects, and that by confining disparate impact analysis to objective criteria, employers could substitute subjective criteria and render *Griggs* "dead letter." Several Rehnquist Court rulings during the 1988 term made job discrimination more difficult to demonstrate, however. One such decision was *Wards Cove Packing Company, Inc. v. Atonio* (104 L. Ed. 2d 733: 1989). *Wards Cove* involved Title VII complaints brought by nonwhite workers at two fish canneries in Alaska. Employment was divided into two classes: cannery and noncannery jobs. The cannery jobs were unskilled and were largely held by local and nonwhite employees. Noncannery jobs were skilled jobs, higher paying, and held by white workers hired at company offices in Washington and Oregon. The minority workers filed an action claiming the companies' practices unfairly divided the work force on racial bases. The Court was highly critical of the data used by the lower courts to establish a prima facie case of disparate impact. Simply comparing percentages of nonwhite workers in the two job classes the Court termed "nonsensical." The "proper" comparison is between the racial composition of the "at issue jobs" and the "qualified population in the relevant labor market." In the Court's view, the cannery work force "in no way reflected the pool of *qualified* job applicants or the *qualified* labor force population" relevant with respect to the skilled noncannery jobs. Accordingly, the methods of recruiting workers or other employment practices "cannot be said to have disparate impact on nonwhites" if the absence of nonwhites holding such skilled jobs reflects a "dearth of qualified nonwhite applicants for reasons that are not the [employers'] fault." Neither did the Court find percentages of nonwhite workers in other positions relevant to work force composition for cannery jobs. So long as there are no "barriers to applying," the selection process probably has no disparate impact on minorities if the percentage of nonwhites hired is "not significantly less than the percentage of qualified nonwhite applicants." Under the comparative method used by the court of appeals, any employer having a "racially imbalanced segment of its workforce could be hauled into court and made to undertake the expensive and time-consuming task of defending the business necessity of its selection methods." The Court also clarified the burden of proof issue. If the nonwhite workers can establish a prima facie case of disparate impact for any of the employers' practices by making the appropriate statistical comparisons, the burden of justifying those practices shifts to the employer. The "ultimate burden of persuasion," however, will remain "at all times" with those challenging the employment practices. Such a rule "conforms with the usual method for allocating persuasion and production burdens in the federal courts." Justices Stevens, Brennan, Marshall, and Blackmun dissented. Justice Stevens said the Court's ruling "turned a blind eye to the meaning and purpose of Title VII." He also said the majority erroneously departed from *Griggs* and those cases that followed. He said *Griggs* had "correctly reflected" congressional intent, a view borne out by absence of congressional attempts to "correct" mistaken construction of Title VII in decisions like *Griggs*.

Housing Discrimination

***Wright v. City of Roanoke Redevelopment and Housing Authority*, 479 U.S. 418, 107 S. Ct. 766, 93 L. Ed. 2d 781 (1987)**   Held that tenants of a public housing authority who were overcharged for utilities have a course of action under 42 USC Section 1983 to enforce rights protected by federal housing laws. At issue in this case was the Brooke Amendment to the Housing Act of 1937, which established a ceiling on rents by limiting them to a percentage of the income of low-income families living in public housing projects. Under rulings of the Department of Housing and Urban Development (HUD), *rent* had consistently been interpreted to include a reasonable amount for the use of utilities. Wright and other tenants brought suit in federal court under Section 1983, claiming the housing authority had overbilled them for utility use and violated the rent ceilings imposed by the Brooke Amendment and the HUD regulations implementing the amendment. The lower courts had ruled that a private course of action under Section 1983 was unavailable to enforce the Brooke Amendment. The Supreme Court reversed in a 5–4 decision, with Justice White delivering the majority opinion. White said that prior cases had shown that Section 1983 can be used against state agents if they violate federal statutes. There are two recognized exceptions, however. The first is when Congress forecloses such enforcement within the enactment. The second is when the statute does not create enforceable rights, privileges, or immunities with the meaning of Section 1983. In order to trigger the first exception, a state must demonstrate by expressed provision or other specific evidence from the statute itself that Congress intended to foreclose private enforcement of the law. White said the Court does not lightly conclude that Congress intended to preclude Section 1983 as a remedy for the deprivation of a federally secured right. Looking at the Brooke Amendment, the Court concluded that its language and legislative history are devoid of any expressed indication that exclusive enforcement was conveyed to HUD. On the contrary, the Court cited both congressional and HUD actions indicating that enforcement authority is not centralized and that private actions were anticipated. Neither are the remedial mechanisms provided to HUD sufficiently comprehensive and effective to raise a clear inference that Congress intended to foreclose a Section 1983 cause of action for the enforcement of tenants' rights secured by the law. The Court was not persuaded that the second exception applied either. The public housing authority contended that the Brooke Amendment gave the tenants no specific or definable rights to utilities enforceable under Section 1983. Further, it asserted that the language providing for reasonable utility allowance was too vague and amorphous to confer an enforceable right. The Court rejected these contentions, saying that the benefits Congress intended to confer on tenants were sufficiently specific and definite to qualify as enforceable rights under Section 1983. Chief Justice Rehnquist and Justices O'Connor, Powell, and Scalia dissented, saying that neither the Brooke Amendment nor HUD interpretations of it supported the view that Congress intended to create an entitlement to reasonable utilities. Furthermore, HUD regulations in themselves, even if they seem to create a right to reasonable utilities, are not judicially enforceable. *See also* EQUITY JURISDICTION, p. 407; JUDICIAL REVIEW, p. 429.

Significance   The Court's decision in *Wright v. City of Roanoke Redevelopment and Housing Authority* (479 U.S. 418: 1987) made the federal courts more accessible for Section 1983 suits by public housing tenants. The Court's decision supplemented HUD enforcement of federal housing laws with the privately initiated lawsuit, thus expanding federal authority over the protection of civil rights. Despite a flurry of federal legislation immediately after the Civil War, civil rights policy was tied until the 1950s to the proposition that only overt state action violating specific federal rights could be reached by federal criminal sanctions. Like actions based on other civil rights laws, civil suits under the old civil rights laws were infrequent. Private actions under Section

1983 are of this kind. This law allows civil suits against persons violating, under color of law, the constitutional rights of others. Long dormant, Section 1983 cases began to be litigated successfully in the early 1960s. In *Monroe v. Pape* (365 U.S. 156: 1961), for example, the Court held that police brutality constituted deprivation of civil rights and could be reached by Section 1983 action. From this decision on, civil rights actions seeking damages or other relief became more numerous. Prescribing the conduct of state and local officials under Section 1983 has serious implications for federal-state relationships, as the Court pointed out in *Rizzo v. Goode* (423 U.S. 362: 1976). In *Rizzo,* the Court restricted the intervention of federal courts into the internal disciplinary policies of a local police department. The Court deferred to principles of federalism in limiting judicial intervention where named municipal officials could not be tightly enough linked to alleged civil rights violations. The trend, however, has been to bring state and local governments under closer federal scrutiny. Illustrative is the decision of *Maine v. Thiboutot* (448 U.S. 1: 1980). In this case, the Court held that Section 1983 suits may be brought against state and local governments for alleged denial of *any* federal law. The controversy in *Thiboutot* arose over loss of certain benefits under the Aid to Families with Dependent Children provisions of the Social Security Act. Cases like *Thiboutot* proved to have a powerful impact on the old doctrine of dual federalism. Given the degree to which federal laws, especially those involving entitlement programs, intertwine with state and local governmental activities, officials responsible for these activities have become more and more subject to direct legal action. Decisions such as *Wright* reflect this trend.

Affirmative Action

Local #28 of the Sheet Metal Workers' International v. Equal Employment Opportunity Commission, **478 U.S. 421, 106 S. Ct. 3019, 92 L. Ed. 2d 344 (1986)**   Sanctioned the use of affirmative action as a means of addressing past racial discrimination. This case involved a court-ordered minority membership target for a local union. Membership in the union came when a person completed a four-year apprenticeship training program. As early as 1964, the local was ordered to cease and desist from its racially discriminatory practices and directed to implement objective standards for selecting apprentices. A series of follow-up proceedings took place, each of which proved ineffective. Recognizing that the record against the local was "replete with instances of bad faith attempts to prevent or delay affirmative action," a federal district court invoked provisions of Title VII of the Civil

Rights Act of 1964 and imposed a 29 percent nonwhite membership goal. The local was subsequently determined to be in noncompliance and twice found in contempt of court and fined. The fine of $150,000 was to be placed in a fund designed to increase nonwhite membership in the apprenticeship program. The local and its apprenticeship committee, supported by the solicitor general of the United States, challenged these rulings with the argument that the membership goal and fund exceeded the scope of remedies available under Title VII. They extended "race conscious preferences" to individuals who are not identified victims of the local's unlawful discrimination. In a 5–4 decision, the Supreme Court rejected the argument and upheld the order containing the membership goal and fund requirements. Speaking for the Court, Justice Brennan said the Congress clearly intended to vest district courts with broad discretion to award appropriate equitable relief to remedy unlawful discrimination. The availability of race-conscious affirmative relief for violations of Title VII furthers the broad purposes underlying the statute. Such affirmative race-conscious relief may be the only means available to assure equality of employment opportunities and to eliminate those discriminatory practices and devices that have "fostered racially stratified job environments to the disadvantage of many minority citizens." In most situations, courts need only order an employer to cease discriminatory practices and make the appropriate award of relief to victimized individuals. In some cases, however, it may be necessary to require an employer or union to take affirmative steps to end discrimination effectively. If an employer or union has been involved with particularly long-standing or egregious discrimination, compelling it to hire or admit to membership qualified minorities roughly in proportion to the number of qualified minorities in the work force may be the only effective way to ensure the full employment of the rights protected by Title VII. Justice O'Connor agreed that federal courts may, under certain circumstances, order preferential relief benefiting individuals who are not the actual victims of discrimination as a remedy for Title VII violations. Chief Justice Burger and Justice Rehnquist believed that remedies should be confined to actual victims of discrimination. Justice White did not subscribe to that proposition. Rather, he saw the court order as establishing a racial quota, something the Court had historically rejected. *See also* EQUAL PROTECTION CLAUSE, p. 313; *REGENTS OF THE UNIVERSITY OF CALIFORNIA v. BAKKE* (438 U.S. 265: 1978), p. 337; REVERSE DISCRIMINATION, p. 447.

Significance   *Local #28 of the Sheet Metal Workers' International v. Equal Employment Opportunity Commission* (478 U.S. 421: 1986) was one of the three important workplace affirmative action rulings made by the Burger Court in the 1985–86 term. The first was *Wygant v. Jackson Board of Education* (476 U.S. 267: 1986), in which the Court determined that the remedy for past discrimination may make it necessary to take race into account even if "innocent persons may be called upon to bear some of the burden of the remedy." In a concurring opinion, Justice O'Connor said that addressing past discrimination is a "sufficiently weighty state interest to warrant the remedial use of a carefully constructed affirmative action program." The Court rejected the view advanced by the Reagan administration that racial preference in employment was to be used only to remedy specifically named victims. Despite the endorsement of affirmative action in general, however, the five-justice majority refused to allow the layoff of white teachers to preserve the employment of less senior black teachers. In order to do so, the racial preference required a showing of a compelling state interest. Given the fact that the Jackson school district was not found to have discriminated against blacks in hiring teachers, the compelling interest test was not met. The other important 1986 affirmative action ruling came in *Local #93 of the International Association of Firefighters v. City of Cleveland* (92 L. Ed. 2d 405). In this case, Cleveland had agreed to resolve employment discrimination suits brought by black and Hispanic fire fighters by promising to promote black and Hispanic workers one-for-one with whites, notwithstanding seniority and test performance. In a 6–3 decision, the Court ruled that Title VII does not preclude federal courts from approving such agreements. The Court saw such consent decrees as a preferred means of achieving voluntary compliance with Title VII.

At issue in *United States v. Paradise* (480 U.S. 149: 1987) was the use of promotion quotas as a race-based remedy for past discrimination. A federal district court had found that the Alabama Department of Public Safety had systematically excluded blacks from employment as state police officers. An order was issued in 1972 calling for the end of such discrimination and establishing a hiring quota. A number of years later it was discovered that none of the blacks recruited under the quota had been promoted. The department agreed to fashion a plan to resolve the problem, but after two years no blacks had been promoted. A test was subsequently devised for promotions, but it was found to have an adverse impact on blacks. When the department failed to submit a satisfactory promotion plan, the court ordered that blacks and whites be promoted on a one-for-one basis until such time as acceptable promotion policies were in place. The Supreme Court, in a 5–4 decision, upheld the one-for-one plan against the claim that the approach was race conscious and violated both the Equal Protection Clause and the Civil Rights Act of 1964. The remedy devised in this case was seen by the Supreme Court as effective, temporary, and flexible. The order was the product of the considered judgment of the district court, which, with its knowledge of the parties and their resources, properly determined that strong measures were required in light of the department's "long and shameful" record of delay and resistance. Similarly, the Court upheld the use of an affirmative action plan giving preference to women in *Johnson v. Transportation Agency* (480 U.S. 616: 1987). The Santa Clara County Transportation Agency designed an affirmative action plan that applied to employee promotions. The plan authorized the agency to consider the gender of a qualified applicant for promotion to positions within traditionally segregated job classifications. The Court upheld the plan, which made consideration of gender a factor in promotion decisions. The Court drew heavily from the rationale in *United Steelworkers of American v. Weber* (443 U.S. 193: 1979). The Court, said Justice Brennan, must be mindful of the consistent emphasis in both the Court and Congress on the value of voluntary efforts to further the objectives of the law when evaluating an affirmative action plan against Title VII's prohibition of discrimination. In this case, the agency identified a conspicuous imbalance in a traditionally segregated job class and undertook a "voluntary effort in full recognition of both the difficulties and the potential for intrusion on males and nonminorities." In *Martin v. Wilks* (104 L. Ed. 2d 835: 1989), the Court ruled that settlements reached in race or gender discrimination cases may subsequently be challenged by persons affected by the settlements, but not party to them. *Martin* arose out of a suit brought against the city of Birmingham, Alabama. The suit claimed racial bias in the hiring and promotion of blacks. A settlement was eventually reached and a federal court embraced its provisions in a consent decree. The order was aimed at producing numbers of black fire fighters roughly reflecting the proportion of blacks in the work force. Under the order, blacks and whites were to be hired and promoted in equal numbers until the result was achieved. A group of white fire fighters later sought to challenge employment decisions made pursuant to the consent decree. Such decrees were generally regarded as immune from subsequent legal challenge, but in a 5–4 decision, the Supreme Court ruled that attack on the decrees was not precluded. The ruling also covered challenges to decrees aimed at relieving gender discrimination. The Court, through Chief Justice Rehnquist, acknowledged that the accepted view in a situation such as this is that persons who do not intervene in a suit likely to affect them should not be permitted to litigate the same issues later. Nonetheless, said Rehnquist, to prohibit challenges contravenes the "general rule" that a person "cannot be deprived of his legal rights in a proceeding to which he is not a party." A judgment among parties to an action "resolves issues as among them, but it does not conclude the rights of strangers to those proceedings."

Minority Preference

Fullilove v. Klutznick, **448 U.S. 448, 100 S. Ct. 2758, 65 L. Ed. 2d 202 (1980)** Allowed a portion of federal construction grant funds to be reserved or "set aside" for businesses owned and operated by racial minorities. *Fullilove v. Klutznick* examined the central affirmative action issue of whether the use of quotas is permissible under the Fourteenth Amendment. The Public Works Employment Act of 1977 contained a minority business enterprise (MBE) section that required at least 10 percent of federal monies designated for local public works projects to be set aside for businesses owned by minorities. Implementation of the policy was designed to come through grant recipients who were expected to seek out MBEs and provide whatever assistance or advice might be necessary to negotiate bonding, bidding, or any other historically troublesome process. The policy was challenged by a number of nonminority contractors, but upheld by the Supreme Court in a 6–3 decision. Chief Justice Burger said the MBE section must be considered against the background of ongoing efforts directed toward deliverance of the century-old promise of economic opportunity. Burger noted that a program using racial or ethnic criteria, even in a remedial context, calls for close examination, "yet we are bound to approach our task with appropriate deference." The Court's analysis involved two steps: the constitutionality of Congress's objectives and the permissibility of the means chosen to pursue the objectives. The Court ruled that Congress had ample evidence to conclude that minority businesses had impaired access to public contracting opportunities, that their impaired access had an effect on interstate commerce, and that the pattern of disadvantage and discrimination was a problem of national scope. Thus Congress had the authority to act. The Court then turned to the means used. Racial or ethnic criteria may be used in a remedial fashion as long as the program is narrowly tailored to achieve the corrective purpose. The Court rejected the view that in developing remedies Congress must act in a wholly color-blind fashion. No organ of government has more comprehensive remedial power than Congress. Where Congress can prohibit certain conduct, "it may, as here, authorize and induce state action to avoid such conduct." The Court recognized that some nonminority contractors who may not themselves have acted in a discriminatory manner may lose some contracts. Such a result, outside the legislative purpose, is an unfortunate but incidental consequence. As

Congress attempts to effectuate a limited and properly tailored remedy to cure the effect of prior discrimination, such a sharing of the burden by innocent parties is not impermissible. Justices Stewart, Rehnquist, and Stevens disagreed. They argued that the "government may never act to the detriment of a person solely because of that person's race." Racial discrimination is invidious by definition, and that rule cannot be any different when the persons injured by a racially biased law are not members of a racial minority. As for the corrective character of the legislation, Justice Stewart remarked that Congress is not a court of equity and has "neither the dispassionate objectivity nor the flexibility that are needed to mold a race-conscious remedy around the single objective of eliminating the effects of past or present discrimination." *See also* EQUAL PROTECTION CLAUSE, p. 313; *REGENTS OF THE UNIVERSITY OF CALIFORNIA v. BAKKE* (438 U.S. 265: 1978), p. 337; REVERSE DISCRIMINATION, p. 447; *WASHINGTON v. DAVIS* (426 U.S. 229: 1976), p. 333.

Significance   *Fullilove v. Klutznick* (448 U.S. 448: 1980) upheld the use of set-asides or reserved funds for minority business enterprises as a method of remedying past discrimination in the construction industry. A year before *Fullilove*, the Court had approved a preferential employment training program in *United Steelworkers of America v. Weber* (442 U.S. 193: 1979). The plan, a component of a collective bargaining agreement, sought to reduce racial imbalances in a corporation's skilled or craft work force. The plan gave preference to unskilled black employees over white employees, even white employees with greater seniority, in admission to training programs that taught the skills needed to become a craft worker. In a 5–2 decision, the Court held that Title VII of the Civil Rights Act of 1964 did not categorically preclude private and voluntary affirmative action plans. To prohibit such plans would produce a result inconsistent with the intent of the Civil Rights Act. It would be ironic if Title VII, "triggered by a nation's concern over centuries of racial injustice," were interpreted as the "legislative prohibition of all voluntary, private race-conscious efforts to abolish traditional patterns of racial segregation and hierarchy." *Fullilove* and *Weber* together adopt the proposition that equal protection allows compensatory policies for groups that have demonstrably been disadvantaged in the past.

The city of Richmond adopted an affirmative action plan requiring prime contractors receiving city construction contracts to subcontract at least 30 percent of the dollar value of the contract to businesses owned or controlled by one (or more) of a number of specified minorities. The plan was designed to "promote wider participation by minority business enterprises in the construction of public projects" and was characterized by the Richmond City Council as "remedial." The Court disallowed the Richmond plan in *City of Richmond v. J. A. Croson Company* (488 U.S. 469: 1989). The principal defect was that Richmond failed to show past discrimination in the city's contract-letting practices or in the conduct of prime contractors toward minority subcontractors. Rather, the city had relied on data that showed that while the city's population was 50 percent black, less than 1 percent of the large construction projects had been awarded to minority businesses. The Court viewed claims based on such data as "generalized" and "amorphous," and ruled that these data could not justify the use of an "unyielding" race-based quota approach. The plan was aimed, said the Court, at remedying the effects of discrimination in the entire construction industry. The data on which the plan was based provided "no guidance for a legislative body to determine the precise scope of the injury it seeks to remedy"; there is no "logical stopping point." Using these kinds of data to define "identified discrimination" would allow local government "license to create a patchwork of racial preferences based on statistical generalizations about any particular field of endeavor." The Court also refused to defer to the city's own designation of the plan as remedial. "Mere recitation of a 'benign' or legitimate purpose for a racial classification is entitled to little or no weight." Racial classifications are "suspect," and that means that "legislative assurances of good intention cannot suffice" in themselves. The Court also found the Richmond plan defective with respect to its scope. The Court said it was "almost impossible to assess" whether the plan was narrowly tailored to remedy prior discrimination because it was not "linked to identified discrimination in any way." Two other aspects of the *Croson* decision are worth noting. First, the Court emphasized that this decision does not preclude state and local governments from "taking action to rectify the effects of identified discrimination." Second, the Court made it clear that striking down the Richmond plan had absolutely no effect on the federal set-aside law upheld in *Fullilove,* after which the Richmond plan had been fashioned. The Court made clear that a different standard applies to congressional action. While the Fourteenth Amendment bars state and local units from discriminating on the basis of race, Congress has a "specific constitutional mandate to enforce the dictates of the Fourteenth Amendment." This power includes authority to define situations that Congress determines threaten principles of equality and to adopt prophylactic rules to deal with these situations. Thus Congress may "identify and redress the effects of society-wide discrimination." States and their political subdivisions are not, on the other hand, "free to decide that such remedies are appropriate."

Decisions as recent as 1990 have suggested that race-based affirmative action programs violate the Equal Protection Clause unless they are designed to promote a "compelling state interest." The only interest that has been compelling enough to justify race-preference initiatives is remediation of demonstrated past discrimination. The Court ruled in *Metro Broadcasting, Inc. v. Federal Communications Commission* (111 L. Ed. 2d 445: 1990) that Congress may mandate "benign" minority preference policies even if those measures "are not 'remedial' in the sense of being designed to compensate victims of past governmental or societal discrimination." At issue in *Metro Broadcasting* (and the companion case of *Astroline Communications Company v. Shurberg Broadcasting of Hartford, Inc.*) were two policies established by the Federal Communications Commission (FCC). The first allows the FCC to consider minority ownership as a factor in licensure decisions. Consideration of this factor enhances minority chances of obtaining new licenses. The second gives minority owners preference in situations where current license holders are likely to lose their licenses—so-called distressed sale situations. Of "overriding" significance in cases such as this, said Justice Brennan for the five-justice majority, is that these minority preference programs "have been specifically approved—indeed mandated—by Congress." The majority based its decision on *Fullilove*. Under terms of *Fullilove*, the Court need not use the strict scrutiny standard when reviewing affirmative action initiatives of the federal government, as opposed to state or local governments. Rather, minority preference programs established by Congress need serve "important governmental objectives" and be "substantially related" to achievement of those objectives. The Court reviewed the need for federal regulation of the "unique medium" of broadcast. The "safeguarding of the public's right to receive a diversity of views and information over the airwaves" was seen as an "integral component of the FCC's mission." On that basis, the Court concluded that "enhancing broadcast diversity is, at the very least, an important governmental objective and therefore a sufficient basis for the commission's minority ownership policies." Justices O'Connor, Kennedy, and Scalia and Chief Justice Rehnquist dissented. Their disagreement focused on the different review standards for the federal government. "The Constitution's guarantee of equal protection," said O'Connor, "binds the Federal Government as it does the states." Justice Kennedy also disagreed with the importance of broadcast diversity as a governmental objective. He said he could not agree with the Court that the Constitution "permits the Government to discriminate among its citizens on the basis of race in order to serve interest so trivial as 'broadcast diversity.'"

Protection of Civil Rights

Patterson v. McLean Credit Union, **109 S. Ct. 2363, 105 L. Ed. 2d 132 (1989)** Reiterated that provisions of the Civil Rights Act of 1866 could be used in legal actions against private racial discrimination. The Civil Rights Act of 1866 guaranteed blacks the right to "make and enjoy" contracts. That provision is currently found in 42 USC Section 1981. For a long time, this language was thought to be applicable only against state action or public discrimination. In the case of *Runyon v. McCrary* (427 U.S. 160: 1976), the Court extended Section 1981 to private discrimination. Since *Runyon,* this section has become a common basis of actions seeking damages for employment discrimination. Brenda Patterson brought such an action against her employer, claiming racial harassment. Following argument of her case before the Supreme Court in February 1988, the Court ordered that the case be reargued. The question to be considered in reargument was whether *Runyon* ought to be overruled. While ruling that the law could be used in private actions, the Court ruled 5–4 that the statute had limited application in the employment setting and did not extend to Patterson's racial harassment claim. The opinion of the Court was authored by Justice Kennedy. He began with the broader question of retaining *Runyon.* He pointed to prior decisions that have been overruled and observed that "our precedents are not sacrosanct." Nonetheless, "departure from the doctrine of stare decisis demands special justification." A special burden must be borne by the party advocating the "abandonment of an established precedent," and that burden is even greater when the Court is asked to overrule a point of statutory construction. *Stare decisis* has "special force" in statutory construction because, unlike with constitutional interpretation, the "legislative power is implicated, and Congress remains free to alter what we have done." The Court concluded that no such "special justification" had been demonstrated necessitating the overruling of *Runyon.* The most common reason for a court to shift position on a precedent is the "intervening development of the law." *Runyon,* said Kennedy, has not been "undermined by subsequent changes or development in the law." Kennedy noted that *Runyon* remains "entirely consistent with our society's deep commitment to the eradication of discrimination based on a person's race." Kennedy then turned to Patterson's specific allegation of discriminatory harassment. He reviewed the language of Section 1981 and pointed out that its "most obvious feature" is the restriction on the scope of the law. If a discriminatory act does not involve "impairment" of one of its specific provisions, Section 1981 "provides no relief." The section cannot, said Kennedy, "be construed as a general proscription of racial discrimination in all aspects of contract relations," for it expressly prohibits discrimination only in the making and enforcement of contracts. The section prohibits refusal to enter into a contract because of race or to make contracts only on discriminatory terms. The right to make contracts does not extend, "as a matter of either logic or semantics, to conduct by the employer after the contract relation has been established." That limitation includes breaching the contract terms or imposing "discriminatory working conditions." Such postformation conduct "does not involve the right to make a contract." Instead, performance of established contract obligations is involved, a matter "more naturally governed by state contract law and Title VII" of the Civil Rights Act of 1964. Justices Brennan, Marshall, Blackmun, and Stevens dissented and criticized the Court's interpretation of Section 1981 as "needlessly cramped" and based on a "most pinched reading of the phrase 'right to make a contract.'" Brennan said the Court's "formalistic" interpretation is "antithetical to Congress's vision of a society in which contractual opportunities are equal." Brennan was also critical of the Court's reaffirmation of *Runyon* on *stare decisis* grounds. In his view, that "glosses over" the most compelling reasons for retaining *Runyon*—that it was "correctly decided" and that Congress had "ratified our construction of the statute" as manifest in subsequent actions by that body. *See also* EQUAL PROTECTION CLAUSE, p. 313.

Significance   *Patterson v. McLean Credit Union* (105 L. Ed. 2d 132: 1989) limited the reach of Section 1981, confining it to those discriminatory employment decisions occurring before someone is hired. Once a person is employed, discriminatory treatment falls under the purview of Title VII of the Civil Rights Act of 1964. *Patterson* can be seen as a decision that retreats from previous civil rights rulings. *Patterson* is important for what it did not do, however. It did not overrule *Runyon v. McCrary* (427 U.S. 160: 1976). *Runyon* had held that Section 1981 reaches private contracts. When the Court agreed to review *Patterson,* it indicated a reconsideration of *Runyon* would be included. *Patterson* affirmed *Runyon,* thus Section 1981 continues to cover private contracts. Section 1983 of Title 42 of the U.S. Code comes from provisions of the Civil Rights Act of 1871 and enables persons to recover damages for violations of their civil rights. The case of *Jett v. Dallas Independent School District* (105 L. Ed. 2d 598: 1989) examined the relationship of these two statutes, and the standard to be used in judging the liability of a school district for damages claimed under Section 1981. Jett, a white male, was a teacher, athletic director, and football coach at a largely black high school in Dallas, Texas. After Jett had a series of conflicts with the school's black principal, the principal recommended that Jett be relieved of his athletic duties.

The school superintendent concurred in the recommendations and reassigned Jett to another school. Jett brought action, claiming his reassignment was the product of racial discrimination on the part of agents of the school district. The Supreme Court ruled against Jett, saying that school district liability under Section 1983 exists only if the principal and superintendent had acted pursuant to a formal policy or "well settled custom that amounted to official policy." It was the Court's view that Congress had limited the liability of public entities based on employee conduct in Section 1983, and that Congress had not intended that such liability previously possible under Section 1981 should remain. In other words, the Section 1983 language on liability, including the "official policy or custom" standard, modified Section 1981 as well. The Court said that Section 1983 provides the "exclusive federal damages remedy" for violations covered by Section 1981 when claims are made against public entities. Under these terms, it must be shown that public employees who allegedly discriminate must possess formally conveyed policy-making authority or have acted pursuant to official "custom or policy." Since most public entities have formally adopted antidiscrimination statements, the effect of *Jett* is largely to insulate local entities from damage awards. Justices Brennan, Blackmun, Marshall, and Stevens dissented. It was their position that Section 1981 afforded an independent cause of action to victims of discrimination by public employees, and that Section 1983 did not restrict Section 1981 remedies.

DeShaney v. Winnebago County Department of Social Services, **489 U.S. 189, 109 S. Ct. 998, 103 L. Ed. 2d 249 (1989)** Ruled that the state is not required to protect the "life, liberty, and property of its citizens against invasion by private actors." Joshua DeShaney was physically abused on a regular basis by his biological father. The Winnebago County Department of Social Services (DSS) received numerous complaints about the abuse and made some effort to protect the child. However, DSS took no steps to remove Joshua from his father's custody. A final beating of Joshua, aged 4 at the time of the incident, was sufficiently severe to leave the child permanently brain damaged and "profoundly" retarded. Action was brought under U.S. Code Section 1983 against DSS by Joshua and his mother for failure to protect him from his father's abusive conduct. It was asserted that DSS's failure to remove Joshua from his father's custody deprived him of his physical safety as protected by the substantive component of the Due Process Clause of the Fourteenth Amendment. A federal district court granted summary judgment for DSS and was affirmed by the court of appeals. The Supreme Court ruled 6–3 that the agency did not violate Joshua's rights under the Due Process Clause. The clause is aimed at limiting the state's power to act, and is not a "guarantee of certain minimal levels of safety and security." It forbids deprivation of life, liberty, and property by the state, but cannot be expanded to impose an "affirmative obligation on the state to ensure that those interests do not come to harm by other means." An argument was also presented on behalf of Joshua that even if there were no due process obligation to act to protect the general public, the state had a particular duty in Joshua's case because of a "special relationship" of DSS to client in this case. DSS was aware that Joshua "faced a special danger of abuse," and caseworkers had specifically indicated an intention to "protect him against that danger." Having "actually undertaken" to protect Joshua from his father, the state "acquired an affirmative 'duty,'" through the Due Process Clause, to "do so in a reasonably competent fashion." The Court rejected these contentions. The state, said the Court, assumes responsibility for a person's "safety and general well-being" only when it formally takes custody of a person and holds that person against his or her will. The affirmative duty to protect arises "not from a State's knowledge of an individual's predicament or from its expressions of intent to help him, but from the limitation which it has imposed on his freedom to act on his own behalf." The harm suffered by Joshua in this case occurred while he was in the custody of his father, "who was in no sense a state actor." While the state may have been aware of the "dangers that Joshua faced in the free world," the state "played no part in their creation," nor did it "do anything to render him any more vulnerable to them." That the state once took temporary custody does not "alter the analysis." When DSS returned Joshua to his father, it "placed him in no worse position than that in which he would have been had it not acted at all." The state, concluded the Court, does not "become permanent guarantor of an individual's safety by once having offered him shelter." Under these circumstances, the state had no "constitutional duty" to protect Joshua. Justices Brennan, Marshall, and Blackmun dissented, stating that Joshua's position deserved consideration under Section 1983.

Significance   Like *DeShaney v. Winnebago County Department of Social Services* (489 U.S. 189: 1989), a large number of cases are currently brought under Section 1983 of Title 42 of the U.S. Code. That section says that liability shall attach to the "deprivation of any right, privileges or immunities secured by the Constitution and laws." This provision remained largely unused for almost a century because it was believed to extend only to officially authorized misconduct. The Warren Court broadened the reach of Section 1983 as a remedy in *Monroe v. Pape* (365 U.S. 167: 1961), ruling that persons are subject to damage suits whenever their conduct violates federal or state law. Under Section 1983, defendants may be liable not only for compensatory damages, but for punitive damages as well. The latter require a finding that the action was reckless or "callously indifferent" to a person's rights. *Monroe* opened the door for a great many damage suits, and the Court has frequently faced questions about such litigation. Several recent examples will illustrate. The Court ruled in *Graham v. Connor* (490 U.S. 386: 1989) that civil rights actions brought under Section 1983 claiming use of excessive force by police should be decided using the "objective reasonableness" standard. Graham's excessive force claim had been rejected by the lower courts because he failed to show that the police used force "maliciously and sadistically for the very purpose of causing harm." The Court unanimously ruled that a less demanding standard should have been used rather than the substantive due process standard. The Court rejected the idea that all excessive force claims are "governed by a single generic standard." Rather, specific constitutional rights allegedly infringed by the challenged use of force must be identified, and claims evaluated against the standards associated with that right. The Fourth Amendment reasonableness standard that applies to "seizures" was seen as appropriate here. It requires inquiry into whether police actions were reasonable in light of "facts and circumstances" facing the officers, without regard to "underlying intent or motivation." The reasonableness of a particular action must be judged "from the perspective of a reasonable officer on the scene," and its "calculus must embody" a recognition that split-second judgments on amount of force are often necessary. This is a different perspective from the "20/20 vision of hindsight." The Court rejected the proposition that the "malicious and sadistic" standard was "merely another way of describing conduct that is objectively unreasonable." The Court remanded the case for reconsideration under the objective reasonableness standard.

In *City of Canton v. Harris* (103 L. Ed. 2d 412: 1989), the Court considered whether a municipality is liable under 42 USC Section 1983 for failing to train an employee who, in turn, allegedly violates a person's civil rights. Harris was taken into custody by Canton police. Soon after, she fell several times. She responded incoherently when asked if she wanted medical assistance, and none was called. Upon her release, she was hospitalized with various emotional ailments. She subsequently filed suit, claiming she had not received proper medical assistance while in police custody. Specifically, she argued that the shift commander with sole responsibility to assess medical needs had not been given sufficient and special training to make medical determinations. Canton argued that liability under Section 1983 could occur only where a municipal policy is "itself unconstitutional." The

Court rejected this argument and ruled that liability under Section 1983 could stem from failure to train sufficiently. The Court went on to establish some guidelines. Liability for adequate police training can occur only where the deficiency "amounts to deliberate indifference to the constitutional rights of persons with whom the police come into contact." Only where a failure to train adequately "reflects a 'deliberate' or 'conscious' choice" by the municipality can the deficiency be "properly thought of as an actionable city policy." It cannot simply be asserted that a training program constitutes policy. Instead, the focus must be on whether the training program is "adequate to the tasks the particular employees must perform." The defect in the training program must also be "closely related to the ultimate injury" suffered by the plaintiff. In other words, the plaintiff must prove that the training deficiency "actually caused the police officers' indifference to the medical needs." Another recent Section 1983 decision came in *National Collegiate Athletic Association v. Tarkanian* (488 U.S. 179: 1988), which addressed the authority of the National Collegiate Athletic Association (NCAA) to enforce rules and standards for intercollegiate athletic programs. The NCAA is a private organization founded in the early 1900s to adopt rules for intercollegiate athletics and to govern the conduct of the public and private member institutions on such athletic policies as eligibility, recruitment, and financial aid. The NCAA has a Committee on Infractions, which conducts investigations and determines whether rule violations have occurred. This committee is empowered to impose penalties on member institutions, but cannot directly sanction employees of member schools. The committee found a number of violations at the University of Nevada, Las Vegas (UNLV), including ten infractions in Coach Tarkanian's basketball program. Sanctions were imposed on UNLV. These sanctions included a two-year probation during which the basketball team would be banned from television appearances and postseason tournament competition. The committee also recommended that Coach Tarkanian be suspended during the probation period. UNLV was requested to show cause why additional sanctions should not be imposed if it failed to comply with the suspension of Coach Tarkanian. Tarkanian commenced suit under 42 USC Section 1983, contending denial of due process. The essence of Tarkanian's claim was that the NCAA and UNLV had a totally interdependent relationship—the university delegated authority to the NCAA, and the NCAA was dependent on the university to enforce its sanctions. As a consequence, the NCAA became a joint participant in state action, thus making its action subject to suit under Section 1983. Tarkanian further contended that since state action was involved, investigations and determinations made by the NCAA are subject to the same due process requirements as those applying to state agencies. The Supreme Court ruled 5–4 that the NCAA did not act "under color of" state law within the meaning of Section 1983. The Court first examined the relationship between the NCAA and UNLV. The Court concluded that neither the university's decision to adopt NCAA standards nor its "minor role" in their formulation was a "sufficient reason" for concluding that the NCAA was acting under color of Nevada law when it promulgated standards. Throughout, UNLV retained power to withdraw from the NCAA and "establish its own standards." Furthermore, the NCAA investigation and subsequent recommendations for sanctions were not state action because UNLV had delegated power directly to the NCAA. Rather than the NCAA acting as an agent of UNLV during the investigation and enforcement proceedings, the NCAA and UNLV had acted as adversaries. Indeed, UNLV had used its "best efforts to retain its winning coach—a goal diametrically opposed to the NCAA's interest in ascertaining the truth of its investigation's reports." The Court said it would be "ironic indeed" to conclude that the NCAA sanctions against UNLV—sanctions that Nevada, through its attorney general, "steadfastly opposed"—could be "fairly attributable to the State of Nevada." Finally, the Court rejected Tarkanian's contention that the power of the NCAA was so great as to give UNLV no "practical alternative to compliance." Even presuming that a "private monopolist can impose its will on a state agency" by threatening to no longer deal with it, it "does not follow that such a private party is therefore acting under color of state law." In the case of *Will v. Michigan Department of State Police* (105 L. Ed. 2d 45: 1989), the Court decided that a state is not a "person" for civil rights liability purposes. The Civil Rights Act of 1871 (42 USC Section 1983) provides that any "person" who injures another person under "color of state law" may be liable for civil damages. Will, a systems analyst in the Department of State Police, brought a Section 1983 action against the department, claiming he was illegally denied promotion. Specifically, Will asserted that he was not promoted because his brother had been classified a political "subversive" by a special investigation unit of the state police known as the "Red Squad." The state law authorizing the surveillance of such political activists and the maintaining of surveillance files on them was eventually held to be unconstitutional. Though Will was highly placed on the promotion register, he was not promoted because of his brother's Red Squad file. The Supreme Court affirmed the state court ruling that a state is not a "person" subject to suit under Section 1983. The Court ruled that neither the language nor the legislative purpose of Section 1983 supported the assertion that subjects the state to liability. Normal usage of the term *person* does not include the state. To argue the contrary, said the Court, would require a "decidedly awkward way of expressing an intent to subject the States to liability." The Court also considered Congress's purpose in enacting Section 1983. It was to provide a "federal forum to remedy many deprivations of civil liberties," but it was not intended to provide a "means for litigants who seek a remedy against a State for alleged deprivation of civil liberties." The latter is bound by the doctrine of sovereign immunity established through the Eleventh Amendment. The Court said it could not conclude that Section 1983 was intended to "disregard the well-established immunity of a State from being sued without its consent." Similarly, the Court ruled in *Ngiraingas v. Sanchez* (109 L. Ed. 2d 163: 1990) that officials in U.S. territories such as Guam are not "persons" under terms of Section 1983 when they are acting in their official capacities. Both federal and state courts have jurisdiction over cases brought under Section 1983. A unanimous Court held in *Howlett v. Rose* (110 L. Ed. 2d 332: 1990) that the defense of "sovereign immunity" is not available to defendants in Section 1983 actions.

Spallone v. United States, 107 L. Ed. 2d 644 (1990)   Considered whether a federal court could order city counsel members to vote as directed on a desegregation matter. The city of Yonkers was found to have acted in a racially discriminatory fashion when it located all its subsidized housing in a nonwhite section of the city. The city and its community development agency were then ordered to facilitate construction of subsidized housing throughout the city. Following an unsuccessful appeal by the city, an agreement, subsequently embraced in a consent decree, was reached between the parties. Included in the order was a provision that the city council would adopt regulations that all future housing constructed anywhere in the city include some portion of subsidized units. The legislation was also to include certain incentives to foster the development of such housing. Reaction from the residents of neighborhoods where such housing was to be built was both extensive and negative. Indeed, the opposition was sufficiently strong that the city council refused to adopt the legislation required under the consent decree. Instead, the council adopted a resolution that declared a moratorium on construction of all public housing. This resolution was adopted in direct defiance of the court decree. The court once again ordered the council to adopt the necessary legislation. The court gave the council only a few days to do so and indicated that failure to act would result in contempt sanctions against both the city and the council members who voted against the legislation. The punishment for noncomplying members was to be $500 in fines per day and imprisonment after the tenth day.

A resolution on intent to comply was defeated by a 4–3 council vote. Following a hearing, the court found the city and the four council members in contempt. Two council members eventually switched their votes in the face of escalating fines against the city. The fines ceased following the second vote, although $820,000 in fines were assessed against the city. While none of the council members was jailed, each paid $3,500 in fines. The Supreme Court refused to review the fines against the city, but consolidated the petitions from the four council members for review. In a 5–4 decision, the sanctions against the individual council members were reversed as an abuse of judicial discretion under "traditional equitable principles." The Court said the council members, as distinct from the city, were not parties to the original action, nor were they found to be "individually liable" for any particular violations on which the remedial order was based. The original corrective order itemizing specific "affirmative steps" was directed only to the city. Furthermore, the Court said there was also a "reasonable probability" that sanctions against the city would have been sufficient to obtain the desired results. Finally, the Court focused on the order requiring council members to vote in a particular way. While not ruling that council members ought to be immune from contempt sanctions, "considerations underlying the immunity doctrine must inform the District Court's exercise of discretion." In particular, the Court pointed out the notion that a restriction on a legislator's freedom "undermines the 'public good' by interfering with the rights of the people to representation in the democratic process." The Court here distinguished between sanctions against the city and the individual council members. The latter causes members to act, "not with a view to the wishes of constituents or to the fiscal solvency of the city, but with a view solely to their own personal monetary interest." This creates a "much greater perversion of the normal legislative process" than sanctions on the city for "failure of these legislators to enact an ordinance." Justices Brennan, Marshall, Blackmun, and Stevens dissented. They did not view the supplementing of sanctions against the city with personal sanctions against the council members as an abuse of discretion. Neither did they think the district court could have reasonably expected that the sanctions against the city alone would have produced compliance with the provisions of the consent decree. *See also* EQUAL PROTECTION CLAUSE, p. 313.

Significance   Legislative bodies possess substantial power to respond to civil rights violations. *Missouri v. Jenkins* (109 L. Ed. 2d 31: 1990) examined the scope of remedial power of the federal judiciary in school desegregation situations. A federal district court found that the state of Missouri had maintained racially segregated schools in

Kansas City and had failed to address the effects of this discriminatory conduct sufficiently. The school district had been unable to generate additional tax revenues for desegregation because of certain
provisions of state law, such as a two-thirds voter approval requirement for tax increases. The court approved a desegregation plan
submitted by the school board, but the district had exhausted all
available means of raising the needed funds. The court then ordered
that the local property tax rate be raised to a level required to yield the
necessary revenue to implement the desegregation plan for the
1987–88 school year. The order was approved by the court of appeals
for that first year, but the district court was directed to take a "less
obtrusive" course for subsequent years. In particular, the appellate
court recommended that the local school board be ordered to impose
any increase itself rather than the court taking action directly. The
Supreme Court ruled, in a 5–4 decision, that the direct increase in the
property tax rate was an "abuse of discretion" on the part of the
district court. Before taking such a "drastic step," the district court
was "obliged to assure itself that no permissible alternative would
have accomplished the required task." The Supreme Court pointed to
the court of appeals decision as containing a permissible alternative.
The district court could have "authorized or required" the school
district to increase property taxes and "enjoined the operation of the
state laws that would have prevented [the school district] from exercising this power." The difference between these approaches, said the
Court, is "far more than a matter of form." Directing local authorities
to "devise and implement remedies not only protects the function of
those institutions but, to the extent possible, also places the responsibility for solutions to the problems of segregation upon those who
have themselves created the problems." Missouri contended that federal courts cannot set aside limits established by state law on local
taxing authorities. The Supreme Court disagreed. A court order of
the kind outlined by the court of appeals is "plainly a judicial act
within the power of a federal court." It is "clear" that a local taxing
authority may be ordered to levy taxes in excess of the limit set by the
state "where there is reason based in the Constitution for not observ-
ing the statutory limitation." Here the order to levy taxes would
"compel the discharge of an obligation imposed on [the school dis-
trict] by the Fourteenth Amendment." To rule otherwise, said the
Court, would "fail to take account of the obligations of local government, under the Supremacy Clause, to fulfill the requirements that
the Constitution imposes on them." Regardless of how much discretion local authorities have to fashion desegregation remedies, if a
state-imposed limit operates to "inhibit or obstruct the operation of a
unitary school system or impede the disestablishing of a dual school

system, it must fall; state policy must give way when it operates to hinder vindication of federal constitutional guarantees." Justice Kennedy issued a dissent for himself, Chief Justice Rehnquist, and Justices O'Connor and Scalia. In Kennedy's view, federal courts could either impose the tax increase directly or reach the same result indirectly through delegation to the local school district. He referred to the majority's distinction between the two approaches as "convenient formalism." A judicial taxation order is "but an attempt to exercise a power that has always been thought legislative in character." "Today's casual embrace of taxation imposed by the unelected, life-tenured Federal judiciary," he said, "disregards fundamental precepts for the democratic control of public institutions." The *Jenkins* decision reflects a very broad view of federal judicial authority. The Court had previously allowed federal courts to intervene in a variety of situations, but had never allowed a federal judge to order a tax increase to remediate constitutional violations.

THE NEW EQUAL PROTECTION
Reapportionment and Race

Mobile v. Bolden, **446 U.S. 55, 100 S. Ct. 1490, 64 L. Ed. 2d 47 (1980)**   Upheld a municipal at-large election process against claims that such a system diluted minority group voting influence. *Mobile v. Bolden* considered whether malapportionment of legislative districts violated the Equal Protection Clause of the Fourteenth Amendment because it debased the value of an individual's vote. A federal district court found a constitutional violation in the election process in Mobile, Alabama, and ordered that a single-member district structure replace the current at-large system. The Supreme Court found the at-large plan to be constitutionally adequate and reversed the district court in a 6–3 decision. Critics of the at-large or multimember district approach argued that some elements of the electorate were unrepresented. The Court noted that criticism of the at-large election is rooted in its winner-take-all aspect and its tendency to submerge minorities. The specific question posed in *Bolden* was whether the at-large scheme had been established for the purpose of reducing the impact of black voters. No finding was made by the trial court that black voters had been deprived of the privilege of voting or hampered in the registration process. The Court had previously found in such cases as *White v. Regester* (412 U.S. 755: 1973) that the multimember election system was not unconstitutional per se. Constitutional violations occur in apportionment systems only "if their purpose were invidiously to minimize or cancel out the voting potential of racial or ethnic minorities." To demonstrate such a violation, a plaintiff must prove that the disputed plan was conceived or operated as a purposeful device to further racial discrimination. A showing that a particular group has not elected representatives in proportion to its members is not sufficient. The Court said that while black candidates in Mobile have been defeated, that fact alone does not work a constitutional deprivation. The Court also rejected the relevance of discrimination by the city in the context of municipal employment and the dispensing of public services. Evidence of possible discrimination by city officials in other contexts is "tenuous and circumstantial evidence of the constitutional invalidity of the electoral system under which they attained their offices." The Burger Court concluded that past cases show "the Court has sternly set its face against the claim, however phrased, that the Constitution somehow guarantees proportional representation." Justices Brennan, Marshall, and White dissented. They argued that a sufficient discriminatory impact had been shown. Justice Marshall said the Court's decision meant that "in absence of proof of discrimination by the State, the right to vote provides the politically powerless with nothing more than the right to cast meaningless ballots." *See also* APPORTIONMENT, p. 384; *BAKER v. CARR* (369 U.S. 186: 1962), p. 343; *REYNOLDS v. SIMS* (377 U.S. 533: 1964), p. 344.

Significance   Mobile v. Bolden (446 U.S. 55: 1980) held that discriminatory intent must be demonstrated before an electoral system can be found unconstitutionally defective. But what if the intent is benevolent? What if an apportionment plan is designed to make more likely the electoral success of minorities? The Court upheld such a plan in *United Jewish Organization of Williamsburgh, Inc. v. Carey* (430 U.S. 144: 1977), where district lines in New York were drawn to enhance the possibility of electing racial minorities to the state legislature. The plan split a group of Hasidic Jews, formerly concentrated in a single state assembly and senate district, into two districts. Suit was brought claiming voter reassignment had been based on race. The Court upheld the redistricting plan, finding that other voters in the county involved were not denied an opportunity to participate in the political process. The Court also held that considerations of race could be made in an attempt to comply with provisions of the Voting Rights Act of 1965, as in *South Carolina v. Katzenbach* (383 U.S. 301: 1966). As long as considerations of race were directed toward the achievement of racial equality, they were permissible. Plans that actually disenfranchise are clearly unconstitutional, however. In *Gomillion v. Lightfoot* (364 U.S. 339: 1960), the Court held that a plan that restructured the boundaries of a city so that most black residents were placed outside the city limits was in violation of both the Fourteenth and Fifteenth Amendments.

The Voting Rights Act of 1965 also requires that any change in voting procedures or conditions that have an impact on voting practices are subject to preclearance by the attorney general of the United States. The full impact of this requirement was seen in *City of Pleasant Grove v. United States* (479 U.S. 462: 1987). Pleasant Grove, a nearly all-white city in Alabama, was denied preclearance to annex a then uninhabited area on the ground that it had refused to annex adjacent black neighborhoods despite petitions by the neighborhood residents. The Supreme Court said an annexation is subject to preclearance under the law. Even the annexation of vacant land on which residential development is anticipated must be precleared. In the Court's view, to allow a state to circumvent the preclearance requirement when annexing vacant land intended for white development would disserve congressional intent to reach the subtle as well as the obvious official actions that have the effect of denying voter groups based on race. Further, preclearance is dependent on a showing that both discriminatory purpose and effect are absent. The burden of proving absence of discriminatory intent and effect, said Justice White, rests with the governmental unit seeking preclearance. Pleasant Grove argued that there were no black voters in the city at the time the annexation decision was made, so the proposals did not deny or reduce existing black voter representation. The Court rejected this contention, saying it was based on an incorrect assumption that relevant provisions of the act can relate only to present circumstances. Its provisions look not only at present effects, but at future effects as well. Similarly, an impermissible purpose under the act may relate to anticipated as well as present circumstances. In other words, annexation cannot be used as a means of preventing integration. An obvious means of thwarting integration is to provide for the growth of a monolithic white voting bloc, thereby effectively diluting the black vote in advance. This is just as impermissible an objective as the dilution of present black voting strength. The New York City Board of Estimate is a body with power relating to, among other things, city contracts, property, and finances. It is composed of eight members, each of whom serves by virtue of other elective office. The board's membership includes the New York City mayor, city counsel president, and city comptroller. All of these persons hold their positions by citywide election. The five other members of the board are the borough presidents elected, respectively, by residents of the Bronx, Brooklyn, Manhattan, Staten Island, and Queens. The board does not establish the city's budget, but does participate with the city council in its preparation. On such matters as contracting, city property use, and franchising, the board has exclusive power. For issues of exclusive jurisdiction, the mayor, city council president, and comptroller have two votes each. The five borough presidents have only one vote each. Thus if the three citywide members vote together, they have a majority regardless of what the borough presidents do. On matters relating to the budget, however, the mayor cannot vote. The consequence in this instance is that a coalition of borough presidents can always control budget issues. In *New York City Board of Estimate v. Morris* (103 L. Ed. 2d 717: 1989), the Court was asked to determine if the one person, one vote rule applied to this board. The contention of the challengers was that the five boroughs were equally represented on the board despite disparate borough populations. The Court ruled that the selection methods used for board membership were local elections and subject to operative reapportionment requirements. The Court further endorsed a population-based methodology for the computation of deviations modified to take into account that voters in each borough vote for and are represented by both their borough president and citywide members. Finally, a provision of the Missouri Constitution authorized creation of a board empowered to reorganize city and county governments in Saint Louis. The constitutional provision limited membership on the board to "freeholders," owners of real estate. The restriction was challenged as a violation of equal protection. A unanimous U.S. Supreme Court held the board of freeholders was not exempt from the reach of the Equal Protection Clause. The clause "protects the right to be considered for public service without the burden of individually discriminatory disqualifications." Membership on the board of freeholders was viewed as a form of public service even though the board did not enact laws directly. The Court then considered whether the land ownership requirement could withstand equal protection scrutiny, and ruled the requirement was a form of invidious discrimination even using the least demanding rational basis test. Missouri sought to defend the policy on the ground that property owners have a "firsthand knowledge" of schools, sewer systems, and other "amenities of urban life." The Court dismissed this argument, saying the ability to understand issues affecting one's community "does not depend on ownership of real property." Second, Missouri contended that a real property owner had a "tangible stake" in the future of the community. The Court rejected the argument that property ownership alone demonstrates such an "attachment" to a community as to serve as the sole condition of service on the board.

Illegitimacy

Weber v. Aetna Casualty and Surety Company, **406 U.S. 164, 92 S. Ct. 1400, 31 L. Ed. 2d 768 (1972)**   Struck down a state classification based on legitimacy as a violation of the Equal Protection Clause. *Weber v. Aetna Casualty and Surety Company* examined the classification of illegitimacy and held that a state handling claims for worker's compensation benefits may not disadvantage the unacknowledged illegitimate child of a deceased worker. Henry Stokes had died from employment-related injuries. At the time of his death, Stokes was living with four legitimate minor children, one unacknowledged minor, and Willie Mae Weber, the mother of the unacknowledged minor. Stokes's wife had been committed to a mental institution prior to his death. After Stokes's death, a second illegitimate child of Stokes and Weber was born. The Louisiana worker's compensation law placed unacknowledged illegitimate children in a class of "other dependents," a class of lower status than that of "children." The "other dependents" class may recover worker's compensation benefits only if the higher class of survivors does not exhaust the maximum benefits. The four legitimate offspring of Stokes were awarded the statutory maximum, leaving nothing to the two unacknowledged illegitimate children. In an 8–1 decision, the Supreme Court said this statutory scheme violated the Equal Protection Clause. Justice Powell's opinion declared the statute to be unacceptable even though it was limited to unacknowledged illegitimate children and did not prohibit recovery altogether. The less favorable position into which the unacknowledged illegitimate child was placed was said to be fatal because "such a child may suffer as much from the loss of a parent as a child born within wedlock or any illegitimate later acknowledged." Louisiana law precluded acknowledgment of the illegitimate child even if the father had wished to do so. Justice Powell observed that "the burdens of illegitimacy, already weighty, become doubly so when neither parent nor child can legally lighten them." He suggested the Court's inquiry into such cases turned on two questions: What legitimate state interest does the classification promote? and What fundamental personal rights might the classification endanger? The Court did not take issue with Louisiana's interest in protecting legitimate family relationships, but it did not feel the challenged statute promoted that interest. "Persons will not shun illicit relations because their offspring may not one day reap the benefits of workmen's compensation." While illegitimacy has been socially condemned through the ages, Justice Powell thought that visiting this condemnation on the head of an infant was illogical and unjust. Penalizing the illegitimate child is simply an ineffectual way of deterring the parent. Justice Rehnquist felt the Court was engaged in a highly subjective review of what constituted legitimate state interests and how those interests might be advanced in relation to fundamental person rights. He would have deferred to Louisiana's distinction between legitimate and unacknowledged illegitimate children. *See also* FOURTEENTH AMENDMENT, p. 412; RIGHT OF PRIVACY, p. 316.

Significance   *Weber v. Aetna Casualty and Surety Company* (406 U.S. 164: 1972) said that a state could not deny equal benefit recovery opportunities to unacknowledged illegitimate children. But the Supreme Court has never been able to determine conclusively the exact character of illegitimacy as a classification or the level of scrutiny it deserves. The Court has scrutinized the problem more closely than the rationality test would require, but it has never found illegitimacy to be a suspect class deserving the strictest scrutiny. Examples of the Court's crisscrossing path in dealing with this classification follow. In *Levy v. Louisiana* (391 U.S. 68: 1968), the Court struck down a law that denied unacknowledged illegitimate children opportunity to recover wrongful death damages for their mothers. The statute was viewed as sufficiently arbitrary that impermissible discrimination could be found by use of standards less demanding than strict scrutiny. In *Labine v. Vincent* (401 U.S. 532: 1972), however, the Court upheld a state succession law that denied illegitimate children inheritance rights equal to those of legitimate children. The Court said a state had the power to protect and strengthen family life as well as to regulate the disposition of property. *Weber* was next in sequence and resembled more closely the approach taken in *Levy*. *Matthews v. Lucas* (427 U.S. 495: 1976) then held that a requirement demanding proof of dependency by illegitimate children seeking social security death benefits was a rational means of protecting against survivor benefits being paid to children who were not dependent. The Court noted in *Lucas* that statutory classifications based on illegitimacy fall into "a realm of less than strict scrutiny." Claiming that such less-than-strict scrutiny was not "toothless," the Court a year later struck down an Illinois statute that precluded illegitimate children from inheriting property from their fathers in *Trimble v. Gordon* (430 U.S. 762: 1977). Using a rationale closely resembling that of *Weber*, the Court found the classification too remote from a legitimate state purpose to pass review. The issue before the Court in *Clark v. Jeter* (486 U.S. 456: 1988) was whether a state's statute of limitations on commencing paternity actions violates the Equal Protection Clause. Clark filed a paternity suit against Jeter ten years after the birth of her illegitimate daughter. Although blood tests conclusively showed Jeter to be the father, judgment was entered on his behalf because state law required that support complaints be filed within six years of the child's birth. The Court struck down the six-year limit. The period for obtaining child support, said the Court, must be "sufficiently long" to offer a "reasonable opportunity" for claims to be filed on behalf of the illegitimate children. If a limitation is placed on that opportunity, it must be "substantially related" to the state's interest in avoiding litigation of "stale or fraudulent claims." The Court concluded that it was "questionable" that the six-year time period was either reasonable or substantially related to an interest in avoiding litigation of stale or fraudulent claims.

Gender: Employment

California Federal Savings and Loan Association v. Guerra, **479 U.S. 272, 107 S. Ct. 683, 93 L. Ed. 2d 613 (1987)**   Upheld a state law requiring employers to grant maternity leave and job reinstatement to women employees. California Federal Savings and Loan (Cal Fed) refused to reinstate Lillian Garland following her pregnancy disability leave. Garland then sought to invoke state law by filing a complaint with the state agency authorized to enforce the law. Cal Fed brought action in U.S. district court, claiming the state law was inconsistent with and preempted by Title VII of the Civil Rights Act of 1964 as amended by the Pregnancy Disability Act of 1978 (PDA). The PDA declared that discrimination on the basis of pregnancy constituted illegal gender discrimination. The PDA also required that pregnant women be treated the same as any other disabled employee. Cal Fed asserted that the PDA therefore prohibited the preferential treatment of pregnant women. The trial court granted summary judgment for Cal Fed, but the court of appeals reversed. The Supreme Court also ruled against Cal Fed in a 6–3 decision. The opinion of the Court was delivered by Justice Marshall. The question presented in the case was whether Title VII, as amended by the PDA, preempted California law. In making such a determination the Court's task was to ascertain the intent of Congress. Federal law may supersede state law by stating so in express terms or where the scheme of federal regulation is sufficiently comprehensive to support the inference that Congress left no room for supplementary state regulation. A third alternative in areas where Congress has not completely displaced state regulation is where federal law may preempt state law to the extent it actually conflicts with federal law. This basis for preemption was involved in *Guerra.* Upon examination of the Civil Rights Act of 1964, the Court found that the preemptive effect of Title VII was narrow in scope and severely limited. The Court said this reflected the importance

Congress attached to state antidiscrimination laws in achieving Title VII objectives. The provisions added by the PDA accomplished the same purpose. The PDA was intended to illustrate how discrimination against pregnancy is to be remedied. Congress intended the PDA to be a "floor beneath which pregnancy disability benefits may not drop—not a ceiling above which they may not rise." In addition, the Court found it significant that Congress was aware of state laws similar to California's, but apparently did not consider them inconsistent with the PDA. In the Court's view, Title VII as amended by the PDA and California's pregnancy disability leave statute shared a common goal. Both sought to promote equal employment opportunity. By requiring reinstatement after pregnancy leave, the California law ensures that women will not lose their jobs because of pregnancy disability. By taking pregnancy into account, California's leave statute allows both men and women to have families without losing their jobs. The state law does not compel employers to treat pregnant workers better than other disabled employees. Rather, it establishes benefits that employers must, at a minimum, provide to pregnant workers. Chief Justice Rehnquist and Justices White and Powell dissented. They felt that Title VII clearly prohibited the preferential treatment of pregnant workers. In their view the California law was necessarily preempted. *See also* CIVIL RIGHTS ACT OF 1964, p. 393; JUDICIAL REVIEW, p. 429; PREEMPTION DOCTRINE, p. 443.

Significance   The Court upheld a state law that required employers to provide unpaid pregnancy leave and reinstatement in *California Federal Savings and Loan Association v. Guerra* (479 U.S. 272: 1987). The case hinged on whether the law gave pregnant women preferential treatment in violation of the provisions of Title VII of the Civil Rights Act of 1964 as amended by the Pregnancy Disability Act of 1978. If the state statute was in conflict with the federal law, it would be invalidated by application of the preemption doctrine, a rule grounded in the Supremacy Clause of Article VI. The Court concluded that there was no substantive conflict between the state law and the federal enactments, thus the doctrine was inapplicable. The *Guerra* decision also broadened the scope of protections available to pregnant employees. Pregnancy as an employment disability has not always fared so well. In *Geduldig v. Aiello* (417 U.S. 484: 1974), for example, the Court allowed a state disability insurance program to exempt coverage of wage losses for normal pregnancies. Rather than finding impermissible gender classification, the Court held that the relevant classes were divided on the basis of pregnancy, and the nonpregnant class consisted of both men and women. Two years later the Court upheld an employee benefit plan that excluded from its coverage pregnancy-related disabilities in *General Electric Company v. Gilbert* (429 U.S. 125: 1976). The *Gilbert* decision prompted Congress to enact the PDA. Indeed, as Justice Marshall said in *Guerra,* when Congress amended Title VII with the PDA, it "unambiguously expressed its disapproval of both the holding and the reasoning of the Court in the *Gilbert* decision." *Guerra* seems compatible with the sentiments of Congress as embodied in the 1978 amendments. In addition to approving state initiatives on the matter of leave and reinstatement rights in connection with pregnancy, the *Guerra* decision enhances the likelihood of federal legislation similar to that of the California statute reviewed in this case. The 1986–87 term also produced a decision less favorable to the interests of pregnant employees. In *Wimberly v. Labor and Industrial Relations Commission of Missouri* (479 U.S. 511: 1987), the Court unanimously held that states may deny unemployment benefits to women who left their jobs because of pregnancy as long as the state disqualified "all persons who leave for reasons not causally connected to the work." For a state to apply such a law, it is not necessary to know that the employee left because of pregnancy. All that is relevant is that she stopped work for a reason bearing no causal connection to her work or her employer. Coupled with the *Guerra* decision, *Wimberly* gives the states a great deal of discretion in establishing policy about how pregnancy is to be managed in the workplace.

In *Roberts v. United States Jaycees* (468 U.S. 609: 1984), the Court upheld the application of a state antidiscrimination law that forced an organization to accept women into its membership. The Court found that the state's interest in promoting gender equality prevailed over the organization's expression and association interests. In a decision similar to *Roberts,* the Court upheld a state law that required all-male, nonprofit clubs to admit women to membership in *Board of Directors of Rotary International v. Rotary Club of Duarte* (479 U.S. 929: 1986). The Court ruled that application of the state law was appropriate and did not interfere with the freedom of private association. Constitutional protection is afforded only those associations that are sufficiently intimate or private. A number of factors are germane in determining whether a particular association warrants protection, including organization size, purpose, selectivity, and whether others are excluded from critical aspects of the relationship. Rotary clubs were found not to qualify for protection because of their potentially large size, their high membership turnover, the inclusive nature of club membership, the public character of their service activities, and the encouragement of nonmember participation and media coverage of their activities. The Court also concluded that even if there were some slight infringement on the association rights of members, such an infringement is justified by the state's compelling interest in eliminating discrimination against women and in assuring them equal access to public accommodations, as well as the acquisition of leadership skills and business contacts. The balance between regulations designed to combat discrimination and the associational rights of private clubs was again considered in *New York State Club Association, Inc. v. City of New York* (487 U.S. 1: 1988). New York adopted a human rights law in 1965 that prohibited discrimination of virtually all kinds. The law specifically exempted clubs and institutions of a "distinctly private" nature. A 1984 amendment to the law known as Local Law 63 provided that a club shall not be considered "distinctly private" and therefore exempt from the original law if it has "more than four hundred members, provides regular meal service and regularly receives payment . . . directly or indirectly from or on behalf of non-members for the furtherance of trade or business." Benevolent orders and religious corporations were not included in the narrowed exemption language of the 1984 amendment. The New York State Club Association, a nonprofit consortium of private clubs and associations, facially challenged the amendments on First and Fourteenth Amendment grounds but was unsuccessful. A unanimous Supreme Court also upheld the constitutionality of the amended law. A number of the large clubs were clearly subject to antidiscrimination regulation under the holding in *Roberts*. The Court did not find any infringement on club members' rights. Absent evidence demonstrating special circumstances, the Court was satisfied that large clubs could "effectively advance their desired viewpoints without confining their memberships to persons having the same sex, for example, or the same religion." Neither was there evidence to demonstrate that the law actually impaired the "ability to associate or to advocate public or private viewpoints." Finally, the Court rejected the facial equal protection challenge aimed at the exemption extended to benevolent orders and religious organizations. The Court said that the city council could have reasonably distinguished among the groups "in the crucial respect of whether business activity is prevalent among them." Local Law 63 reflects a legislative judgment that benevolent orders and religious corporations are "unique," a finding that provides a rational basis for their exemption. The Court concluded that the association had not shown such a judgment to be erroneous.

County of Washington v. Gunther, 450 U.S. 907, 101 S. Ct. 2242, 68 L. Ed. 2d 751 (1981) Held that Title VII of the Civil Rights Act of 1964 covered more than equal pay for equal work claims. *County of Washington v. Gunther* allowed the Court to clarify the relationship between two federal enactments treating sex-based wage discrimination. Title VII barred employment discrimination. The Equal Pay Act of 1963 prohibited wage differentials based on sex for persons performing equivalent work. Title VII contained a reference to the Equal Pay Act through a provision of the Bennett Amendment, which exempted from the Equal Pay Act differences in wages stemming from seniority, merit, or work quantity. The question in *Gunther* was whether or not the Bennett Amendment made Title VII and the Equal Pay Act coextensive relative to wage discrimination, or whether Title VII provided broader protection than situations in which unequal pay for equal work were involved. Gunther, a female guard at a county jail, brought suit under Title VII claiming wage disparity between male and female guards for substantially similar, but not identical, work. In a 5–4 decision, the Court ruled that the Bennett Amendment permitted Title VII litigation to go beyond equal pay for equal work claims. Justice Brennan's opinion stressed that the objective of the Bennett Amendment was to make the two statutes compatible by specifying some affirmative defenses that would apply in situations where pay disparities existed for equal work. To confine Title VII to the equal work standard of the Equal Pay Act would mean that a woman who is discriminatorily underpaid could obtain no relief, no matter how egregious the discrimination might be, unless her employer also employed a man in an equal job in the same establishment at a higher rate of pay. The majority rejected the view that Congress had intended the Bennett Amendment "to insulate such blatantly discriminatory practices from judicial redress under Title VII." Rather, Title VII was used by Congress "to strike at the entire spectrum of disparate treatment of men and women resulting from sex stereotypes." Chief Justice Burger and Justices Stewart and Powell joined in a vigorous dissent written by Justice Rehnquist. The dissenters felt the intent of Congress in Title VII was that claims of gender-based wage discrimination were contingent on a showing of equal work. The minority was highly critical of the majority's judicial activism. Rehnquist said the Court's decision was based on the majority's "unshakable belief that any other result would be unsound public policy." He charged that the Court "is obviously more interested in the consequences of its decision than in discerning the intention of Congress," and that the Court "relies wholly on what it believes Congress should have enacted." The decision was "simply a case where the Court superimposed on Title VII a gloss of its own choosing." *See also* CIVIL RIGHTS ACT OF 1964, p. 393; EQUAL PROTECTION CLAUSE, p. 313; *FRONTIERO v. RICHARDSON* (411 U.S. 677: 1973), p. 359; *ROSTKER v. GOLDBERG* (453 U.S. 57: 1981), p. 361.

Significance   *County of Washington v. Gunther* (450 U.S. 907: 1981) held that Title VII challenges of sex-based wage discrimination are not limited to claims of unequal pay for equal work. While the Court explicitly said that its decision did not embrace the comparable worth concept, *Gunther* did mean that women bringing wage discrimination suits need only show that gender was used in a discriminatory fashion in setting rate of pay. *Gunther* also reflected the broadening view of the Burger Court about what constitutes sex discrimination. In *Geduldig v. Aiello* (417 U.S. 484: 1974), the Court had allowed a state disability insurance program to exempt coverage of wage losses from normal pregnancies. Rather than finding a classification by gender, the Court held that the two classes were divided on the basis of pregnancy, and the nonpregnant class consisted of both men and women. Three subsequent cases, however, found the Court moving away from the *Geduldig* position. In *Newport News Shipbuilding and Dry Dock Company v. Equal Employment Opportunity Commission* (462 U.S. 669: 1983), the Court struck down a health plan that did not provide the same pregnancy coverage for the wives of male employees as it provided for female employees. In *Los Angeles Department of Water and Power v. Manhart* (435 U.S. 702: 1978), the Court held that requiring female employees to make higher contributions to retirement programs than men violated Title VII despite the statistical probability that a woman would collect more retirement benefits because of greater longevity. The counterpart to *Manhart* came in *Arizona Governing Committee for Tax Deferred Annuity and Deferred Compensation Plans v. Norris* (463 U.S. 1073: 1983), in which the Court invalidated an employer-sponsored retirement plan that provided smaller benefits to women by using sex-based actuarial tables reflecting greater longevity for women. The Court said the classification of employees on the basis of sex was no more permissible at the payout stage of a retirement plan than at the stage when the money was paid in. In *Hishon v. King & Spalding* (467 U.S. 69: 1984), the Court unanimously held that law firms may not discriminate on the basis of gender in making decisions on promotion to partnership. The Court rejected two arguments advanced by the law firm. First, the firm contended that such promotion decisions were exempt from the job discrimination provisions of Title VII. Second, the firm maintained that the right of association insulated partnership decisions. The Court disagreed on both points. A similar decision came in *Price Waterhouse v. Hopkins* (490 U.S. 228: 1989). Hopkins was an officer in an office of Price Waterhouse, a national accounting firm. She was proposed for partnership, but the decision was postponed for a year. At the end of the year, her partnership was never reconsidered. She resigned the firm and filed suit under Title VII of the Civil Rights Act of 1964, claiming gender discrimination. The Supreme Court ruled that Price Waterhouse bore the burden of proof, but need only prove its case by a preponderance of the evidence. Title VII, said the Court, "eliminates certain bases for distinguishing among employees while otherwise preserving employers' freedom of choice." This "balance" of employee rights and employer prerogatives "turns out to be decisive" in this case. While an employer may not take gender into account in making employment decisions, the employer must be "free to decide against a woman for other reasons." Accordingly, once a plaintiff in a Title VII action "shows that gender played a motivating part" in a decision, the defendant "may avoid a finding of liability only by proving that it would have made the same decision even if it had not allowed gender to play such a role." This "balance of burden," said the Court, is the "direct result of Title VII's balance of rights." As to the standard of proof, the Court said it was "persuaded" that the preponderance of evidence standard was more appropriate than the "clear and convincing standard." The issue before the Court in *Lorance v. AT&T Technologies, Inc.* (104 L. Ed. 2d 961: 1989) was the timing of job discrimination actions under Title VII. Prior to the collective bargaining agreements of 1979, seniority at AT&T Technologies was based on plantwide service and could be transferred upon promotion to other positions. Lorance and several other women were promoted to the more skilled position of "tester." The 1979 agreements entered subsequent to Lorance's promotion provided that seniority in tester positions was dependent exclusively on time as a tester. The women, all of whom were promoted between 1978 and 1980, were notified of work force reductions requiring their demotions in 1982. They were demoted because they were least senior under the new seniority rules, but would not have been least senior if their years of plantwide service had been considered. The women filed charges contending that the new system was adopted to protect incumbent male testers. The Supreme Court ruled that the 300-day filing limitation for Title VII actions dates from the adoption of the discriminatory system, not from when its effects become manifest. The Court said that a seniority system, even one that has a disparate impact on male and female employees, must also have a "discriminatory purpose." On its face, the new agreement was not discriminatory as it did not "treat similarly situated people differently." The basis of the claim was that it was an attempt to protect male employees by an intentional change in the seniority rules. In other words, the women claimed "intentionally discriminatory alteration of their contract rights." This change took place with the adoption of the new system in 1979. Accordingly, the limitations period "commenced at that point."

Finally, the Court held in *University of Pennsylvania v. Equal Employment Opportunity Commission* (107 L. Ed. 2d 571: 1990) that universities can be compelled to disclose previously confidential peer reviews in cases where discrimination is charged in the making of tenure and promotion decisions. Title VII of the Civil Rights Act of 1964 prohibited employment discrimination and empowered the Equal Employment Opportunity Commission (EEOC) to investigate claims of such discrimination. The EEOC was given the power to subpoena needed documents as part of its enforcement authority. Here, the EEOC requested materials relating to an allegedly discriminatory tenure decision. The Court unanimously declined to protect the peer review process. The Court said that the process is not entitled to privileged status unless it "promotes sufficiently important interests to outweigh the need for probative evidence." Justice Blackmun, speaking for the Court, noted a particular reluctance to recognize a privilege in an area where Congress itself had thoroughly considered the possibility and chosen against it. He referred to congressional judgment to extend Title VII to educational institutions and provide the EEOC with broad subpoena power. The Court agreed that the role of universities is significant and that confidentiality is important to the peer review process. The "costs that ensue from disclosure, however, constitute only one side of the balance." The cost associated with racial and gender discrimination "is a great if not compelling governmental interest." Often, peer review documents are indispensable in determining the presence of illegal discrimination. "Indeed, if there is a 'smoking gun' to be found that demonstrates discrimination in tenure decisions, it is likely to be tucked away in peer review files."

Handicapped

***Massachusetts Board of Retirement v. Murgia*, 427 U.S. 307, 96 S. Ct. 2562, 49 L. Ed. 2d 520 (1976)** Upheld a mandatory retirement age of 50 for uniformed police officers against Fourteenth Amendment challenge. *Massachusetts Board of Retirement v. Murgia* illustrates the rationality test for invalidating classifications. In reviewing challenged classification schemes, the Supreme Court has used different evaluative criteria or standards, the least stringent of which is the rationality test. It would invalidate classifications only if they are arbitrary and have no demonstrable justification. The rationality test is typically used in reviewing age-based classifications. In *Murgia*, a provision of state law required that uniformed state police officers retire at age 50. Key to the Court's holding in this case were the criteria used to assess the mandatory retirement policy. Murgia argued that the age classification was a "suspect class" and entitled to a "strict scrutiny" review, a more stringent review than that associated with the rationality test. The Court disagreed and held that Murgia did not belong to a suspect class. His claim could be reviewed using the rationality test. In a 7–1 decision (Justice Stevens not participating), the Court upheld the mandatory retirement law and determined that the strict scrutiny approach should be used only when the classification impermissibly interferes with the exercise of a fundamental right or operates to the particular disadvantage of a suspect class. In the Court's view the Massachusetts policy involved neither situation. The Court proceeded using the rationality standard, a relatively relaxed test reflecting the Court's awareness that the drawing of lines creating distinctions is peculiarly and unavoidably a legislative task. The legislature's actions are presumed to be valid under this approach, and "perfection in making the necessary classification is neither possible nor necessary." In this instance, the legislature sought "to protect the public by assuring the physical preparedness of its uniformed police." Given the fact that physical ability generally declines with age, the Court found the mandatory retirement policy rationally related to the state's objective. The Court concluded by saying the choice of policy by Massachusetts may not be the best means, nor that a more just and humane system could not be devised, but under the rationality test the enactment did not deny equal protection. Justice Marshall dissented from the use of the less demanding test because of its failure to safeguard equal protection interests sufficiently. He would have preferred a flexible standard that would have examined more carefully the means chosen by Massachusetts. To Justice Marshall, the means chosen "forced retirement of officers at age 50 and is therefore so overinclusive that it must fall." *See also* CLASSIFICATION, p. 394; EQUAL PROTECTION CLAUSE, p. 313; FOURTEENTH AMENDMENT, p. 412.

Significance   *Massachusetts Board of Retirement v. Murgia* (427 U.S. 307: 1976) stated that a mandatory retirement policy for uniformed police officers was rational. Soon after *Murgia*, the Court upheld a mandatory retirement policy for Foreign Service officers in *Vance v. Bradley* (440 U.S. 93: 1979). Again the Court found a retirement policy rationally related to the legislative goal of assuring the professional capacity of persons holding critical public service positions. In this case, Foreign Service officers have to undergo special rigors associated with overseas duty. Justice Marshall dissented and reiterated his call for a more demanding standard in reviewing such legislation. Not all age discrimination suits have been unsuccessful, however. In *Trans World Airlines, Inc. v. Thurston* (469 U.S. 111: 1984), the Court unanimously held that an airline's policy of not permitting the automatic transfer of age-disqualified captains to other positions with the company was a violation of the Age Discrimination in Employment Act of 1967. The *Thurston* decision was soon followed by two other important rulings on the same federal law. In *Western Air Lines, Inc. v. Criswell* (472 U.S. 400: 1985), the Court unanimously held that an airline could not require mandatory retirement of flight engineers at age 60. Unlike the situation of pilots and copilots, where age was considered a bona fide occupational qualification, the Court felt that flight engineers could be individually assessed rather than subjected to blanket early retirement rules. In *Johnson v. Mayor and City Council of Baltimore* (472 U.S. 353: 1985), a unanimous Court refused to permit a municipality to require mandatory retirement of fire fighters at age 55. Key to this decision was the Court's rejection of Baltimore's contention that Congress had approved mandatory retirement when it retained such a policy for federal fire fighters at the time it amended the statute in 1978. The Court held that retention of the provision was only for expediency and did not reflect a legislative judgment that youth was a bona fide qualification for the job. In *Equal Employment Opportunity Commission v. Wyoming* (460 U.S. 226: 1983), the Court ruled that state and local governments are not immune from provisions of the Age Discrimination in Employment Act. The act prohibits employer discrimination against any employee or potential employee because of age. The Court made it clear, however, that the judgment did not compel a state to abandon policies that can demonstrate age as a bona fide occupational qualification. Central to the decisions in both *Murgia* and *Bradley* was the holding that compulsory retirement would better ensure good job performance by limiting the age of employees. Both cases sought to maximize the physical capabilities of persons performing certain functions.

The question of physical qualifications for professional training programs was addressed in *Southeastern Community College v. Davis* (440 U.S. 979: 1979). Davis sought admission to a registered nursing program at a state community college despite a hearing disability. She was denied admission. She filed suit under the Rehabilitation Act of 1973, which prohibits discrimination against "an otherwise qualified handicapped person, solely by reason of his handicap." The Court unanimously held that an educational institution may impose reasonable physical qualifications for admission to a clinical training program. The Court did not require the college to make program adjustments to accommodate handicapped persons. The Court ruled in *School Board of Nassau County v. Arline* (480 U.S. 273: 1987) that the Rehabilitation Act also prohibits discrimination against persons with contagious diseases. The act provides that no otherwise qualified person shall be excluded from participation in any program receiving federal funding solely by reason of his or her handicap. Among the several ways a handicapped person is defined in the act is as one who has a record of impairment that substantially limits one or more major life activities. Subsequent administrative regulations have included work as a major life activity. Arline, a teacher, had been hospitalized for tuberculosis in 1957 before the disease went into remission. In 1977 and 1978 Arline suffered relapses and was suspended with pay at the end of the school year. She was then discharged because of the continued recurrence of the disease. Failing to obtain relief from state administrative agencies, Arline commenced action in federal court under the Rehabilitation Act. The Supreme Court concluded that Arline had established a record of impairment from the point of her initial hospitalization. The school district argued, however, that this fact was irrelevant since Arline was dismissed not because of diminished physical capabilities, but because of the threat her relapse posed to others. The Court rejected the contention that the contagious effects of Arline's tuberculosis could be meaningfully distinguished from the disease's physical effects. Arline's contagiousness and her impairment were both caused by her disease. It would be unfair to allow an employer to seize upon the distinction between the effects of a disease on others and the effects of a disease on a patient and use that distinction to justify discriminatory treatment. Allowing discrimination based on the contagious effects of an impairment would be inconsistent with the meaning of the act. The purpose of the act was to protect the handicapped from denial of employment or other benefits because of the prejudiced attitudes or ignorance of others. By broadly defining *handicapped persons,* Congress was acknowledging that "society's accumulated myths and fears about disability and disease are as handicapping as the physical limitations that flow from the actual impairment." The fact that some persons who have contagious diseases may pose a serious health threat to others does not justify excluding all persons with actual or perceived contagious diseases. The *Arline* case had generated some public interest because of its implications for persons with AIDS. Justice Brennan's opinion did not discuss AIDS, but two footnotes made reference to it. One responded to the contention that some carriers of a disease may not suffer any physical impairment, as in the case of AIDS. Accordingly, discrimination solely on the basis of contagiousness cannot be handicap discrimination. Justice Brennan said *Arline* did not require the Court to consider whether the carrier of a contagious disease such as AIDS could be considered to have a physical impairment because Arline's tuberculosis produced impairment independent from contagiousness. A second footnote indicated that a person who poses a significant risk of communicating an infectious disease to others in the workplace is not otherwise qualified for his or her job if reasonable accommodation will not eliminate that risk.

Irrebuttable Presumptions

Vlandis v. Kline, **412 U.S. 441, 93 S. Ct. 2230, 37 L. Ed. 2d 63 (1973)** Invalidated a classification based on residency because it constituted an irrebuttable presumption. *Vlandis v. Kline* examines whether equal protection issues may be assessed by using a framework in which a classification is permitted to exist, while those affected by the classification are prohibited from disputing their status. In *Vlandis,* the Court struck down an irrebuttable presumption. Connecticut required nonresident state university students to pay higher tuition and higher fees than state residents. If the legal address of a married student was outside the state at the time of application for admission to the university, such a person would forever remain a nonresident student. Similarly, if an unmarried person had a legal address outside Connecticut at any time during the year prior to seeking university admission, that person would permanently and irrebuttably retain nonresident status. At issue in the case was not the residency classification per se, but rather the "conclusive and unchangeable presumption" attached to it. Kline and others claimed that they had a constitutional right to controvert that presumption of nonresident by presenting evidence that they were bona fide residents. Connecticut sought to justify the presumption through its interest in equalizing the cost of public higher education between state residents and nonresidents. The Court ruled that rather than ensuring that only its bona fide residents receive their full subsidy, the Connecticut presumption also ensured that some bona fide residents, like Kline, do *not* receive their full subsidy. They can never do so while they remain students. The Court also refused to allow Connecticut to turn its classification into a policy that "favors with the lower rate only its established residents, whose past tax contributions to the State have been higher," because the statutory provisions are "so arbitrary as to constitute a denial of due process of law." Finally, the Court rejected Connecticut's justification of administrative convenience and certainty. Such an interest "cannot save the conclusive presumption from invalidity where there are other reasonable and practicable means of establishing the pertinent facts on which the State's objective is premised." Thus *Vlandis* held that irrebuttable presumptions are prohibited when the presumption is not necessarily or universally true, and when there are reasonable alternative means of making the crucial determination. Chief Justice Burger and Justices Rehnquist and Douglas dissented, taking issue with application of the language of strict scrutiny to a Due Process Clause issue. The dissenters also felt Connecticut was free to pursue a policy that favored established state residents. *See also* EQUAL PROTECTION CLAUSE, p. 313; IRREBUTTABLE PRESUMPTION, p. 427; *MASSACHUSETTS BOARD OF RETIREMENT v. MURGIA* (427 U.S. 307: 1976), p. 355.

Significance   *Vlandis v. Kline* (412 U.S. 441: 1973) struck down a state residency requirement because it was based on a conclusive or irrebuttable presumption. A provision of the Food Stamp Act was likewise invalidated in *United States Department of Agriculture v. Murry* (413 U.S. 508: 1974). The act withheld food stamp eligibility from households with an 18-year-old "who is claimed as a dependent child for Federal tax purposes by a taxpayer who is not a member of an eligible household." The Court ruled that the provision created a conclusive presumption that such a household was not in need, and that the presumption was not a rational measure of need. In *Cleveland Board of Education v. LaFleur* (414 U.S. 632: 1974), the Court struck down a requirement that teachers take an unpaid leave at least five months prior to their child's expected date of birth and not return to work until the semester following the child's attaining an age of three months. The Court noted the failure of the regulation to make individual determinations of a teacher's capacity to continue teaching. The rule served no legitimate purpose, and it unnecessarily penalized the female teacher for asserting her right to bear children. An irrebuttable presumption is not categorically prohibited, however. In *Weinberger v. Salfi* (422 U.S. 749: 1975), the Court upheld a duration-of-relationship requirement for survivor benefits under social security. By law, benefits are denied to wives and stepchildren in cases where the marriage occurred less than nine months prior to the death of the wage earner. The Court ruled that Congress could reasonably conclude that a broad prophylactic rule could protect against the possibility of persons entering marriages simply to claim benefits upon the anticipated early death of the wage earner. The restriction also obviated the necessity for large numbers of individual determinations. Further, it protected large numbers of claimants who satisfy the rule from the uncertainties and delays of administrative inquiry into the circumstances of their marriages. In *Massachusetts Board of Retirement v. Murgia* (427 U.S. 307: 1976), the Court upheld a mandatory retirement age against arguments that individual fitness determinations were a more reasonable approach.

A slightly different kind of presumption was reviewed in *Michael H. and Victoria D. v. Gerald D.* (105 L. Ed. 2d 91: 1989). Under provisions of California law, a child born to a married woman living with her husband, absent a showing of sterility, is conclusively presumed to be an issue of the marriage. The statute permitted only limited rebuttal to this presumption and only by the husband or wife. A challenge to the law was brought by a man (Michael H.) who fathered a child (Victoria D.) during an affair with a married woman (Carole D.) who, at the time of the affair, was separated from her husband (Gerald D.). The husband and wife later reconciled. Test results demonstrated to a certainty in excess of 98 percent that the plaintiff (Michael H.) was the child's father. The law was also challenged on behalf of the child, who wished a filial relationship with both Michael and Gerald. The Court rejected Michael's procedural due process claims because they were based on a "fundamental misconception" of the statutory presumption. While phrased as a presumption, the evidentiary rule was seen as the "implementation of a substantive rule of law." The law makes "irrelevant for paternity purposes" whether a child conceived or born into an existing marriage was fathered by anyone but the husband. The presumption not only expresses substantive policy, but "furthers it, excluding inquiries into the child's paternity that would be destructive of family integrity and privacy." The Court then turned to the substantive issue, whether Michael had a constitutionally protected liberty interest in his relationship with Victoria. Michael contended that the state's interest in protecting the union of Gerald and Carole was insufficient to justify termination of his parental relationship. Considerations of substantive due process hinge on a liberty interest's being "fundamental," and on its being an interest "traditionally protected by our society." The legal issue in this case, said the Court, "reduces to whether the relationship between persons" in the situation of Michael and Victoria has been treated as a "protected family unit under the historic practices of our society," or whether on any other basis it has been accorded "special protection." The Court ruled that "it is impossible to find that it has." Indeed, the Court found the reverse to be true. Rather, "our traditions have protected the marital family against the sort of claim Michael asserts." Noted in particular was the common law presumption of legitimacy. The Court then rejected the child's due process claim as "if anything, weaker than Michael's." She had claimed the right of maintaining a legal relationship with both Michael and Gerald. The Court found that a claim that a state "must recognize multiple fatherhood has no support in the history or traditions of this country."

RIGHT OF PRIVACY

Abortion Regulation

Webster v. Reproductive Health Services, **106 L. Ed. 2d 410 (1989)** The 1988 term found the Supreme Court once again addressing the highly divisive issue of abortion. The Court's ruling in *Webster v. Reproductive Health Services* (106 L. Ed. 2d 410) provided the Court with an opportunity to reconsider fully and possibly overrule the controversial ruling of *Roe v. Wade* (410 U.S. 113: 1973). The Court rendered a decision in *Webster* that substantially modified *Roe,* but did not explicitly overrule it. The origin of the case was a Missouri statute enacted in 1986. Several components of the statute were challenged in federal court by a number of doctors and nurses and two nonprofit medical corporations, one of which was Reproductive Health Services (RHS). The challenged provisions included the following: (1) a preamble that states that life begins at conception, and that the "unborn" have life interests requiring protection; (2) a requirement that before an abortion can be performed on any woman a physician has "reason to believe" is 20 or more weeks pregnant, the physician must determine whether the fetus is "viable" by performing specified medical examinations and tests; (3) an informed-consent requirement that included information on abortion alternatives; and (4) prohibitions on use of public funds, public facilities, or public employees in "performing or assisting" an abortion. This restriction included public employees counseling pregnant women to have nontherapeutic abortions. A U.S. district court upheld only the viability testing, but in doing so eliminated many of the viability tests specified in the law. Missouri, through State Attorney General William Webster, challenged each element of the district court decision except for the portion that struck down the informed-consent requirement. The Court of Appeals for the 8th Circuit affirmed the district court, relying on *Roe v. Wade.* In a fragmented 5–4 decision, the Supreme Court allowed the restrictions, but did not explicitly reverse *Roe.* The opinion of the Court was delivered by Chief Justice Rehnquist. The Court did not rule on the preamble. The preamble was seen as an "abstract proposition" rather than an operating regulation. Since the preamble did not restrict the activities of RHS in "some concrete way," the Court concluded RHS had no standing to challenge the preamble language. This ruling was a rejection of the RHS argument that the preamble was an "operative part" of the statute intended to "guide the interpretation of other provisions of the Act." Rehnquist then turned to the ban on the use of public funds, facilities, and employees. The court of appeals had seen this regulation as possibly preventing a woman's doctor from performing an abortion if the doctor did not have privileges in another hospital. Increased costs and possible delays were also attributed to the regulation. The Supreme Court disagreed, using much of the same analysis as can be found in Medicaid cases such as *Maher v. Roe* (432 U.S. 464: 1977) and *Harris v. McRae* (448 U.S. 297: 1980). As with those cases, the Court recognized the state's decision to "encourage childbirth over abortion," and that policy preference "places no governmental obstacle in the path of a woman who chooses to terminate her pregnancy." Missouri's refusal to allow public employees to perform abortions or to allow abortions to be performed in public facilities leaves a pregnant woman "with the same choices as if the State had chosen not to operate any public hospitals at all." Having already ruled that state refusal to fund abortions (in *Maher* and *Harris*) does not violate *Roe v. Wade,* it "strains logic to reach a contrary result for the use of public facilities and employees." Rehnquist then turned to the most critical aspect of the decision, the viability testing requirements. Rehnquist said the statute required physicians to perform "only those tests that are useful to making subsidiary findings as to viability." Key, however, was the presumption of viability at 20 weeks, which must be directly rebutted by viability test results before an abortion can be performed. The *Roe v. Wade* decision is based on the concept of trimesters. Under *Roe,* the interests of the fetus are not recognized until the final trimester, which occurs about 24 weeks into the pregnancy. Specification in the Missouri law of methods for determining viability "does superimpose state regulation on the medical determination of viability." This section was struck down by the court of appeals on this basis. The Supreme Court was less convinced that the law was flawed, however. Rather, the problem, said Rehnquist, was the "rigid trimester analysis of the course of a pregnancy enunciated in *Roe.*" The "rigid *Roe* framework is hardly consistent with the notion of a Constitution cast in general terms." The Court simply should not function as the "country's ex officio medical board with powers to approve or disapprove medical and operative practices and standards." Thus the "web of legal rules" developed through application of *Roe* could be loosened. More important, the Court did not see "why the State's interest in protecting potential human life should come into existence only at the point of viability," and that there should be a "rigid line allowing state regulation after viability but prohibiting it before viability." The Court acknowledged that the tests "increase the expense of abortion and regulate the discretion of the physician in determining viability of the fetus." Nonetheless, the Court was "satisfied" that the requirement "permissibly furthers the State's interest in protecting potential human life" and is constitutional. Justice O'Connor agreed that the viability testing requirement was constitutional, but came to that conclusion because she did not see the requirement as incompatible with *Roe v. Wade.* Justice Scalia was also among the majority, but said, in his concurring opinion, that *Roe* had been effectively overruled. Indeed, he was critical of Rehnquist for not acknowledging that result. By hanging on to *Roe,* Scalia said the Court "needlessly" prolonged its "self-awarded sovereignty over a field where it has little proper business" since responses to most of the critical questions are "political and not juridical." Justices Blackmun, Brennan, Marshall, and Stevens dissented. Blackmun, the author of the *Roe v. Wade* opinion, was most outspoken in criticizing the decision. He spoke of the "feigned restraint" of the plurality opinion claim that it "leaves *Roe* undisturbed." "But this disclaimer is totally meaningless." The plurality opinion, he contended, is "filled with winks, nods, and knowing glances to those who would do away with *Roe* explicitly." Blackmun "fear[ed] for the liberty and equality of millions of women who have lived and come of age in the sixteen years since *Roe* was decided." Blackmun was very troubled by the viability testing and what it meant to the *Roe* trimester framework. He was even more troubled by Rehnquist's decision to uphold viability testing because it "permissibly furthers the State's interest in protecting potential human life." The "newly minted" standard is "circular and totally meaningless." Whether a challenged regulation "permissibly furthers" a legitimate interest is the "question that courts must answer" in abortion cases, not the "standard for courts to apply." The standard has "no independent meaning," and consists of "nothing other than what a majority of this Court may believe at any given moment in any given case." Blackmun opined that the Court had effectively overruled *Roe* when he wrote, "Thus, 'not with a bang, but with a whimper,' the plurality discards a landmark case of the last generation, and casts into darkness the hopes and visions of every woman in this country who had come to believe the Constitution guaranteed her right to exercise some control over her unique ability to bear children." Blackmun concluded, however, by saying that "for today, at least, the law of abortion stands undisturbed. For today, the women of this Nation still retain the liberty to control their destinies. But the signs are evident and very ominous, and a chill wind blows."

Significance   *Webster v. Reproductive Health Services* (106 L. Ed. 2d 410: 1989) signaled state legislatures that the Court would be receptive to additional restrictions on abortion. Three additional abortion regulation cases were docketed for the 1989–90 term. One of these cases, *Turnock v. Ragsdale* (107 L. Ed. 2d 530: 1989), was settled before argument, however. The case involved an Illinois regulation requiring that abortion clinics be equipped and staffed at levels comparable to hospital operating rooms. The regulation was challenged on the grounds that it would produce extensive increases in the cost of performing abortions, which, in turn, would effectively preclude many women from being able to obtain abortions. The state agreed to drop the regulation, but retained broad inspection authority over abortion clinics. While the Court was prevented from ruling on the substantive issue in the Illinois case, it is likely that other states will enact similar if not identical requirements in the wake of *Webster*. *Hodgson v. Minnesota* (111 L. Ed. 2d 344: 1990) and *Ohio v. Akron Center for Reproductive Services* (111 L. Ed. 2d 405: 1990) examined parental notification statutes from Minnesota and Ohio. The Minnesota statute had two key parts. First, the state required notification of both biological parents when a minor daughter sought an abortion. In a 5–4 decision, the Court struck down this requirement. The statute contained contingency language that if a court enjoined enforcement of the notification requirement, the statute would be amended automatically to provide a judicial bypass as an alternative to parental notification. This alternative allowed a minor to petition a court for permission to obtain an abortion without notifying her parents. The Court upheld this alternative, again by a 5–4 vote. Justice O'Connor provided the decisive vote in both instances. She joined Justices Marshall, Brennan, Blackmun, and Stevens in striking down the statute without judicial bypass. She was joined by Chief Justice Rehnquist and Justices Kennedy, White, and Scalia in upholding the alternative. The Ohio statute required notification of only one parent. It also contained judicial bypass language, but the Court upheld the one-parent notice requirement on its own by a 6–3 vote—Justice Stevens joining the five justices who had upheld the Minnesota alternative. The defect with the Minnesota statute absent the judicial bypass arose from the fact that only about half of Minnesota's minors reside with both biological parents. Justice Stevens spoke of the "particularly harmful effects" of the two-parent notification requirement on "both the minor and custodial parent when parents were divorced or separated." In addition, the Court concluded the requirement "does not reasonably further any legitimate state interest." The principal justification for notification is that it "supports the authority of a parent who is presumed to act in the minor's best interest and thereby assures that the minor's decision to terminate her pregnancy is knowing, intelligent, and deliberate." To the extent "such an interest is legitimate," it could be "fully served" by the notification of one parent, who can then seek counsel from the other parent or anyone else. The state has no legitimate interest in questioning the one parent's judgment on whether to seek wider counsel. The Court concluded that the two-parent requirement actually "disserves" any state interest in protecting a minor in "dysfunctional families." Two-parent notice in such situations is "positively harmful to the minor and her family." As in cases involving judicial hearings as an alternative to securing parental consent for an abortion, the Court found the bypass alternative constitutionally sufficient for notification as well. The judicial bypass feature allows a minor to demonstrate she is fully capable of making the abortion decision. The Court decided the Ohio case without actually ruling on whether the judicial bypass provision is necessary in the one-parent notice situation. Rather, it upheld the one-parent notification requirement as a "rational way" for a state to assist a pregnant minor who is considering abortion. "It would deny all dignity to the family," said Justice Kennedy, "to say that the State cannot take this reasonable step . . . to ensure that, in most cases, a young woman will receive guidance and understanding from a parent." In the Court's view, Ohio's requirement did not impose an "undue, or otherwise unconstitutional, burden on a minor seeking an abortion."

Right To Terminate Medical Treatment

***Cruzan v. Director, Missouri Department of Health*, 111 L. Ed. 2d 224 (1990)** Ruled that a person has a right to discontinue life-sustaining medical treatment. At the same time, the Court ruled 5–4 that a state can require maintenance of the treatment in the absence of "clear and convincing" evidence the person wanted the treatment stopped. Nancy Cruzan was injured in an automobile accident in 1983. Since that time, she has remained in a "persistent vegetative" state. She is administered food and water through a tube in her stomach. Cruzan's parents, acting as legal guardians, requested that the life-sustaining feedings be stopped. The hospital refused to stop the feedings, and the Cruzans initiated legal action. A state trial court found that a person had a right to refuse procedures that were "death prolonging." Cruzan, of course, was incompetent to stop the feedings herself. The issue then became whether statements uttered by Cruzan prior to the accident constituted sufficient evidence of her desire to discontinue medical treatment under the postaccident circumstances. The trial court concluded that all medical treatment should be terminated. The Missouri Supreme Court reversed, however. It ruled that Missouri's "living will" statute favored "preservation of life" in the absence of "clear and convincing" evidence for withdrawal of treatment. The "clear and convincing" standard is the highest standard of evidence used in a civil proceeding. The Missouri Supreme Court decided that Cruzan's preaccident statements were "unreliable" for determining her intent. The issue before the U.S. Supreme Court was whether the federal Constitution precludes a state "from choosing the rule of decision which it did." The Court rested its decision on Fourteenth Amendment due process grounds rather than on the right of privacy. It was the Court's view that a "competent person has a constitutionally protected liberty interest in refusing unwanted medical treatment." That, however, said Chief Justice Rehnquist, "does not end our inquiry." Whether constitutional rights have been violated requires that liberty interests be weighed against the "relevant state interests." The problem in this case was that Nancy Cruzan was herself incompetent to "make an informed and voluntary choice." Rather, the right "must be exercised for her . . . by some sort of surrogate." Missouri recognizes actions by surrogates, but also has "established a procedural safeguard to assure that the action of the surrogate conforms as best it may to the wishes expressed by the patient while competent." A five-justice majority held that Missouri's proof by clear and convincing evidence in such cases was not forbidden by the Constitution. This procedural requirement was established in furtherance of the state's interest in the "protection and preservation of human life, and there can be no gainsaying this interest." Furthermore, the state has an even "more particular interest" in situations like Cruzan's. The choice between "life and death is a deeply personal decision of obvious and overwhelming finality." Accordingly, Missouri may "legitimately seek to safeguard the personal element of this choice through the imposition of heightened evidentiary requirements." Rehnquist concluded by focusing on the issue of surrogate decision making. He did so by characterizing the Cruzans as "loving and caring parents." Were the Constitution to require states to "repose a right of 'substituted judgment' with anyone, the Cruzans would surely qualify." But, he said, the Court does not think the Fourteenth Amendment "requires the state to repose the judgment on these matters with anyone but the patient herself." Family members may possess a "strong feeling—a feeling not at all ignoble or unworthy, but not entirely disinterested, either—that they do not wish to witness the continuation of the life of a loved one which they regard as 'hopeless, meaningless, and even degrading.' But there is no automatic assurance that the view of the close family members will necessarily be the same as the patient's would have been had she been confronted with the prospect of her situation while competent." That being the case, the Court concluded that Missouri could reasonably defer to the patient's own wishes rather than those of close members by imposing a clear and convincing standard of evidence. Justices Brennan, Marshall, Blackmun, and Stevens dissented. The decision, said Brennan, "robs a patient of the very qualities protected by the right to avoid unwanted medical treatment." While the right "may not be absolute, no state interest could outweigh the rights of an individual in Nancy Cruzan's position." The state's "general interest" in life "must accede" to Nancy Cruzan's "particularized and intense interest in self-determination in her choice of medical treatment. There is simply nothing legitimately within the state's purview to be gained by superseding her decision."

Significance   *Cruzan v. Director, Missouri Department of Health* (111 L. Ed. 2d 224: 1990) was the Supreme Court's first "on the merits" response to the so-called right to die issue. In 1976 the Burger Court had declined to review the New Jersey case involving Karen Ann Quinlan. Unlike *Cruzan*, the *Quinlan* case involved discontinuation of the use of life-support machinery as opposed to discontinuing administration of food and fluids. It may prove to be of consequence that the Court in *Cruzan* did not distinguish between feeding and other kinds of medical treatment. What is clear from *Cruzan* is that persons who provide discontinuation of any form of treatment in "living wills" can effectively protect their wishes. Currently most states have living will laws, although they vary substantially. The *Cruzan* case makes it almost certain that every state will soon have such a law. Living wills convey a person's instructions on how physicians and family are to handle life-sustaining treatment decisions in the event the person becomes incapable of making those decisions. Had Nancy Cruzan documented her wishes in a living will, her treatment could have been terminated by her parents because the will would have provided a "clear and convincing" expression of her preference under the circumstances.

APPENDIX C: JUSTICES OF THE SUPREME COURT

CHIEF JUSTICES CAPITALIZED

	TENURE	APPOINTED BY	REPLACED
JOHN JAY*	1789–1795	Washington	
John Rutledge	1789–1791	Washington	
William Cushing	1789–1810	Washington	
James Wilson	1789–1798	Washington	
John Blair	1789–1796	Washington	
James Iredell	1790–1799	Washington	
Thomas Johnson	1791–1793	Washington	Rutledge
William Paterson	1793–1806	Washington	Johnson
JOHN RUTLEDGE	1795	Washington	Jay
Samuel Chase	1796–1811	Washington	Blair
OLIVER ELLSWORTH	1796–1800	Washington	Rutledge
Bushrod Washington	1798–1829	John Adams	Wilson
Alfred Moore	1799–1804	John Adams	Iredell
JOHN MARSHALL	1801–1835	John Adams	Ellsworth
William Johnson	1804–1834	Jefferson	Moore
Brockholst Livingston	1806–1823	Jefferson	Paterson
Thomas Todd	1807–1826	Jefferson	(new judgeship)
Gabriel Duval	1811–1835	Madison	Chase
Joseph Story	1811–1845	Madison	Cushing
Smith Thompson	1823–1843	Monroe	Livingston
Robert Trimble	1826–1828	John Q. Adams	Todd
John McLean	1829–1861	Jackson	Trimble
Henry Baldwin	1830–1844	Jackson	Washington
James Wayne	1835–1867	Jackson	Johnson
ROGER B. TANEY	1836–1864	Jackson	Marshall
Phillip P. Barbour	1836–1841	Jackson	Duval
John Catron	1837–1865	Jackson	(new judgeship)
John McKinley	1837–1852	Van Buren	(new judgeship)
Peter V. Daniel	1841–1860	Van Buren	Barbour
Samuel Nelson	1845–1872	Tyler	Thompson
Levi Woodbury	1846–1851	Polk	Story
Robert C. Grier	1846–1870	Polk	Baldwin
Benjamin R. Curtis	1851–1857	Fillmore	Woodbury
John A. Campbell	1853–1861	Pierce	McKinley
Nathan Clifford	1858–1881	Buchanan	Curtis
Noah H. Swayne	1862–1881	Lincoln	McLean
Samuel F. Miller	1862–1890	Lincoln	Daniel
David Davis	1862–1877	Lincoln	Campbell
Stephen J. Field	1863–1897	Lincoln	(new judgeship)
SALMON CHASE	1864–1873	Lincoln	Taney
William Strong	1870–1880	Grant	Grier
Joseph P. Bradley	1870–1892	Grant	Wayne
Ward Hunt	1872–1882	Grant	Nelson
MORRISON R. WAITE	1874–1888	Grant	Chase
John Marshall Harlan	1877–1911	Hayes	Davis
William B. Woods	1880–1887	Hayes	Strong
Stanley Matthews	1881–1889	Garfield	Swayne
Horace Gray	1881–1902	Arthur	Clifford
Samuel Blatchford	1882–1893	Arthur	Hunt
Lucius Q. C. Lamar	1888–1893	Cleveland	Woods
MELVILLE W. FULLER	1888–1910	Cleveland	Waite
David J. Brewer	1889–1910	Harrison	Matthews
Henry B. Brown	1890–1906	Harrison	Miller
George Shiras, Jr.	1892–1903	Harrison	Bradley

	TENURE	APPOINTED BY	REPLACED
Howell E. Jackson	1893–1895	Harrison	Lamar
EDWARD D. WHITE	1894–1910	Cleveland	Blatchford
Rufus W. Peckham	1895–1909	Cleveland	Jackson
Joseph McKenna	1898–1925	McKinley	Field
Oliver Wendell Holmes	1902–1932	T. Roosevelt	Gray
William R. Day	1903–1922	T. Roosevelt	Shiras
William H. Moody	1906–1910	T. Roosevelt	Brown
Horace H. Lurton	1909–1914	Taft	Peckham
Charles Evans Hughes	1910–1916	Taft	Brewer
Edward D. White	1910–1921	Taft	Fuller
Willis Van Devanter	1910–1937	Taft	White
Joseph R. Lamar	1910–1916	Taft	Moody
Mahlon Pitney	1912–1922	Taft	Harlan
James McReynolds	1914–1941	Wilson	Lurton
Louis D. Brandeis	1916–1939	Wilson	Lamar
John H. Clark	1916–1922	Wilson	Hughes
WILLIAM H. TAFT	1921–1930	Harding	White
George Sutherland	1922–1938	Harding	Clarke
Pierce Butler	1922–1939	Harding	Day
Edward T. Sanford	1923–1930	Harding	Pitney
Harlan F. Stone	1925–1941	Coolidge	McKenna
CHARLES EVANS HUGHES	1930–1941	Hoover	Taft
Owen J. Roberts	1932–1945	Hoover	Sanford
Benjamin N. Cardozo	1932–1938	Hoover	Holmes
Hugo L. Black	1937–1971	F. Roosevelt	Van Devanter
Stanley F. Reed	1938–1957	F. Roosevelt	Sutherland
Felix Frankfurter	1939–1962	F. Roosevelt	Cardozo
William O. Douglas	1939–1975	F. Roosevelt	Brandeis
Frank Murphy	1940–1949	F. Roosevelt	Butler
James F. Byrnes	1941–1942	F. Roosevelt	McReynolds
HARLAN F. STONE	1941–1946	F. Roosevelt	Hughes
Robert H. Jackson	1941–1954	F. Roosevelt	Stone
Wiley B. Rutledge	1943–1949	F. Roosevelt	Byrnes
Harold H. Burton	1945–1958	Truman	Roberts
FRED M. VINSON	1946–1953	Truman	Stone
Tom C. Clark	1949–1967	Truman	Murphy
Sherman Minton	1949–1956	Truman	Rutledge
EARL WARREN	1954–1969	Eisenhower	Vinson
John M. Harlan	1955–1971	Eisenhower	Jackson
William J. Brennan	1957–1990	Eisenhower	Minton
Charles E. Whittaker	1957–1962	Eisenhower	Reed
Potter Stewart	1959–1981	Eisenhower	Burton
Byron R. White	1962–	Kennedy	Whittaker
Arthur J. Goldberg	1962–1965	Kennedy	Frankfurter
Abe Fortas	1965–1969	Johnson	Goldberg
Thurgood Marshall	1967–	Johnson	Clark
WARREN E. BURGER	1969–1985	Nixon	Warren
Harry A. Blackmun	1970–	Nixon	Fortas
Lewis F. Powell	1971–1988	Nixon	Black
William H. Rehnquist	1971–1986	Nixon	Harlan
John P. Stephens	1975–	Ford	Douglas
Sandra Day O'Connor	1981–	Reagan	Stewart
WILLIAM H. REHNQUIST	1986–	Reagan	Burger
Antonin Scalia	1986–	Reagan	Rehnquist
Anthony M. Kennedy	1988–	Reagan	Powell
David H. Souter	1990–	Bush	Brennan

APPENDIX D: COMPOSITION OF THE SUPREME COURT SINCE 1900

The table below represents the members of the Supreme Court since 1900. By locating the term in which a particular case was decided, the names of the justices on the Court at the time of the decision may be readily determined.

THE FULLER COURT (1900–1909 terms)

1900–01	Fuller	White	Gray	Peckham	Brown	Shiras	Brewer	Harlan	McKenna
1902	Fuller	White	Holmes	Peckham	Brown	Shiras	Brewer	Harlan	McKenna
1903–05	Fuller	White	Holmes	Peckham	Brown	Day	Brewer	Harlan	McKenna
1906–08	Fuller	White	Holmes	Peckham	Moody	Day	Brewer	Harlan	McKenna
1909	Fuller	White	Holmes	Lurton	Moody	Day	Brewer	Harlan	McKenna

THE WHITE COURT (1910–1920)

1910–11	White	VanDevanter	Holmes	Lurton	Lamar	Day	Hughes	Harlan	McKenna
1912–13	White	VanDevanter	Holmes	Lurton	Lamar	Day	Hughes	Pitney	McKenna
1914–15	White	VanDevanter	Holmes	McReynolds	Lamar	Day	Hughes	Pitney	McKenna
1916–20	White	VanDevanter	Holmes	McReynolds	Brandeis	Day	Clarke	Pitney	McKenna

THE TAFT COURT (1921–1929)

1921	Taft	VanDevanter	Holmes	McReynolds	Brandeis	Day	Clarke	Pitney	McKenna
1922	Taft	VanDevanter	Holmes	McReynolds	Brandeis	Butler	Sutherland	Pitney	McKenna
1923–24	Taft	VanDevanter	Holmes	McReynolds	Brandeis	Butler	Sutherland	Sanford	McKenna
1925–29	Taft	VanDevanter	Holmes	McReynolds	Brandeis	Butler	Sutherland	Sanford	Stone

THE HUGHES COURT (1930–1940)

1930–31	Hughes	VanDevanter	Holmes	McReynolds	Brandeis	Butler	Sutherland	Roberts	Stone
1932–36	Hughes	VanDevanter	Cardozo	McReynolds	Brandeis	Butler	Sutherland	Roberts	Stone
1937	Hughes	Black	Cardozo	McReynolds	Brandeis	Butler	Sutherland	Roberts	Stone
1938	Hughes	Black	Cardozo	McReynolds	Brandeis	Butler	Reed	Roberts	Stone
1939	Hughes	Black	Frankfurter	McReynolds	Douglas	Butler	Reed	Roberts	Stone
1940	Hughes	Black	Frankfurter	McReynolds	Douglas	Murphy	Reed	Roberts	Stone

continued

THE STONE COURT (1941–1945)									
1941–42	Stone	Black	Frankfurter	Byrnes	Douglas	Murphy	Reed	Roberts	Jackson
1943–44	Stone	Black	Frankfurter	Rutledge	Douglas	Murphy	Reed	Roberts	Jackson
1945	Stone	Black	Frankfurter	Rutledge	Douglas	Murphy	Reed	Burton	Jackson
THE VINSON COURT (1946–1952)									
1946–48	Vinson	Black	Frankfurter	Rutledge	Douglas	Murphy	Reed	Burton	Jackson
1949–52	Vinson	Black	Frankfurter	Minton	Douglas	Clark	Reed	Burton	Jackson
THE WARREN COURT (1953–1968)									
1953–54	Warren	Black	Frankfurter	Minton	Douglas	Clark	Reed	Burton	Jackson
1955	Warren	Black	Frankfurter	Minton	Douglas	Clark	Reed	Burton	Harlan
1956	Warren	Black	Frankfurter	Brennan	Douglas	Clark	Reed	Burton	Harlan
1957	Warren	Black	Frankfurter	Brennan	Douglas	Clark	Whittaker	Burton	Harlan
1958–61	Warren	Black	Frankfurter	Brennan	Douglas	Clark	Whittaker	Stewart	Harlan
1962–65	Warren	Black	Goldberg	Brennan	Douglas	Clark	White	Stewart	Harlan
1965–67	Warren	Black	Fortas	Brennan	Douglas	Clark	White	Stewart	Harlan
1967–69	Warren	Black	Fortas	Brennan	Douglas	Marshall	White	Stewart	Harlan
THE BURGER COURT (1969–1985)									
1969	Burger	Black	Fortas	Brennan	Douglas	Marshall	White	Stewart	Harlan
1969–70	Burger	Black		Brennan	Douglas	Marshall	White	Stewart	Harlan
1970	Burger	Black	Blackmun	Brennan	Douglas	Marshall	White	Stewart	Harlan
1971	Burger	Powell	Blackmun	Brennan	Douglas	Marshall	White	Stewart	Rehnquist
1975	Burger	Powell	Blackmun	Brennan	Stevens	Marshall	White	Stewart	Rehnquist
1981	Burger	Powell	Blackmun	Brennan	Stevens	Marshall	White	O'Connor	Rehnquist
THE REHNQUIST COURT (1986–)									
1986	Rehnquist	Powell	Blackmun	Brennan	Stevens	Marshall	White	O'Connor	Scalia
1988	Rehnquist	Kennedy	Blackmun	Brennan	Stevens	Marshall	White	O'Connor	Scalia
1990	Rehnquist	Kennedy	Blackmun	Souter	Stevens	Marshall	White	O'Connor	Scalia

INDEX

Cross-references to dictionary entries are located in the text at the end of each definition paragraph. Page references in bold type indicate dictionary entries.

Index

Harvey. See Michigan v. Harvey
Hass. See Oregon v. Hass
Hayes. See Bordenkircher v. Hayes
Hayes v. Florida, 89
Hazelwood School District v. Kuhlmeier, **33**
Heffron v. International Society for Krishna Consciousness, Inc., 16
Hicks. See Arizona v. Hicks
Hill. See Houston v. Hill
Hishon v. King & Spalding, 223
Hobbie v. Unemployment Appeals Commission of Florida, 22
Hodgson v. Minnesota, 235
Hoffman Estates, Village of v. Flipside, Inc., 31
Hogan. See Malloy v. Hogan
Hopkins. See Price Waterhouse v. Hopkins
Horton v. California, 82
Houston v. Hill, 32
Howlett v. Rose, 209
Hudson v. Palmer, 95
Hunt v. McNair, 11
Hustler Magazine v. Falwell, **36**

Idaho v. Wright, 138
Illinois v. Allen, 134
Illinois v. Perkins, 127
Illinois v. Rodriguez, 92

Jackson. See Michigan v. Jackson
Jackson Board of Education. See Wygant v. Jackson Board of Education
Jacobsen. See United States v. Jacobsen
Jaffree. See Wallace v. Jaffree
James v. Illinois, 121
Jeffers. See Lewis v. Jeffers
Jenkins. See United States v. Jenkins
Jenkins v. Georgia, 43
Jenness v. Fortsen, 67
Jeter. See Clark v. Jeter
Jett v. Dallas Independent School District, 203
Jews for Jesus. See Board of Airport Commissioners v. Jews for Jesus
Johnson. See Ohio v. Johnson; Texas v. Johnson
Johnson v. Mayor and City Council of Baltimore, 227
Johnson v. Mississippi, 177
Johnson v. Transportation Agency, 197
Jones v. Thomas, 110

Katzenbach. See South Carolina v. Katzenbach
Keller v. State Bar of California, 56
Kemp. See McCleskey v. Kemp

Kendrick. See Bowen v. Kendrick
Kentucky v. Stincer, 136
Kentucky Bar Association. See Shapero v. Kentucky Bar Association
Kentucky Department of Corrections v. Thompson, 95
Keyishian v. Board of Regents, **54**
King & Spalding. See Hishon v. King & Spalding
Kline. See Vlandis v. Kline
Klutznick. See Fullilove v. Klutznick
Kokinda. See United States v. Kokinda
Kuhlmeier. See Hazelwood School District v. Kuhlmeier

Labine v. Vincent, 217
LaFleur. See Cleveland Board of Education v. LaFleur
LaFollette. See Democratic Party v. LaFollette
Lakewood v. Plain Dealer Publishing Company, 34
Lassiter v. Department of Social Services, 148
Leake. See Perry v. Leake
Lemon v. Kurtzman, 13
Leon. See United States v. Leon
Levy v. Louisiana, 217
Lewis v. Jeffers, 179
Lightfoot. See Gomillion v. Lightfoot
Local #28 of the Sheet Metal Workers' International v. Equal Employment Opportunity Commission, **194**
Local #93 of the International Association of Firefighters v. City of Cleveland, 196
Lockett v. Ohio, 165
Lockhart v. Nelson, 109
Long. See Michigan v. Long
Lorain Journal. See Milkovich v. Lorain Journal
Lorance v. AT&T Technologies, Inc., 224
Los Angeles Department of Water and Power v. Manhart, 223
Lowenfield v. Phelps, 177
Lucas. See Matthews v. Lucas
Lynaugh. See Penry v. Lynaugh
Lynch v. Donnelly, 19
Lyng v. Northwest Indian Cemetery Protective Association, 23
Lyng v. United Automobile Workers, 55

Maher v. Roe, 233
Maine v. Thiboutot, 194
Maine v. Thornton, 73
Mallard v. United States District Court for the Southern District of Iowa, 149

246

Malley v. Briggs, 75
Malloy v. Hogan, 128
Manhart. See Los Angeles Department of
Water and Power v. Manhart
Mapp v. Ohio, 114
Maroney. See Chambers v. Maroney
Marsh. See Richardson v. Marsh
Martin. See Schall v. Martin
Martin v. Wilks, 197
Martinez. See Procunier v. Martinez
Maryland v. Buie, 89
Maryland v. Craig, 137
Maryland v. Garrison, 72
Massachusetts Board of Retirement v.
Murgia, **225,** 230
Massachusetts Citizens for Life. See
Federal Elections Commission v.
Massachusetts Citizens for Life
Massiah v. United States, 151
Mathews. See Morris v. Mathews
Matlock. See United States v. Matlock
Matthews v. Lucas, 217
Mauro. See Arizona v. Mauro
Maynard v. Cartwright, 177
McCarty. See Berkomer v. McCarty
McCleskey v. Kemp, **167**
McCoy v. Court of Appeals of Wisconsin,
153
McCrary. See Runyon v. McCrary
McKoy v. North Carolina, 166
McLean Credit Union. See Patterson v.
McLean Credit Union
McPherson. See Rankin v. McPherson
Memoirs v. Massachusetts, 42
Mempa v. Rhay, 152
Mergens. See Westside Community Schools,
Board of Education of v. Mergens
Metro Broadcasting, Inc. v. Federal
Communications Commission,
201
Meyer v. Grant, 61
Michael H. and Victoria D. v. Gerald D.,
231
Michigan v. Clifford, 80
Michigan v. Harvey, 120
Michigan v. Jackson, 117, 120
Michigan v. Long, 89
Michigan v. Thomas, 86
Michigan v. Tyler, **78**
Michigan Department of State Police. See
Will v. Michigan Department of State
Police
Michigan Department of State Police v.
Sitz, 102
Milkovich v. Lorain Journal, 39
Miller v. California, **42**
Miller v. Fenton, 117

Mills v. Maryland, 174
Millsap. See Quinn v. Millsap
Mimms. See Pennsylvania v. Mimms
Mincey v. Arizona, 120
Minnesota v. Olson, 77
Miranda v. Arizona, **113,** 151
Missouri v. Jenkins, 210
Mistretta v. United States, **182**
Mobile v. Bolden, **212**
Monroe v. Pape, 194, 205
Monsanto. See United States v. Monsanto
Montalvo-Murillo. See United States v.
Montalvo-Murillo
Moran v. Burbine, 124
Morris. See New York City Board of
Estimate v. Morris
Morris v. Mathews, 108
Morrison v. Olson, **156**
Mosley. See Chicago Police Department v.
Mosley
Muniz. See Pennsylvania v. Muniz
Munro v. Socialist Workers Party, **65**
J. H. Munson Company. See Secretary of
State of Maryland v. J. H. Munson
Company
Murdock v. Pennsylvania, 9
Murgia. See Massachusetts Board of
Retirement v. Murgia
Murray v. Giarratano, 152
Murry. See United States Department of
Agriculture v. Murry
Myers. See Florida v. Myers

Nassau County, School Board of v. Arline,
228
National Collegiate Athletic Association v.
Tarkanian, 207
National Conservative Political Action
Committee. See Federal Election
Commission v. National Conservative
Political Action Committee
National Federation of the Blind of North
Carolina. See Riley v. National
Federation of the Blind of North
Carolina
National Treasury Employees Union v. Von
Raab, 99
Nelson. See Lockhart v. Nelson
New Jersey v. T.L.O., 89
New York v. Ferber, 43, 49
New York v. Harris, 77
New York City Board of Estimate v.
Morris, 215
New York State Club Association v. City
of New York, 221
New York Times v. Sullivan, 39, 40,
41

251